Men
Without
Masks

Men Without Masks

Writings from the Journals of Modern Men

Michael Rubin

ADDISON-WESLEY PUBLISHING COMPANY

Reading, Massachusetts • Menlo Park, California
London • Amsterdam • Don Mills, Ontario • Sydney

We gratefully acknowledge the following for permission to reprint previously published material:

SONS

Page 3: From *Diary of a Black Sheep* by Colonel Richard Meinhertzhagen. London: Oliver & Boyd Ltd., 1964.

Page 12: From *The Diaries of Franz Kafka 1910–1913* by Franz Kafka, edited by Max Brod. Copyright © 1948 by Schocken Books Inc. Copyright © renewed 1975 by Schocken Books Inc.

Also from *The Diaries of Franz Kafka 1914–1923*, edited by Max Brod. Copyright © 1949 by Schocken Books Inc. Copyright © renewed 1976 by Schocken Books Inc.

Page 23: From *The Journal of Andrew Bihaly*, edited by Anthony Tuttle (Thomas Y. Crowell). Copyright © 1973 by Josephine Bihaly. Permission granted by Harper & Row.

Page 32: From *In the Middle of Things* by Michael Rubin. New York: G.P. Putnam's Sons. Copyright © 1973 by Michael Rubin.

Continued on page 311

Library of Congress Cataloging in Publication Data
Main entry under title:

Men without masks.

1. Men--Biography. 2. Men--Psychology. I. Rubin,
Michael.
HQ1090.M45   305.3'092'2   80-18923
ISBN 0-201-06342-5
ISBN 0-201-06343-3 (pbk.)

INTERIOR BOOK DESIGN BY SUSAN MARSH

Copyright © 1980 by Addison-Wesley Publishing Company, Inc. Philippines copyright 1980 by Addison-Wesley Publishing Company, Inc.

ABCDEFGHIJ-DO-89876543210

ISBN 0-201-06342-5
ISBN 0-201-06343-3 (pbk.)

To the editors of
Revelations: Diaries of Women
Mary Jane Moffat
and
Charlotte Painter
for their inspiration, guidance,
and encouragement

With special thanks to Nora Gallagher

The help of Brian Crockett, Martha Drumm, Robert Ehrlich,
John L'Heureux, Stuart Miller, Joseph Portnoy,
Roger Sorrentino, Ruth M. Taylor, Bill Taylor, and
Anthony Tuttle has also been deeply appreciated
and is gratefully acknowledged.

Contents

Introduction

PART ONE: SONS

1 Richard Meinhertzhagen   3
2 Franz Kafka   12
3 Andrew Bihaly   23
4 Michael Rubin   32

PART TWO: IDEALISTS

5 Otto Braun   45
6 Alan Seeger   54
7 Alfred Hassler   64
8 Arthur Bremer   74
9 John L'Heureux   83

PART THREE: LOVERS, HUSBANDS, FATHERS

10 Edward Weston   95
11 Ned Rorem   107
12 W.N.P. Barbellion   117
13 Peter Marin   128
14 David Steinberg   138
15 Josh Greenfeld   147

PART FOUR: WORKING MEN

16 Fred Bason   159
17 Jerry Kramer   169
18 Martin Siegel   180
19 Walter Morris   190
20 Basile Yanovsky   199
21 Raphael Soyer   211

PART FIVE: EXPLORERS

22 Richard E. Byrd   225
23 Tobias Schneebaum   233
24 Thomas Merton   242
25 Howard Nemerov   253
26 Frederick S. Perls   263

PART SIX: AGING, OLD, AND DYING MEN

27 James Dickey   275
28 Gamaliel Bradford   281
29 Angelo Roncalli (Pope John XXIII)   292
30 William Soutar   301

Introduction

MEN OF COURAGE fill this book. Oh, not with the kind of courage we ordinarily prize in men, though some of the men here show that, too. They bust their heads in football games and lose their lives in war. They go to jail for their convictions, endure the isolation of a polar winter, survive among a tribe of cannibals. But even the most audacious of these individuals share a courage of a different kind. In a world where self-reflection still does not much count among the more "manly virtues," all the men in this collection have also been brave enough to confront the feelings evoked by their lives in order to be more wholly themselves.

The risks involved in such feats are clear. For one thing, this emotional process can be very painful. For another, its revelations are often appalling. What son wants to realize, as Richard Meinhertzhagen does here, that his mother will never love him in the way he so sorely needs? What worker, like Walter Morris, that his salary has largely determined his self-esteem? And, like the long-doubting lover, W. N. P. Barbellion, that his life is to end just when it is being enchanted at last by his new wife? For even a man's ecstasies—his ardor, his zeal, his sense of transcendence—may be hard to bear when felt to the full.

What's more, for a man to experience his emotions is an effort that doesn't always meet with approval of our particular culture. Whether our lessons are explicit or implied, as boys we men are taught early on to dampen certain feelings, to deny other feelings almost entirely, certainly to control them. Emotions deemed inappropriate or too apparent, we learn young, will speak to others of our weakness, our vulnerability, our everlasting shame. To be considered "one of the boys," we must often force a show of enthusiasm for what is frightening or repugnant to us. To be counted among the brave, we boys are often made to walk through fire and pretend it doesn't burn. Allowing ourselves the full ebb and flow of our feelings, then, often runs against the social tide.

Just as surely, taboos against our looking too much within are traditional with us. Introspection is awarded few laurels—unless it has managed to produce some marketable commodity. Movement is the name of our more manly games, the forward march toward tangible goals, the successful pay-off of some predetermined destination. For example, to keep a journal that is not a mere account of such travels, but rather an impulsive, undetermined, inner exploration, whose only goal is a deeper engagement with oneself, is for poets and philosophers, not "real" men.

But even if approved occasions for acceptable expressions of our feelings are allowed us, we boys are encouraged from the start to have our emotions take a backseat to our intellects. Subjectivity, intuition, imaginative embroidery, we are made to assume, are more appropriate to girls, and as such as frivolous and self-concerned—though not, of course, without a certain charm we soon learn to cater to or patronize. No, for us men it is analysis, objectivity, the rigors of logical thinking that are values not equal but superior to responsiveness, spontaneity, the fancies of the dreaming mind. The intellect, uninfluenced by feeling, is not regarded as only one of our essential tools, but as the best possible instrument of perception and the highest judge of all truth.

This control of our emotions—and often of our bodies—in the service of our intellect is only part of a larger pattern of control we men are made to exercise from an early age. We are encouraged not only to dominate our own felt lives and reflections but also to control the direction of other lives as well. Though lip-service is given at school to cooperative effort, our schooling more clearly teaches us that other boys, other men, are our competitors, to be played against, not with, and not for the joy of the game itself, but for the joy of winning it. Women? Objects for further conquest. And as we might have been made to serve our father's will, so our children are often made to grow up serving ours.

Even the natural world we inhabit must come under our heavy thumbs. Men in this culture are seldom taught to tread lightly upon the grounds we move through, but to cut them up and pull them apart, to possess them until they are exhausted. Not to dominate, or at least not to try to, is tantamount to failure—to be thought a passive, dreamy sort, feminized and cowardly. The mystical and quixotic among us might eschew such lessons of control (and we tougher-minded, more active men can certainly tolerate those "ineffectual" types with no loss to ourselves), but to lay down our *own* weapons of domination for long is to call our very masculinity into question, which is harder—much harder—to tolerate. By regularly putting aside such controls in the interests of more spontaneous self-reflection, the men in this anthology have often braved that hard question regarding the nature of their sex.

These social determinations of our masculinity often cast us men into roles we assume are natural to us, and so, ironically, strive harder to perfect—since they are not. The rewards for this performance are certainly enticing: a clear-cut definition of ourselves and the ready acceptance of like-minded men.

But any narrowed conception of our nature obviously has its price. The man who labors hard to live by such limiting assumptions puts on a stiffish mask that he may soon have trouble seeing through. These masks, which often glorify his inexpressiveness, inevitably come to alter the quality of his relationship to himself and his participation in the world.

Perhaps the greatest courage of the men in this anthology is revealed in their determination to take a frequent look at the more marvelous though fearfully mutable face that moves beneath the mask.

The men in here, however, partake in no common rebellion against the cultural requisites of manhood. These lives are too varied for that. It's the journals they keep—and the nature of the journal itself—that compel them to set aside their social poses and enter their own lives more thoroughly. For the journal, whether kept over a period of weeks, months, years, or the course of an entire lifetime, is a private act. Usually meant for nobody's eyes but the writer's, the journal releases him from his need for public posturing—that arch controller making him feel he must master his body and soul and the world about him or else go unapproved.

Like a child left for a time to play alone, the journal writer is also set free from the eyes of his parents and peers. Impulsively, he may take up his pen without concern for the figure he cuts, no matter how foolish it seems. Spontaneously, he may write whatever occurs to him with no need to attend to the obligations of subject or structure or style. And when he dares, he will follow the flow of his thoughts and feelings wherever their depths and fancies may lead; attend to his daydreams no matter how futile; pursue his nightmares to their worst revelations; dwell on his pleasures and pains in a way that his world, and the conscience it has helped to create, too often discredits.

Does such writing suggest only some sort of sad psychological compensation? Possibly. For often the journal *is* a defensive act of the emotions, a way of coping with an uncongenial world, an oasis of freer reflection in a desert of the deaf and hard-hearted. Franz Kafka, you will soon see, often uses his diaries as such while he listens to his parents at cards out in the parlor; so does Rabbi Martin Siegel after another frustrating day trying to serve his congregation.

The journal might even come to be our only friend, granting the intimacy we would much prefer to find in another human being—in that ideally compatible other who would be willing to share (though he or she cannot repair for us) the nature of the lives we lead. Alfred Hassler in prison, John L'Heureux at his Jesuitical studies, Fred Bason with his barrow of second-hand books often confide in their diaries when no intimate is able to hear them out.

And keeping a journal might even prove to be a far more desperate necessity: confiding our passionate confusions to a journal might stop us from destroying ourselvves or others by acting out those emotions in an effort to avoid feeling them through. So it is for Ned Rorem after the end of a love affair, and for Andrew Bihaly until, pitiably, not even his journal can save him any longer from suicide.

But anyone who keeps a journal usually finds the endeavor more creative than compensatory. The confessional aspect of such work not only proves an expressive outlet for emotion, and perhaps for its catharsis, but is also a sensitive instrument of self-analysis that can only deepen our understanding of our lives. Recognizing recurrent patterns of concern and responsiveness through such writing leads us toward a greater awareness of our own psychology so that our strengths and weaknesses, our desires and abhorrences may be more thoughtfully evaluated. I count myself among those men like Howard Nemerov, Frederick Perls, Peter Marin, and David Steinberg, who have used their journals as a form of self-help. For the privacy and freedom of the journal invites unconscious material to come to fuller consciousness, which may often help shake us loose from early reactions no longer useful in our adulthood, though still habitually employed.

And if change of this sort is not what we particularly seek through our diaries, the very act of journal keeping may allow us, as it does Tobias Schneebaum and Gamaliel Bradford, to appreciate our own complexity and mystery more fully, enhancing our sense of personal significance in a world that often flattens out those meanings we seek to design for ourselves.

As a vehicle of self-exploration, the journal may be of particular importance to men. As suggested before, exercises in spontaneity, such as the journal provides, allow men to recognize that our reasoning processes are not the sum total of our minds. Our visceral and irrational responses are equally valuable to a fuller understanding of ourselves and the world that we make. Giving up our control for the free play of the journal, we may begin to recover certain powers lost long ago: our tenderness, perhaps; our ability to absorb more from our experiences; a more creative receptivity. Amorphous states of mind may eventually come to clearer definition—the origin of that unfathomable sense of dread, the significance of that disquieting fantasy. As these disowned aspects of our capacities become more apparent, we can only acknowledge them as parts of ourselves because they have been made manifest by our writing. And as we accept more of those features that have been disenfranchised in the name of masculinity or maturation, we may come to appreciate not only our fluid natures but also sense a greater wholeness in ourselves.

If this smacks of self-indulgence or a convenient escape from our larger responsibilities, it is perhaps ironic to find that paying attention to our own lives has once more become suspect. After a full decade of psychological and social advances through the activities of women's liberation, gay consciousness, and the human potential movement, explorations of our reflective and emotive life are again being called into question with catch-phrases like The Me Generation or the classier Culture of Narcissism. Such excess self-absorption at the expense of social commitment is considered a political danger.

Certainly an excessive dedication to *any* pursuit might be open to similar criticism. The journals of some of our idealists here suggest just that. But the social critic might give more thought to the benefits of such self-concerned work as journal writing. The journal is not necessarily a ticket-of-leave from social action. Often, it may prove to be a more valid passport *into* the community one chooses to serve. Creative solutions to public as well as personal problems often come out of such private reflections; new directions for a more effective life may be discovered. A reading of the complete journals of some of these men, such as Thomas Merton, Alfred Hassler, Martin Siegel, and Pope John, will make this function apparent.

More important, I believe that our action in the world is better predicated upon a fuller understanding of the motives for that involvement, an admission of our doubts and expectations, the recognition of the sacrifices it might entail, and the limitations of its possible success. Without confronting our own devils, how are we to do honest work with the devils we find out there? And since the journal helps us to accept our own ambiguities, it also enables us to accept the ambiguities of others. Such a lesson in compassion can only be valued in our continuing exchanges with the world.

In this regard, I hope my book will make more women as well as men aware of the particular difficulties that we men face in a world claimed to be dominated by masculine interests and values. The belief that men have inherited one set of natural tendencies while women have inherited another has led to a divisiveness between the sexes that continues to limit our understanding of each other. Though the women's movement has done much to break down myths and stereotypes about women in the interests of their complexity, it does not often recognize a similar complexity in men. I hope this collection increases the insight of women into the lives of their counterparts.

The particular journals found in this anthology were chosen for several reasons. Although research took me through hundreds of men's diaries, my main intent lay in finding the journals of men who had used their hearts as much as their heads as they wrote about their daily lives. I also wanted examples of men still close to the events they describe—men who, unlike the autobiographer, were not yet influenced by the passage of time, the cosmetics of memory, or the postures of reputation. With the question of audience and esthetics largely set aside, these individuals may often be seen living through the actual course of their feelings as they explore their deepest concerns and most difficult revelations. This might help the general reader and the serious diarist achieve a better understanding of that process, and perhaps encourage a similar exploration in themselves. To experience your feelings is often an unpleasant risk, but it's a risk that must be undertaken as part of the way to achieve a deeper connection between yourself and your world.

Stunning examples of such dynamic personal writing may be found throughout Western history, from Augustine and Abelard to Descartes and Amiel, from Boswell and Swift to Montaigne and Rousseau. But these are rare; earlier journals too often prove to be mere calendars, descriptions of public events, notes on household expenses and travels jotted down for future reference, or acts of penitence and self-discipline offered up to some higher power. The notion of a "self" not substantially identified with church, state, or class is a relatively modern conception; a greater sense of individualism, the recourse, perhaps, of an era of discontinuity, cultural fragmentation, and a multiplicity of possible beliefs. Since many more relevant examples of the self-reflective journal may be found in more recent times, I decided to limit my selection to useful illustrations from men of this century.

Then, too, I tried to include individuals who, though they address themselves to the concerns of most modern men, were either living especially interesting lives or were probing their lives in especially interesting ways. With this in mind, I hoped not to overload the anthology with professional writers (notoriously good journal keepers), but with men for whom writing was a secondary interest—men who, whether renowned or unknown, were engaged in a wide range of personal and worldly pursuits, and so might raise a richer variety of issues that could be addressed in any serious search of self-discovery.

And like the variety of individuals I finally selected, the many forms that these journals take will show, I hope, the variety of ways the self-reflective journal might be used, and so serve as further inspiration.

The arrangement of these selections follows a simple plan. Although we are all many men—sons, lovers, workers, seekers—to ourselves and to others, during the courses of our lives certain concerns seem to demand more of our attention than others. With our natural inclination to grow up both safe and free, our early developmental tasks are undertaken almost unawares. But this insistence upon our independence and our security must soon also deal with the specific contingencies of our particular environment. SONS, the first section of this anthology, offers examples of several young men still involved in their relationships to their parents. This continuing engagement with childhood's primary struggle between dependence and autonomy illustrates several degrees of success and failure with a task that, in some measure, is never concluded no matter how long we may live.

Our maturing also entails a continual fashioning of our personal meaning in this world, a meaning we often seek to achieve through an emulation of role models or a commitment to exemplary ideals. Although many of us continue throughout our lives to seek identification with some cause larger than ourselves, younger men seem especially zealous in this pursuit. IDEALISTS, our next section, concerns boys and men who feel the urgent need to serve these higher purposes. We may question their motives, share their confusions, even be shocked in some cases by their dreams of the greater glory, but it is hard to deny this common impulse toward dedication to a more significant social or spiritual cause.

But the evolving structure of our individual lives is built just as much upon our capacities for love and for work, whatever forms these may take. LOVERS, HUSBANDS, FATHERS turns us toward the more amorous and domestic sides of our natures. These excerpts try to illustrate the lives of several men immersed in the age-old problem of balancing their own needs against the needs of those whom they love. Certainly it shows that men have the capacity for loving others deeply despite their doubts—and in many different ways.

For many men, their personal meaning is felt more thoroughly through the work they undertake. Yet the nature of much modern labor often alienates a man from any significant interaction with the job at hand. Its demands may also define the man too well. The WORKING MEN offered next all make that strategic effort to maintain an active involvement with their labors as well as their own identity apart from it. Though their occupations may vary, their commitments differ, and their satisfactions be not necessarily great, all are examples of men who often refuse to acquiesce to the image their work tends to exact, or to become automatons at their tasks.

Though some of our claims upon life may be carried out to our contentment, we find that we must contain others in some uncertain balance, while still others we bring painfully unresolved into our futures. Our EXPLORERS perhaps best exemplify this predicament. A deliberate blend is presented here of three adventurous individuals who discover more about themselves than they do about the exotic lands they explore, along with two others who stay closer to home to explore their inner lives through more innovative use of their journals.

And through all these urgencies, we are forever aware that life never stands still, that time always sits on our weakening backs. This inevitable pressure is most evident in our final section, AGING, OLD, AND DYING MEN—men who dare look time in the face, a task that always seems to entail a struggle to avoid despair while seeking a greater sense of integrity to one's entire life. It comes as no surprise that the various ways these men employ their latter days on earth, or contrive to deal with death, also seem integral to the ways they have experienced their lifetime.

Even the most casual reader will quickly sense that an anthology like this is bound to distort the lives with which it deals. Slicing into a journal for a few excerpts to illustrate a theme never does justice to the life thus invaded. I certainly agree. In self-defense let me say that I never tried to turn a journal keeper's minor concern into a major issue for him. The thread that was finally pulled from each life for closer examination was always a strong one within the whole cloth of the journal.

Still, I learned early in this work that there was no way I could avoid not seeing these men through my own eyes; responding to them out of my own interests, prejudices, and limitations. This will become even more apparent to the reader in my preface to each figure. I can only hope that these brief selections will lead many of you back to their original sources where you might come to appreciate more completely all the complexities and concerns of the individuals introduced here.

A further warning: The nature of the journal itself often distorts the life it encloses. Even if the journal is examined in its entirety, the reader can never be sure if it truly reflects the life as lived. No matter how honest the journal keeper may try to be about himself, he generally sits down to write when he most needs to—when he is feeling oppressed, when he is searching for some new understanding, when he must rid himself of a painful impression. Self-reflective diaries most often register the anguish and doldrums of a life, not its more inspiring excitements. As one of our writers, W. N. P. Barbellion, says to his friend, the journal, "I haven't written to you for ever so long, and my silence as usual indicates happiness."

But a necessarily problematic engagement with these men's journals is perhaps its greatest value. Appraising each excerpt for its possible truth forces the reader to pit his or her own system of values against each diarist's. Whether you are sympathetic to an action, idea, or emotion, or shocked to a sure antipathy, I hope that your own responsiveness will be used to tell you something more about yourself. Obviously, I want this collection to encourage its readers to regard their emotional lives in a more acceptable light. I want them to understand that no feeling fully experienced is inappropriate; that its expression, whether within the privacy of the journal or among trusted intimates, may well be a matter of mental health, an important tool of adjustment, or a creative solution to the difficulties of any life. To restrain or deny feelings limits our depth of perception, loses empathy for other people, and leads to an inner disunity. And for us men especially, to become a man of more conscious feeling is to become more fully human.

San Francisco, California   M. R.
August 1980

Part One

Sons

Chapter One

Richard Meinhertzhagen
1878-1967

I F YOU HAVE managed to survive your own childhood with some sense of your true feelings intact, you might agree that, for better or worse, the lessons in love learned at home remain with you for the rest of your days. At the age of eighty-five Richard Meinhertzhagen set out to describe for his own descendants the influence of his early environment upon the subsequent course of his life. In so doing he drew upon his boyhood diaries, which were begun at the age of six at the suggestion of Ethel Huxley, daughter of Thomas Huxley, and later, as a schoolboy, were further encouraged by Herbert Spencer, "who stressed the importance of observing, recording, explaining."

The Huxleys and Spencers, the Potters, the Churchills, Sidney Webb, and Oscar Wilde are among the famous friends and relations who visit at Mottisfont, the Meinhertzhagens' country manor in Romsey, England, during Richard's privileged childhood—privileged by comfort, position, and culture, but short on parental affection. The prevailing Victorian attitudes and mores might have something to do with the way that the family's love is displayed, but Richard does see demonstrable affection in his large family, and he feels a special warmth for his beloved brother Dan, as well as great respect for his kind though distant father. No, it is his mother's confounding attitude toward him as he first tries to win her heart, then hardened by failure, begins to refute it, that leaves a lifelong legacy of unfulfillment.

Compounding his difficulty with his mother is the rank injustice he suffers during his terms at Fonthill, a boarding school run by vicious schoolmasters who seem straight out of Dickens. That his mother is the last one to listen to his pleas for release from the place, or even to acknowledge the welts from his beatings, is astounding. In his later years, Meinhertzhagen is able to find reasons for his mother's behavior among the difficulties of her own life, and he is content with the reconciliation they manage to make after the death of his father. But that cannot change the perceptions of the boy Richard. The residue of this disastrous relationship between mother and son remains evident in the man.

"Observing, recording, explaining." Herbert Spencer's advice became the habits of Colonel Richard Meinhertzhagen's long life. He put them to good use in his published ornithological studies, and in his timely accounts of his career in the British Army in Kenya and the Near East during the early part of the century. But nowhere do his experiences seem to count for more than during the formative years he describes in his *Diary of a Black Sheep*.

1884

This is my DAIRY
by Dick

and nobody knows it but Dan and Miss Huxley and Grandpapa and it is very secret. I was born on March 3rd, 1878 and today is March 3rd, 1884 and I will write everythings that happen but Miss Huxley says I must not talk about the weather or food which is a pity because it is easy. Today Bardie and me and Olivia Bevan rode in the row and my feet were very cold.

1889

13 SEPTEMBER. I think mother sees I do not want to go back to school; she tells me I am behaving very foolishly and that Fonthill is doing me a lot of good. She says I am sulking and brooding and that she will be glad when I go back to school. She is glad to see me go back to torture and beatings. Oh God, please take care of me. I shall never talk to Mother again about Fonthill because she does not want to understand.

18 SEPTEMBER. Mother is always telling me I must not lose my temper, a thing I have never done. I took a toss off the Grey this morning and came home feeling rotten. There was some mud on my boots when I came to lunch, not very much and not nearly so much as Bardie had on hers, and mother told me to go and take them off. So I went and when I got upstairs I felt sick so I went to bed. Mother came up after lunch and was very angry, told me I must not lose my temper and that I must get up at once. So I did and was sick. If I had told Mother why I was sick she would have said I was shamming or would have laughed.

24 SEPTEMBER. I saw Dan off to Harrow from Baker Street and asked him what would happen if I killed Walter [Walter Radcliffe, a master and co-owner of Fonthill]. He said I would be expelled and probably hung. Well, I don't mind a bit and if I kill him I shall run away and not go home and I don't mind if I am hung if I kill him and I told Dan so and he asked me not to do it because Father would mind very much. Dan also told me he would make Mother take me away if Walter was horrid.

8 OCTOBER. Walter has started again, the beast. I feel I have nothing left now but myself, no friends but Dan and I shall fight the

beast with what I can find. I feel as though my body were an empty shell wandering about with no desire beyond to kill, my little soul, if I have one left, tucked away somewhere inside, smothered in shame, killed by cruelty, starved and bruised for lack of love. Oh God, release me from this torment and give me back my mother's love.

10 OCTOBER. I hit Walter and shall be expelled. I dont care for I feel rejected by Mother and forsaken by God.

18 NOVEMBER. There are two ME's, the outward and visible one, gloomy, argumentative, intolerant and suspicious. The other ME is right inside me fighting against all these things, longing for a little encouragement and appreciation, hoping that some day and somewhere I shall find love and peace.

14 DECEMBER. The end of the term is near but I feel I dont care if I go home or not. I feel so unattractive, such a wanderer and outcast and only half alive. I believe there is good in me somewhere but it is all trampled down and crushed. I have horrid dreams of Walter still.

1890

18 AUGUST. Mother had a garden party at Mottisfont today and Dorothy came looking lovely. When I was talking to her on the lawn Mother came up and boxed me on the ears and knocked my cap off, accusing me of not having taken off my hat to her when I met her. Dorothy at once said "Oh, but he did when we met" but Mother only walked away. I was so ashamed of this happening before Dorothy that I left her at once and went to the Duck Ground where I remained for the rest of the afternoon. Dorothy went very red.

1 SEPTEMBER. Mother spoke to me about being nearly drowned at Longfords. She told me not to be such a humbug for I could swim alright if I wanted to and that Bill [Bill Playne, eight years Richard's senior, and a frequent visitor at Mottisfont] had done quite right in making me swim. I know I can swim a little but I have never swum before in deep water. I wish Mother would not take Bill's part against me and use him as a sort of schoolmaster. Mother treats Bill much better than she treats me. I wish I was somebody's else's little boy and had a mother who cared for me, then I would be happy.

1891

29 JULY [*Fonthill*]. What is the object of life and is prayer useless, these are questions which upset me. Why have I been born to suffer so? Is God listening to my prayers? The Bible says that real happiness can only be got through suffering. That is not my experience. All this cruelty and unhappiness has changed me from a happy person when I left Aysgarth to a tortured person now. I never hated anyone before I came here. I did not know what evil was till I came here. I am clearer about the value of prayer. There is no living God, but that does not prevent prayer being a comfort. I no longer pray to God for he has forsaken me. I pray to some little divine spark within me, in other words I am calling to everything that is good in me if there is anything left. Nobody listens to my prayers except me. I confess my sins to myself hoping to see light and truth. Fonthill has knocked all ideas of a living God out of me but there is a living devil called Walter. I must fight my battles by myself. I shall never find God because there is none, but I can make my own God out of some little bit of good which still remains with me. And I have also lost mother which is more awful than losing God.

11 AUGUST [*Mottisfont*]. A victory over Herbert Spencer! At lunch today he said that the swift was the fastest of all the swallow

tribe. Dan at once told him that the swift was not a swallow. Mother intervened and told us not to contradict our elders and betters. But after lunch we produced Gould and Yarrell and several other books to convince Mr. Spencer, but he would not look at them; so then we fetched the skin of a swallow and of a swift and showed him the difference in the feet and wings but even so he would not listen. So we went to Dunbridge and caught a swift on its nest and we caught a swallow in the stables and then showed him the different mouths and he then told us we were right. I think he was very angry and so is Mother, who says we must not argue so much with Mr. Spencer, so we won't.

1892

6 JANUARY. Mr. Brooksbank is staying here and at breakfast this morning Mother blamed me for being out late last night and leaving the basement door open. I had not been out late. I was hurt at this constant accusation for things I have never done. Then Mother said, "You are my naughtiest but favourite son," to which Brooksbank added—"There, Dick, that's a tremendous compliment." It certainly was and it took my breath away. I thought about Mother's remark all day and wondered if she really meant it so when she was dressing for dinner I went into her room and asked her if it was true. I just longed to hear that it was and would have hugged her if she had just shown that she meant it, but all she said was—"Now run away, I'm busy just now"—and so the chance has gone. Shall I ever hear from my mother's lips that she loves me?

23 AUGUST. This afternoon Margie [Richard's sister] told Mother that the Slococks were afraid of her and they are. Lots of people are afraid of Mother for she is so critical and proud. Later on mother asked Dan if it was true that the Slococks were afraid of her and he said they were and then Mother asked Dan if we were afraid of her and Dan

said he was afraid of being left in the room alone with Mother because he never knew what she was going to say. And Mother didn't like it but it's true. Neither Dan nor I will ever be left alone with Mother though we both adore her; it's very sad and all wrong.

1893

4 SEPTEMBER. After dinner I was surprised to see Dan sitting on the arm of Mother's chair. It gave me a shock for I should not have dared to do it. I have not even held my mother's hand since I can remember though I have often longed to do so. Why cannot I get on to terms of affection with my mother? Whenever I try I am snubbed. But now that I have seen Dan sitting on Mother's chair I really must try something. I am sure that if I were to sit on Mother's chair I should be told to get off and as for taking her hand—I don't know what would happen.

1896

7 JANUARY. I am visiting the Holts at Ullett Road. Aunt Lallie is a very dear, kind old lady, just like an old hen clucking around chickens. She has given me a lovely travelling clock, just one of the things I wanted. She also told me that I had been a most agreeable surprise to her for Mother had told her that I was bad-mannered and morose. She told me she will write to Mother and tell her she is quite wrong about me, so I kissed her for that; I do love appreciation and so seldom get it at home. I know things are all wrong between me and Mother, but whenever I try and show her some affection I am just pushed away with a snub. Whenever I think about it and pray for some miracle to happen to put it right I get terribly worried and brood about

it and then I am told I am sulking. But I do wish Mother would not tell her sisters about me for if she tells her sisters she must tell other people, which accounts for many things. Why does she hate me so?

1897

3 SEPTEMBER. Aunt Maggie surprised me this evening by telling me she wished I was one of her children. I was so embarrassed that I blushed for the first time in my life. She then told me that Mother was quite wrong about me and that she would write and tell her so. I asked her what Mother had said but she would not tell me. Dear Aunt Maggie, she has been a wonderful godmother to me, generous, kind and always most affectionate. I have always regarded Aunt Maggie as the best company, the most human and the least abnormal of all the Potter sisters. But she has some odd children about whom she cannot resist talking to people like me, just like all the other Potter sisters. I like them all better than I like most of my first cousins though some of them are a bit indigestible. Jack and Paul are delightful children.

1898

26 JANUARY. Dan and I dined with Aunt Kate and Uncle Leonard this evening. After dinner Aunt Kate said she wanted to have a little talk with me and I knew at once what was coming—a lecture. Dan giggled when he saw me being dragged off. I have no doubt Aunt Kate means well but she is too condescending and won't come off her pedestal of righteousness and superiority. She harped on my bad manners, my bad temper and all the same old things. I asked her if she had ever seen me bad tempered or bad mannered and she said she had not and she finally admitted that Mother had told her. It is too horrible and I felt that sinking feeling, all alone, deserted and forsaken. It made me so

depressed and spoiled my whole evening. Dan goes to Bremen tomor-row. I wish he was not going for he is the only one who really understands me.

1899

22 MARCH. Tomorrow I leave England for India to join my regiment. More than I can express in words, I desired to show my mother my deep affection for her before I went but I have failed and I hate myself for it. I believe Mother really loves me at the bottom of her heart but her nature forbids her showing it by word or gesture. And I find all my pent-up love for Mother crushed under an unbreakable crust of shyness and moral cowardice. My soul has been frozen in the ice of criticism and estrangement. I knew Mother would speak to me this evening and I was prepared to throw myself into her arms. But she started by telling me I must learn not to sulk and that I must restrain my temper and cultivate better manners. I am not sulky, nor bad tempered nor bad mannered. This renewal of criticism when I expected love, froze me to silence and I at once became icy cold, desperately cold. My lips felt sealed by steel. There is no ostentation in frozen steel. If only mother had taken my hand or put her arms around me I should have responded at once and I believe she would have done so also; but there it is and neither of us could make that vital gesture which might have brought us together. I remained silent and could say nothing though something in me was bursting with a desire to kiss my mother over and over again, a thing I have never done. In the end my mother said, "Well, I suppose there is nothing more to be said" and I left the room in floods of tears. It is now nearly midnight and I should like to go down to mother's room but dare not; I know she must be awake and feeling just as I do now, in the depths of misery. It's Hell for us both and all so silly. And now I shall have to go to India and I don't know when I shall ever see Mother again.

Chapter Two

Franz
Kafka
1883-1924

PERHAPS THE SAD but supportable separation that Richard Meinhertzhagen finally makes from his mother is to some measure due to an English gentry tradition that demands a son's cool display of his independence, whatever the emotional cost. In contrast, the bourgeois household of the Kafkas in Prague, Czechoslovakia suggests an emotional hothouse deliberately designed to make dependence flourish: A father who uses his wife and children to cater to his psychosomatic ailments, his troublesome business, his oppressive patriarchy; a mother given to false cheer and bootless fretting, unwilling to deal with any hard truths; and a son—Franz Kafka—who, out of his own unresolved need for parental support, lingers on in his childhood home year after year, fitfully playing all roles assigned him: difficult son, frail neurasthenic, undutiful employee, incorrigible artist. Kafka's special agony lies in his recognition of his own participation in this family conspiracy without ever being able to make a separate peace with it. His special genius, of course, lay in his ability to turn this prosaic domestic absorption into the unique serio-comic nightmares of his astonishing fiction.

Long before Kafka wrote his pained and problematic *Letter to his Father* in 1919, entries in his many haphazard notebooks directly recorded his distress with himself and his family, or indirectly reflected upon these feelings through pertinent dreams, imagery, narrative experiments, letter drafts, and analyses of his own creative work. Often in the process Kafka's reasonable rage is reasoned away; and even in his famous letter, he manages to condemn himself by delivering up to his father the argument that his father might make against him: ". . . you cannot stand up to life, but in order to set yourself up in it comfortably, free from care and without self-reproach, you prove that I robbed you of your capacity to stand up to life, and shoved it in my pocket."

His father never received Kafka's letter. Before she was to deliver it *for* him, Kafka's mother read it at her son's request. She did so and returned it to him, upon which Kafka retained it. Nowhere is the family conspiracy more apparent, nowhere more pathetic. While reading Kafka's diaries and letters, one cries out for angry confrontation, explosion, release—just as, while reading Kafka's novels, one so wants K to discover the crime for which he is some day to stand trial, or a way out of the castle that comes to consume his whole life.

1910

His gravity is the death of me. His head in its collar, his hair arranged immovably on his skull, the muscles of his jowls below, tense in their places—

1911

AUGUST 26. . . . Father has been unable to fall asleep these evenings because of excitement, since he has been completely caught up in his worries about the business and in his illness, which they have aggravated. A wet cloth on his heart, vomiting, suffocation, walking back and forth to the accompaniment of sighs. My mother in her anxiety finds new solace. He was always after all so energetic, he got over everything, and now. . . . I say that all the misery over the business could after all last only another three months, then everything will have to be all right. He walks up and down, sighing and shaking his head. It is clear that from his point of view his worries will not be taken from his shoulders and will not even be made lighter by us, but even from our point of view they will not, even in our best intentions there is still something of the sad conviction that he must provide for his family. By his frequent yawning or his poking into his nose (on the whole not disgusting) Father engenders a slight reassurance as to his condition, which scarcely enters his consciousness, despite the fact that when he is well he usually does not do this. Ottla confirmed this for me. Poor Mother will go to the landlord tomorrow to beg.

OCTOBER 24. Mother works all day, is merry and sad as the fancy strikes her, without taking advantage of her own condition in the slightest, her voice is clear, too loud for ordinary speech but does you good when you are sad and suddenly hear it after some time. For a long time now I have been complaining that I am always ill, but never have any definite illness that would compel me to go to bed. This wish certainly goes back chiefly to the fact that I know how comforting Mother can be when, for example, she comes from the lighted living-room into the twilight of the sick room, or in the evening, when the day begins to change monotonously into night, [she] returns from business and with her concerns and hurried instructions once more causes the day, already so late, to begin again and rouses the invalid to help her in this. I should wish that for myself once more, because then I should be weak, therefore convinced by everything my mother did, and could enjoy childish pleasure with age's keener capacity for grati- fication. . . .

OCTOBER 26. . . . Because it consoles me I write down an autobiographical remark of Shaw's, although it actually is the opposite of consoling: As a boy he was apprentice in the office of a real-estate agency in Dublin. He soon gave up this position, went to London and became a writer. In the first nine years, from 1876 to 1885, he earned 140 kronen in all. "But although I was a strong young man and my family found itself in poor circumstances, I did not throw myself into the struggle for a livelihood; I threw my mother in and let her support me. I was no support for my old father, on the contrary, I hung on to his coattails." In the end this is little consolation for me. The free years he spent in London are already past for me, the possible happiness becomes ever more impossible, I lead a horrible synthetic life and am cowardly and miserable enough to follow Shaw only to the extent of having read the passage to my parents. How this possible life flashes before my eyes in the colors of steel, with spanning rods of steel and airy darkness between!

In order not to forget it, should my father once again call me a bad son, I write it down that, in the presence of several relatives, without special occasion, whether it may have been simply to put me in my place, whether it was supposedly to rescue me, he called Max a *meshuggener ritoch,*" and that yesterday when Löwy was in my room, ironically shaking his body and contorting his mouth, he referred to these strange people who were being let into the house, what could interest one in a strange person, why one enters into such useless relationships, etc. After all, I should not have written it down, for I have written myself almost into a hatred of my father, for which after all he has given no occasion today and which, at least as far as Löwy is concerned, is out of all proportion to what I have written down as having been said by my father, and which even increases because I cannot remember what was really wicked in my father's behavior yesterday.

Löwy. My father about him: "Whoever lies down with dogs gets up with fleas." I could not contain myself and said something uncontrolled. To which Father with unusual quietness (to be sure, after a long interval which was otherwise occupied): "You know that I should not get excited and must be treated with consideration. And now you speak to me like that. I really have enough excitement, quite enough. So don't bother me with such talk." I say: "I make every effort to restrain myself," and sense in my father, as always in such extreme moments, the existence of a wisdom of which I can grasp only a breath.

Today at breakfast I spoke with my mother by chance about children and marriage, only a few words, but for the first time saw clearly how untrue and childish is the conception of me that my mother builds up for herself. She considers me a healthy young man who suffers a little from the notion that he is ill. This notion will disappear by itself with time; marriage, of course, and having children would put an end to it best of all. Then my interest in literature would also be reduced to the degree that is perhaps necessary for an educated man. A matter-of-fact, undisturbed interest in my profession or in the factory or in whatever may come to hand will appear. Hence there is not the slightest, not the trace of a reason for permanent despair about my future. There is occasion for temporary despair, which is not very deep, however, whenever I think my stomach is upset, or when I can't sleep because I write too much. There are thousands of possible solutions. The most probable is that I shall suddenly fall in love with a girl and will never again want to do without her. Then I shall see how good their intentions toward me are and how little they will interfere with me. But if I remain a bachelor like my uncle in Madrid, that too will be no misfortune because with my cleverness I shall know how to make adjustments.

It is unpleasant to listen to Father talk with incessant insinuations about the good fortune of people today and especially of his children, about the sufferings he had to endure in his youth. No one denies that for years, as a result of insufficient winter clothing, he had open sores on his legs, that he often went hungry, that when he was only ten he had to push a cart through the villages, even in winter and very early in the morning—but, and this is something he will not understand, these facts, taken together with the further fact that I have not gone through all this, by no means lead to the conclusion that I have been happier than he, that he may pride himself on these sores on his legs, which is something he assumes and asserts from the very beginning, that I cannot appreciate his past sufferings, and that, finally, just because I have not gone through the same sufferings I must be endlessly grateful to him. How gladly I would listen if he would talk on about his youth and parents, but to hear all this in a boastful and quarrelsome tone is torment. Over and over again he claps his hands together: "Who can understand that today! What do the children know! No one has gone through that! Does a child understand that today!" . . .

1912

In the large room there was the clamor of card playing and later the usual conversation which Father carries on when he is well, as he is today, loudly if not coherently. The words represented only small shapes in a formless clamor. Little Felix slept in the girls' room, the door of which was wide open. I slept across the way, in my own room. The door of this room, in consideration of my age, was closed. Besides, the open door indicated that they still wanted to lure Felix into the family while I was already excluded.

Dreamed recently:

I was riding with my father through Berlin in a trolley. . . . We came to a gate, got out without any sense of getting out, stepped through the gate. On the other side of the gate a sheer wall rose up, which my father ascended almost in a dance, his legs flew out as he climbed, so easy was it for him. There was certainly also some inconsiderateness in the fact that he did not help me one bit, for I got to the top only with the utmost effort, on all fours, often sliding back again, as though the wall had become steeper under me. At the same time it was also distressing that (the wall) was covered with human excrement so that flakes of it clung to me, chiefly to my breast. I looked down at the flakes with bowed head and ran my hand over them.

When at last I reached the top, my father, who by this time was already coming out of a building, immediately fell on my neck and kissed and embraced me. He was wearing an old-fashioned, short Prince Albert, padded on the inside like a sofa, which I remembered well. "This Dr. von Leyden! He is an excellent man," he exclaimed over and over again. But he had by no means visited him in his capacity as doctor, but rather only as a man worth knowing. I was a little afraid that I should have to go in to see him too but this wasn't required of me. Behind me to the left, I saw, sitting in a room literally surrounded by glass walls, a man who turned his back on me. It turned out that this man was the professor's secretary, that my father had in fact spoken only with him and not with the professor himself, but that somehow or other, through the secretary, he had recognized the excellences of the professor in the flesh, so that in every respect he was as much entitled to an opinion on the professor as if he had spoken to him in person.

Hopeless evening with the family today. My brother-in-law needs money for the factory, my father is upset because of my sister, because of the business, and because of his heart, my unhappy second sister, my mother unhappy about all of them, and I with my scribblings.

SEPTEMBER 24. My sister said: The house (in the story) is very like ours. I said: How? In that case, then, Father would have to be living in the toilet.

1913

FEBRUARY 11. While I read the proofs of *The Judgment,* I'll write down all the relationships which have become clear to me in the story as far as I now remember them. This is necessary because the story came out of me like a real birth, covered with filth and slime, and only I have the hand that can reach to the body itself and the strength of desire to do so:

The friend is the link between father and son, he is their strongest common bond. Sitting alone at his window, Georg rummages voluptuously in this consciousness of what they have in common, believes he has his father within him, and would be at peace with everything if it were not for a fleeting, sad thoughtfulness. In the course of the story the father, with the strengthened position that the other, lesser things they share in common give him—love, devotion to the mother, loyalty to her memory, the clientele that he (the father) had been the first to acquire for the business—uses the common bond of the friend to set himself up as Georg's antagonist. Georg is left with nothing; the bride, who lives in the story only in relation to the friend, that is, to what father and son have in common, is easily driven away by the father since no marriage has yet taken place, and so she cannot penetrate the circle of blood relationship that is drawn around father and son. What they have in common is built up entirely around the father, Georg can feel it only as something foreign, something that has become independent, that he has never given enough protection, that is exposed to Russian revolutions, and only because he himself has lost everything except his awareness of the father does the judgment, which closes off his father from him completely, have so strong an effect on him. . . .

AUGUST 15. Agonies in bed toward morning. Saw only solution in jumping out of the window. My mother came to my bedside and asked whether I had sent off the letter and whether it was my original text. I said it was the original text, but made even sharper. She said she does not understand me. I answered, she most certainly does not understand me, and by no means only in this matter. Later she asked me if I were going to write to Uncle Alfred, he deserved it. I asked why he deserved it. He has telegraphed, he has written, he has your welfare so much at heart. "These are simply formalities," I said, "he is a complete stranger to me, he misunderstands me entirely, he does not know what I want and need, I have nothing in common with him."

"So no one understands you," my mother said, "I suppose I am a stranger to you too, and your father as well. So we all want only what is bad for you."

"Certainly, you are all strangers to me, we are related only by blood, but that never shows itself. Of course you don't want what is bad for me."

Through this and several other observations of myself I have come to believe that there are possibilities in my ever-increasing inner decisiveness and conviction which may enable me to pass the test of marriage in spite of everything, and even to steer it in a direction favorable to my development. Of course, to a certain extent this is a belief that I grasp at when I am already on the window sill.

1914

JANUARY 4. We had scooped out a hollow in the sand, where we felt quite comfortable. At night we rolled up together inside the hollow, Father covered it over with the trunks of trees, scattering underbrush on top, and we were as well protected as we could be from storms and wild beasts. "Father," we would often call out in fright when it had already grown dark under the tree trunks and Father had still not appeared. But then we would see his feet through a crack, he would slide in beside us, would give each of us a little pat, for it calmed us to feel his hand, and then we would all fall asleep as it were together. In addition to our parents we were five boys and three girls; the hollow was too small for us, but we should have felt afraid if we had not been so close to one another at night.

The parents and their grown children, a son and a daughter, were seated at table Sunday noon. The mother had just stood up and was dipping the ladle into the round-bellied tureen to serve the soup, when suddenly the whole table lifted up, the tablecloth fluttered, the hands lying on the table slid off, the soup with its tumbling bacon balls spilled into the father's lap.

MAY 27. Mother and sister in Berlin. I shall be alone with my father in the evening. I think he is afraid to come up. Should I play cards [Karten] with him? (I find that letter K offensive, almost disgusting, and yet I use it; it must be very characteristic of me.) How Father acted when I touched F.

NOVEMBER 12. Parents who expect gratitude from their children (there are even some who insist on it) are like usurers who gladly risk their capital if only they receive interest.

DECEMBER 19. Yesterday I wrote "The Village Schoolmaster" almost without knowing it, but was afraid to go on writing later than a quarter to two; the fear was well founded, I slept hardly at all, merely suffered through perhaps three short dreams and was then in the office in the condition one would expect. Yesterday Father's reproaches on account of the factory: "You talked me into it." Then went home and calmly wrote for three hours in the consciousness that my guilt is beyond question, though not so great as Father pictures it. Today, Saturday, did not come to dinner, partly in fear of Father, partly in order to use the whole night for working; yet I wrote only one page that wasn't very good.

1916

OCTOBER 18. *From a letter to F.:* . . . I am descended from my parents, am linked to them and my sisters by blood, am sensible of it neither in my everyday affairs nor, as a result of their inevitable familiarity to me, in my special concerns, but at bottom have more respect for it than I realize. Sometimes this bond of blood too is the target of my hatred; the sight of the double bed at home, the used sheets, the nightshirts carefully laid out, can exasperate me to the point of nausea, can turn me inside out; it is as if I had not been definitively born, were continually born anew into the world out of the stale life in that stale room, had constantly to seek confirmation of myself there, were indissolubly joined with all that loathsomeness, in part even if not entirely, at least it still clogs my feet which want to run, they are still stuck fast in the original shapeless pulp. This is how it sometimes is.

But at other times again, I know that they are my parents after all, indispensable elements of my own being from whom I constantly draw strength, essential parts of me, not only obstacles. At such times I want them to be the best parents one could wish for: if I, in all my viciousness, rudeness, selfishness, and lack of affection, have nevertheless always trembled in front of them (and in fact do so today—such habits aren't broken), and if they again, Father from one side, Mother from the other, have inevitably almost broken my spirit, then I want them at least to be worthy of their victory. They have cheated me of what is mine and yet, without going insane, I can't revolt against the law of nature—and so hatred again and only hatred . . . .

1922

DECEMBER 2. Writing letters in my parents' room—the forms my decline takes are inconceivable! This thought lately, that as a little child I had been defeated by my father and because of ambition have never been able to quit the battlefield all these years despite the perpetual defeats I suffer . . . .

Chapter Three

Andrew Bihaly
1935-1968

AT THE AGE of thirty-three Andrew Bihaly attached a rubber tube to the jet of his two-burner stove, fastened a plastic bag around his head, ran the tube into it, and turned on the gas. The mass of written material found in his tenement on the Lower East Side of Manhattan supplied all the motives for the anxiety and despair that led to his suicide. But perhaps more important, it also recorded his heroic struggle to come to terms with a childhood whose traumas still haunted him as an adult.

Out of the repetitive welter of Andrew's undated notes, the novelist Anthony Tuttle has masterfully edited *The Journal of Andrew Bihaly* to produce not only a moving portrait of a child of the Holocaust, but also of a young man of the 1960's who placed his faith in the promises of the "Aquarian Age," with its ideals of communal generosity and unconditional love.

As Andrew seeks to live by these principles, sustaining himself with odd jobs and volunteer work, he uses his journal as his confessor, his analyst, his enspiriting friend. Among the deepest concerns of his writing is the influence of his mother upon his adult relations with women.

During World War II, Andrew's mother had him sent to a hostelry for delinquents to protect him from the Nazis. After her own internment in several concentration camps (Andrew's father having already been murdered during the Eichmann Death March), she and Andrew were finally rejoined and able to emigrate to the United States. Both that early abandonment and their uncertain new life in America exacted a terrible price.

As we read of Andrew's desperate efforts to draw the appropriate distinction between his old feelings and his present reality, we recognize in this extreme every boy's struggle toward autonomy. And through Andrew we understand once again that our parents are also the unwilling victims of their own histories.

English was Andrew's second language, learned as a teenager; under his pen his faulty syntax and vocabulary often yield a poetry all their own, which further illuminates the innocence of a vision unconscionably darkened by the times into which he and his parents were born.

. . . I was folding the laundry and Alfred comes in. He brings pot and we take a 'little' drag on the pipe and start talking. By the time we stop, it is darkening already. I said, "I have to free myself from my mother, and it is very difficult to stop believing what my mother told me to believe and to learn to do what I myself want to do." He told me, it is also very difficult to get away from his mother; he often wanted to kill her, now he is glad he doesn't have urges like that. I told him, I love my mother, but I have to be free from her. And he said, some of his friends remembered parts of their mother, a breast, a buttock, and they masturbated while they were thinking about it . . . .

This must be just another aspect of some people's lives. Some people dare to be more explicit about it, some people less so. But I am not hung up that way, and perhaps I am just allowing myself to realize the truth, that I've liberated myself from my mother for the first time in my life.

Actually for a while I was thinking about my mother, and what I would say to her if we got into an honest conversation. I want eventually to become friends with my mother.

A whole era of my life was with her and I must have inherited and later had to fight my mother's personality, and still must combat the kinds of images she gave me about society, women, and principles. The effect is coming out now.

It is evening. Mignone was just here for the last time. A big step to see whether I am healthy or whether I get depressed as when Alma left me. This may be the last love relationship where the girl was an image, a beautiful image upon whom I can project the image of my mother, love them with the innocence and devotion and tearfulness of falling in love with my mother—I, my subconscious.

The chief activity during these love encounters is crying. I cry because I am happy because I am with my mother again. I feel I must be protected again because I am afraid in the world. I am still a little boy and it is difficult for me to make the kind of steps that are possible in this land and at the same time love a woman with the thirst and patience and beneficence of wow.

Mignone came and packed her belongings in her luggage and took the diaphragm out of her bag and threw it in the garbage with a deft motion, with an intimate knowing smile she deftly put the diaphragm into the garbage bag. My former chick whom I supposedly showed how to make love . . . . And she kissed me, sadly it seemed, with her sad, long-drawn silent smile, a beautiful shimmer over her eyes—and I loved that in her, it reminded me of my mother. Now that I see it, I am crying—my mother's face makes me cry. Everything is happening today. Everything is coming together upon me today.

. . . I don't dare poke my head into the past, it is too daring, it will hurt and I am postponing it . . . . But I have to go back into my past, to 1944. During the Nazi occupation I was nine years old. On a hot summer day my mother told me that I had to leave home with a lady for a strange place, but she would come for me in a few days. She kissed me and hugged me and gave me a big bag of delicious candy.

And I saw her smile as I went away with the strange lady, who was a nurse.

The nurse took me by train from Budapest to a place called Visegrad and from the train, after a long walk up on a hill under the hot sun, to a huge, strange-looking building complex. There I saw priests in long robes, and many boys dressed in long gray uniforms which were too small on some boys, on the others too big. All the boys had their hair almost completely cut off, but not evenly cut. I had on well-cut summer shorts with sandals, and my blond hair was cut in style.

The lady who took me there turned me over to a priest, and she left.

The priest told me to go to the boys outside, and I did. When the boys saw that I had candy, they all asked for it. In the evening we went to sleep and nobody kissed me good-night. I cried in the dark.

I found out the boys were delinquents and I had been left in a reformatory. I was waiting for my mother to come for me, but she never came. I was punished there, so I thought I was a delinquent. I must have done something bad, that my mother had sent me there to be punished. She sent me away from her, she did not love me, she did not want me anymore. But what did I do? I didn't know.

After the war, I got back to our house. I rang our door-bell. A strange lady opened our door, and when she saw me she said to me, go away. She didn't let me in. And Alma didn't let me in either. I knew then that she did not love me anymore. But why? What did I do to her?

Beth, Anny's roommate, called me up, and she came over. I treated her beautifully. I placed on the tape recorder Renaissance music, prepared gourmant food, and put it down upon the rug. We ate and conversed in a pleasant way. But gradually something went wrong. I did not know what, but something was wrong with my mood. I got a sleepy, listless, sad feeling. I became glum. I stood up and moved the dishes from the carpet, and lay down next to her. I put my head upon her thigh and looked up at her; she reminded me of my mother. I wanted to tell her that but at first I couldn't find the language to say it.

I tried. I explained that this is one of my greatest troubles and I am trying to get over it, that whenever I am under a strain or tension,

I look up at a woman and, no matter how young she is, how unlikely the association, I feel she is my mother, she reminds me of my mother. She held my head close to herself, caressing it. We made a date for the following week at her place.

I became emotional again after Beth left.

It is a religious morning, made religious by incense and Baroque music, and a beautiful stream of white light streaming into the room from the window, my window, the window that somehow means life to me. My tree is alive in the summer with its green leaves just under my window. I feel closer to myself, I feel the existence in its most genuine form, that of pleasure, not orgiastic, but quiet and inner. Life at such times touches us, and our emotions surge forth. Now in the gleaming sunlight I perceive the tiniest Daliesque details; and everywhere I look my eyes become like magnifying instruments. I see the tree; now it is dizzy-looking in winter nature. I see the droplets of condensation upon the glass in which I poured the cold milk for my breakfast alone.

. . . Do I have an inferiority complex when I am with USA girls? I might have hit something potent here. An inferiority complex plus hate for myself . . . .

. . . Who am I? Where have I been? I push away the layers of memories. I repress them, I do not want to see old visions. I do not want to remember the summers with my governess in Hungary, in Budapest, our home there. Is it alright to remember? Is it alright to love your mother? Is it alright to remember the pain when my mother left me in the monastery? Is it alright to cry when the past hurts? Is it alright to cry when you feel the warm tits of a woman? No more sitting around. I want to do something about my life. Where am I? What am I doing?

. . . I must go back finally to the realities of my life, to the realities of the war. If it has to be, I have to intentionally bad-trip myself, because now I can do it. And if this is the thing that I need, let it be. Perhaps it is the way it must be; self-knowledge is freedom. But I was a little boy then, and yet, that is the thing, I still am the little boy. But I do not have to be that anymore. I can be a man now. But first I must describe as much about the war years as I can remember, and the more

I feel the more I will benefit by it. The first thing that occurs to me is
to cry, to desperately cry . . . .

. . . Oh, I'd love to be free, as free as when I was a child. I hate to
be afraid of life, I hate to be afraid of impotence when I am in bed with
a woman. If I can live my life just one year, no matter how old I am,
sexually free, really free, then I have worked for good ends. But let me
see how I feel about such things in one year. Life will pick up, there
is nowhere for it to go but to pick up. My fear has to give, I know my
fear will give, as I try more and more to relax, to make love perhaps
to the same woman repeatedly . . . . When I am confident, I will be
confident always. But I must keep working at it, every day, and then
I hope that by spring, when everything in nature is in love, the sun
with the sky, the earth sucking the raindrops, the birds calling for their
mates in my garden in the spring, then I will be free for love, I will be
a good lover . . . .

. . . here I am, having had a beautiful woman in my room—she
was friendly, telling me her most personal inner worries, and she
listened as I tried to give her a soothing answer from my personal point
of view. She left me with an inner quiet peace which she said I made
her feel, and to extend my hopes, she kissed me warmly before she
left. Yet why do I run from the realization that I become gloomy with
women? My gloom, in spite of all my efforts, pervades the atmosphere
and reverberates between us. It is fear in me. Fear also makes me
insensitive to the reactions of women. I cannot sense how they feel, so
I cannot easily respond to, or judge their reactions. I have a notion that
I leave a woman ice cold sexually, because I feel ice cold. It is the effect
of fear. But what am I afraid of? Am I afraid they will run away if I
touch them, that I will be left alone, like I was left alone by my mother
when she was taken to concentration camps? Then I had the awareness,
'I must have done something wrong,' otherwise she could not have left
me. It is like an echo, 'Chicks must be on a pedestal, not to be fresh
with. You must keep your hands to yourself,' and I feel the pain and
I cannot touch the girl. I hear a muffled echo, I cannot cry, the pain
chokes me, I am left alone . . . .

And the fear descends upon me like a net, pulling my head down-
ward, to my limbs . . . .

28

. . . Erotic comfort shimmers in every one of my ligaments. I remember Mira. I told her last night, "Your ass is oval, white, gently curving, round with little cheeks, and I love it." She is so girlish, a little girl-woman. I told her about the war. She understands me, she is Jewish. She listened last night as I told her about my life. She held me tight. I writhed with my memories for a long time. But slowly I became tranquil, and gradually I began to tingle with passion. It was phenomenal, I enjoyed her so much. And oh, it was an erotic night. In the morning we took a bath and she caressed my softly washed hair, which brought back memories of my childhood. While we were eating breakfast I told her, "My personality disintegrates if I limit myself to an exclusive relationship with one woman; I become frightened that she will leave me, because of my bad experience during the war with my mother. I become insecure, I become impossible to relate to." I talked about my writing, how it had a therapeutic value for me.

We walked the few blocks from her house to the subway with a friendship bond between us, a love. She was wearing a nice, warm wintercoat. But I kind of like the feeling of disintegration in clothing. Torn things are somehow nice to wear, it represents your sentiment.

A long, long time ago, when I arrived at Visegrad, the correction house, 'Javitointézet,' I had candy with me. The boys, who were marched in columns, seeing that the priests said it was all right, surrounded me, and I gave away all my candy. A whole bagful. Some of the boys stuffed candy into their mouths and stuck their hands repeatedly in front of me for as long as I had candy . . . . But when I did not have any more candy, I was alone for the first time in my life all alone and I was only nine, a little blond boy, skinny, frightened. I needed a friend then very much. And a boy came over, put his hand on my shoulder and acted as my friend, and soon he asked me: "Do you have any more candy?" and I told him, "No, I gave it all out." He turned immediately and left me standing. I had friends later, but it is hard for me to trust anyone, and it is very hard for me to give anything to anyone, to share my things.

Anny and Honey and Beth came to visit me . . . someone . . . gave them each a box of all sorts of rich, expensively wrapped candies . . . . As I was unwrapping and eating the candies, gradually the past started to haunt me. They were the same kind as those that my mother had given me before she sent me away. And I remembered the pain those candies caused me in the correction house.

Yesterday I took the candies and walked with the box through Christy Street, one of the poorest Puerto Rican slum streets. The box fell and all those beautifully wrapped candies scattered upon the gray, dusty sidewalk. I picked them all up and gave one to each of the kids who came over to watch—they were dressed up prettily for Sunday. Their mothers stood close by, gossipping together in a little group. They stared at me. I was rich and they were poor, since I gave away the shiny candies. But then I became scared and started to run—running out from the monastery . . . .

At Tompkins Square, breathless, with my heart throbbing, clutching what was left of the candies, I gave them to the young people who looked like hippies, and I became calm.

On the Lower East Side, boys and girls, 'hippies' who have long hair, sit in a group in the middle of Tompkins Park. When they accumulate, they sing and get high. Then the cops come. They don't like what the hippies enjoy, it does not suit them and they pull these young people apart and drag them away. The rules do not have to be so exact, friends. Fellow species, the rules can be looser. We must give freedom to hug and kiss. We must speak to each other, and laugh together instead of being strangers to each other; we must be able to look our friends eye to eye, we must not teach that you must mistrust your brother, he might take your candies away, or the man might rape you . . . .

LOVE IS LIFE—Hate and Fear is chaos.

. . . I sit in a small psychedelic shop on Avenue A, off Tompkins Square Park . . . Her eye catches mine. She sings the song that her accompanist is playing on an organ. It is haunting, meandering—it brings back memories from a church, a church in Visegrad. I look in the eyes of the woman, she smiles at me, I am unable to communicate with her. I am sad, I feel tears around the edges of my eyes. I smile, I am possessed by her smiling eyes, her beautiful lips. I don't know what to do. She sees someone, goes to talk to him. I close my eyes. When I open them she is gone.

I feel my emotions. My pain is real to me, it is intense, choking, prolonged. I am literally squeezing back tears. The reason for my feelings, I don't see the woman . . . . Whenever I come in contact with a woman, I become melancholy, blue, sad. I feel tired, very tired. Oh how very much I want to bury my head in a soft woman's lap and cry and say how deeply lonely I feel.

I come home. It's drizzling. I cry a little, goading myself to let my feelings go; I want to be free of it, of this sadness.

My depressions are very forceful, but on the other side of them lies a world of adventure and fascination. Warmth, a friendliness for the world. But in my world there is pain and a consciousness that is gray and green and mean. Full of fear and worry and punctuated by a wish to commit suicide. It often comes in the morning, I wake up with it.

I write words in my uncertainties. What can words express?

I sit in the garden. The house is neglected now, no one sweeps it. I pick up the papers from the yard, but people on the higher floors throw down paper cups, bones, bread and cigarette butts, and I pick them up again. Alfred left a gas range in the yard, it has been here for many weeks. Then came a broken refrigerator and other junk.

I shall have to call up the Sanitation Department. I will put out the junk in front of the house, to be taken away, and I will sweep out the house again.

Chapter Four

Michael Rubin

URING MY OWN prolonged struggle to put the past in its
place in order to live with a greater sense of independence
from family influences, in 1972 I underwent a form of intensive therapy
whose initial phase prescribed three weeks of social isolation. Long,
empty, inactive hours alone surrounded each day's open-ended private
therapy session and twice-weekly group meetings. Those hours spent
without recourse to my usual defenses against my feelings were as
revealing to me as those hours spent with my therapist. Though written
against direct orders, the journal I kept during these three weeks in
"isolation" also proved to be a valuable tool for this work. Offered here
from *In the Middle of Things* are excerpts dealing with aspects of my
relationship with my parents as understood through this therapy.

Eight previous years of orthodox psychoanalysis did not give me
nearly as much practical help as did this intensive approach. The difference lay for me in its deliberate emphasis on the direct expression
of feelings, both current and abreactive. The endless talk of psychoanalysis had only enhanced my skill at the verbal games that kept me
from the heart of many unresolved problems. But Rhoda, my intensive

therapist, insisted on an emotional response to every dredged memory which, when expressed, brought me astounding new insights into its impact on my life. With these techniques I also began to learn how to "feel my feelings" as they arose instead of acting them out in self-destructive or ineffectual ways in order to avoid feeling their significance. This belated rite of passage has helped me to deal more wisely with the legacies of my past. Though my life is still informed by my childhood, I no longer live a life so deeply designed to satisfy childhood needs that were not and will never be met.

Monday

1:05 P.M.   . . . Rhoda knocked at my door at 9:30. Asked me to come upstairs. Immediate dislike for her noncommittal sternness— a professional manner she's probably learned from some gaddamn textbook, or finds necessary to keep her protected from the maniacs. . . .

In the semi-darkened office she tells me to lie down on a black leather mat, a box of tissues nearby. She asks me to breathe deeply— arms spread out, legs spread out, making me feel awfully vulnerable. Always dutiful, I do as directed and feel myself beginning to get dizzy from so much deep breathing.

Does she sense it? She says, "Say, 'Mama.'"

Like a baby doll, I say, "Mama."

She says, "Again."

"Mama," I say. Then again. And again.

I don't know how or why, but eventually I begin to say it for its own sake, and at Rhoda's suggestion, louder and louder: "Mama. Mama! Mama!!"

And before I know what's happening I find myself weeping and then screaming it out, calling for her: "Mama. Mama. Mama!!"

Rhoda tells me to pound the mat.

I scream louder. I pound. Pound. Pound.

Eventually she asks, "What are you feeling?"

I have to think to define the heat and the constrictions in my body. "Anger," I tell her, though I'm not sure *why* I feel angry. "Fear," I say, though I'm not sure why I should be feeling afraid.

"Let it out!" Rhoda shouts. "Feel it. Feel it!". . .

Tuesday

9:15 P.M. . . . I got into hell tonight more quickly than I'd imagined I could. Rhoda, who was one of the therapists working this evening, helped me get there fast. As usual she asked me to start by breathing deeply, then she simply said, "Let it out."

It came. Oh, it came. My weeping, howling, cursing, and exhausted pauses lasted close to an hour and a half. I started by calling out my need for my mother again. Felt my gorge rise. Got angry and blamed the knots in my stomach on her once more. Asked her again how much I had to hurt to make her know I loved her? Why didn't she return it? On and on. The same stuff as this morning, but just as deeply felt. Tissues, damp and crumpled tissues everywhere.

Then I began to realize—no, to *feel*— that everything, all those childhood fears of mine were the result of not having had enough of her. I begged her for more attention, more love, screamed with rage when I couldn't have it. And this new insight: All the crying I'd done during childhood, in adolescence, on into my twenties and even after her death had come out of that one damned theme: my original unfulfilled need of her.

Why else did I feel such misery all my life or go to such extremes to try to believe she was mine? No, she was no Jewish Mother as Rhoda would have me think. I was not her Little Man. She didn't smother me. But I clung to her, all right! I clung to her because I was never sure of ever *having* her. . . .

Wednesday

10:45 A.M.   Rhoda just told me to take the night off but not to talk to anyone. "Don't talk away these feelings, Mike." I suppose I shouldn't be writing them away either, but I'm feeling so much even as I write this down that it seems impossible to do so. Right now I'm shaking like a leaf with cold, and crying, crying as I hear someone upstairs screaming for his life as I just now screamed for mine.

It's true. God, at least it *feels* so true! I can't recall any order to all this now, but I know we started today by my telling Rhoda about my feelings for her last night (something I didn't even admit to myself yesterday while it was actually happening); that is, my angry feeling of unwillingness during group to share her with anyone else there, the jealousy I felt when she went away from me. And then when she came near me again, the immediate resentment for feeling called on to *perform* for her to keep her there. Mother, Mother, of course—instant transference. Rhoda made me rage at that. Then to call for my mother's love again. Call. Rage at its never coming. Call again. Rage again for having to earn attention by performing for it. Call for it. And rage. It was endless, endless, but I didn't want it to stop. . . .

Then once more I find myself insisting that my mother had *real* grief. I saw it in her eyes. She was a terribly unhappy woman. And I always felt so responsible for adding to her misery. But then I'm suddenly angry again because it was *her* grief, *her* sick life, and not my fault at all! . . .

I remembered then how often she used to go to the movies alone in the afternoon when I was a kid. Somehow I sensed she always went when she was unhappy. At the time I could only assume—or did she somehow imply it?—that my sister and I had made her miserable and driven her away. We were her grief. We made her unhappy. But of course I could win her back again by being extra-specially good to her when she came home, couldn't I? Always the good one, being what she wanted me to be, being *her*, God damn it, suffering *her* pain instead of my own.

Rhoda asks if I ever cried at the movies as I'd seen my mother do sometimes when she took me along with her. Instantly I recall the final scenes from the original version of that Fanny Hurst tear-jerker *Imitation of Life*: While watching her dead black mother go by in a hearse, the daughter who's been passing for white, breaks out from the crowd to scream, "Mammy! Mammy!" and begins tearing at the coffin to get to her mother.

The memory makes me roll on the floor in agony. When I first saw that movie, I'd wept my heart out. But I was only around ten at the time. Already I must have felt a complicated identification with both figures—the daughter, guilt-ridden for having hurt her mother so, and the mother in the coffin who had suffered her daughter's cruel denial of love. I was both mother and child.

But when I tell Rhoda this, she says I was crying for *myself*, not for the daughter, not for the mother—not even for my own dead mother. We can't really feel anyone's pain but our own, she insists, and I denied this by taking up my mother's grief as my own, the movie mother's for mine. . . .

Thursday

6:20 P.M. A full afternoon. Around three I took to the floor of my room for a long warm-up before my session upstairs. Several motives I see for doing this kind of preparation now: It keeps me closely in touch with my pain. It also makes it easier to get into a greater intensity later on—again today I went into Rhoda's office with eyes already streaming and tissues to the nose. But I'm afraid that's where a baser reason shows through: Within me still is the neurotic little boy saying, "Look, Mommy, look how hard I'm trying for you, look how good at my therapy I am!" I want to earn my gold medal from Rhoda. I want to be her model patient just as I wanted to be my mother's model son. I did the same damn thing with Dr. M, playing the good little analysand and doing his dream homework for his analyst's love. And, oh, how I resented it when the reward wasn't forthcoming. But *knowing* that didn't stop me from doing it then and doesn't seem to stop me from doing it now. It just adds an edge of irony, damn it! If, maybe, this time I can feel deeply enough the pain of so desperately needing my mother's approval, maybe I'll find this less-than-helpful motive diminishing more and more. Maybe, maybe. . . .

And another movie came to mind while I was up there on the floor today. *Little Men.* One of Jo's orphaned boys does something wrong. To punish him, she gives him a ruler and asks him to hit her hands hard, to *hurt* her with the ruler by hitting her hands. He can barely lift the stick to do it. She insists. Slowly he begins to hit her and is crying out his heart for hurting her this way. Goddamn it, when I saw that scene in a TV rerun once long ago, I thought, "What a beautiful and fitting punishment." That little kid would never do that bad thing again, not when it meant hurting the only woman in the world he loved and who loved him! Oh, but today I suddenly felt the awful tyranny in it! Even now as I write it down, I'm feeling the brute injustice against that little boy! The coercion, the emotional blackmail, the crime committed against his tenderness in the name of virtue! Up against the wall, Louisa May Alcott!

I told Rhoda that that was exactly the kind of pressure my mother practiced on me. And I *accepted* it, turned myself into a guilty sinner for her—for making her sad, for hurting her! Rhoda told me to tell dear old Mom. I did, again and again—screamed it out until I was sure she was hearing it in her grave. . . .

Then, damn it, my rational mind intruded again. How could I blame her for it? How—when she was fucked up by *her* mother who must have been fucked up by *her* mother somewhere in the wilds of the Ukraine.

"A little kid doesn't know that," Rhoda said.

"That's right!" I shouted. "A little kid doesn't know that, Mother!"

Sure, sure, as an adult I can forgive her her sorry ignorance of herself, her awful misery. But as a little boy inside still, the little boy who's always been there looking for what he never had, I can only hate her for it still. Hate her! . . .

"Oh God, I have no one to hold onto but *me*, Rhoda. If I don't hold myself, no one will."

And that's when the worst of it began today. As I lay there on the mat I finally knew that I really had to hate my mother as fully as possible in order to let myself live on my own terms at last. The thought alone was enough to drown me in tears again.

"I don't want to hate you!" I cried. My God, to say "I hate you!" and *mean* it? "I can't say it, Rhoda."

"Why not?"

"It would be like killing her." Like killing my own mother! I never had her the way I needed her, I know that now, but I couldn't kill the little I *did* have. "But I have to—I have to—". . .

And when I was done, felt desolately alone. The aloneness that was always there, but which I could never admit to for fear it would destroy me. The aloneness I defended myself from with acts of piety, silence, obedience. Incorporating my mother into myself like some fucking holy wafer.

"Get out of me!" I cried over and over in one more frenzy.

An effective exorcism? The dybbuk removed? I don't know. I knew she couldn't hear. Hadn't heard it while she lived, wouldn't hear it in her coffin. But I screamed it all out at her anyway. . . .

When I lay there spent and sweating, Rhoda asked, "How do you feel now, Mike?"

"I don't know if there's any lasting value in this," I said, "but right now it's sure as hell therapeutic."

"More of it tonight," she said with a lovely laugh.

Saturday

8:30 A.M. Slept well enough last night but found myself up at first light. Immediately flooded by memories of Dad. The power of yesterday's session? Tossed and turned on the verge of tears but foolishly fought them back. The old survival operation.

Deliberately I searched my mind for good times with Daddy: Trips to Prospect Park Zoo on Sunday morning. Running between his legs to be caught and allowed to escape, then running in for the playful struggle again. Being carried out on his shoulders into the "deep water" at Riis Park or Brighton Beach. Feeling very secure and proud up there. Climbing the highest hill in Brooklyn with him one afternoon. . . .

One most important good memory: summer at the Hermitage. Age seven or eight. One Friday evening after the daddies had come up from the city, mine said, "Let's go for a swim." It was past swimming time and had started to rain a little; no one else was in that pool but my father and I. Delicious. Sinful. He was a great swimmer . . . . But I was swimming well and seemed to be impressing him. God, it was so quiet there—just the two of us—and that delightful threat as the rain hit the water. To make him laugh I said, "Hey, we'll get wet!" And he laughed. I never wanted it to end. . . .

Hell, so much of this seems trivial now. So much a deliberate wish to make a *case* against my father. Every kid goes through similar trials, doesn't he? Why should I bring in so overwhelming an indictment on such slim evidence. It makes me feel fraudulent, ungrateful. Do I really want to get angry at these unavoidable disasters?

(But that little kid knew them only as disasters, Dad! "Be that little kid, Mike. Feel it as you truly felt it then," I hear Rhoda saying in my mind. . . .)

When my two-year-old sister came nosing around the table while my parents were having dinner one night, Daddy pushed a cupcake in her face. Little Mickey wouldn't snoop near Daddy's dessert like that. Not he. He doesn't want to be hurt by Daddy like sister was. He's older. Better. He'll steal a cupcake later when no one's looking.

"Let's find out what's inside the beanbag, Sister."

We open it together and oops—the beans spill out.

"They're beans. That's interesting. That's what makes the noise and feels so funny."

Uh-oh—Daddy's coming. He doesn't like what we've done. He's sending us to bed.

"But we just wanted to see—"

He's coming at us with a strap now. He's hitting me with his belt—because I opened a beanbag!

Sister's throwing another tantrum and now Daddy is pushing her face down near her own vomit to make her smell her mess like a dog. Little Mickey will never throw up. He doesn't want his face in vomit.

39

He won't scream like sister does. She's the bad one. Mickey's good. Mickey will be loved. Look how good I'm being, Mommy. Look, Daddy! Stay away from me, Daddy! . . .

10:00 P.M. When it grew colder tonight, I returned to my room on the run . . . feeling fully that endlessly welling grief for never having had enough love, and often fooling myself into thinking if I worked hard enough for it I would find it.

More tears. Deep breaths. The tingling feeling. More pain.

During a lull I wanted to look at my watch—and realized what I was looking for again was elapsed time, hoping it was late enough to end my torture. I laughed and screamed aloud: "It's never going to end! It's there—that emptiness—and it'll always be there! *Now* you know why you're so conscious of the goddamn clock! You think that there's a time limit to this pain! That Mommy will make the hurt go away, that if you wait long enough, are *good* enough, you're going to be granted happiness! That's why your head's always living in the future! Well, you know what your happiness is going to be? Knowing that there's no hope for that kind of happiness and being able to feel your outrage as deeply as you're feeling it now! At least you won't be searching for illusions of relief from that terrible knowledge anymore! At least you'll know the goddamn score! Zero! Zero! Feel that zero! *Feel it!*"

More tears and more.

It came and went, not with greater intensity than it first had, and often with just vaguely hurting lulls. But I knew what the pain was and I sat with it until now. . . .

Monday

5:30 P.M. Rough start to today's session. Went in complaining again about my incessant need to organize things, imagining how the sessions should go, so fearful of a life unplanned, of spontaneity, of imperfection. . . .

Began thinking how my mother always kept my father and me apart—never allowing me to say a straight word to him or to make him angry—and realized how similar it must have been in her own life with her own domineering father. . . .

Suddenly I felt my whole lifetime of unfairness to my father and sobbed. Then I realized that my first erotic fantasies had obliquely been about him. Relating him to the picture of an ogre in a book of fairy tales at the age of eight, I'd wanted to crawl up the hairs of the giant's leg.

"Why?" asked Rhoda.

"To get into his arms. To feel his strength. I needed him. His muscles.". . .

"You wanted him to hold you. You needed him. That's a feeling. Feel it!"

Oh, boy, I felt it. Cried out in need of him. Wanted my father to hold me. To hold me. To love me. Protect me. To make me feel loved by him. And behind those tears and screams of need, hating the sense that he never was, never would be mine, and that the feeling had to be felt like this and accepted as did the futility of that need ever being fulfilled.

Sunday

10:15 A.M. A morning in the park to watch the Fathers and Sons. . . .

One father is reading his Sunday paper while pushing his daughter's swing. . . .

Oh God, another father is not handling at all well his little son's fear of a swing! The boy won't attempt one whose height is really more suitable for him, but his father doesn't seem to care. The boy's younger sister is swinging nicely on one the same height as his, and the father is indicating this by a disregard for his son's declaration that he's swinging higher.

The boy's physical cowardice reminds me of my own. His father's indifference *my* father's.

"Hey, Daddy, watch how fast I go!" the boy shouts now. . . .

That fuck-up is *still* across the park with his daughter while the boy now sits forlornly on the lower swing repeating, "Daddy, Daddy, Daddy. . . ."

I'm not making this up, damn it! It's happening right before my eyes. I'm holding back a sudden swell of tears. What can I do? Rush to the swing to push the kid, which would probably frighten him to death, or create hostility in his father, and at best give the boy only a sorry substitute for what he needs? . . .

"Push me, Daddy!"

"Get on the higher one," the father stipulates.

The boy goes. Tries it—doesn't seem too frightened. But stops as soon as the father turns away after registering again only the scantest interest in his son's brave attempt to do his bidding. Back to the lower swing now, calling, "Push me, Daddy!"

He doesn't want to go high! He doesn't even want to be pushed! He wants to be *loved,* you fucker!

The father comes over at last and pushes, but with the question: "How come you switched swings?"

The boy doesn't answer. It would be a forced confession of cowardice. And he's fool enough now to be happy that his bastard of a father is near him for a little. Stay with him, please, damn you! Don't desert him again. Your daughter's perfectly content over there, not even looking for you. Push *him.* Push *him!* Not too high!

Damn it, you pushed too *hard!*

The boy's afraid now. He scuffs his shoes to stop.

"What are you doing to your shoes?" the fuck-up complains.

"I want to go on the slide." The boy runs away from his father.

The father looks at the sky.

I'm the only one crying around here!

42

Part Two
Idealists

Chapter Five

Otto
Braun
1897-1918

DURING HIS SHORT but enviable life, Otto Braun considered his parents to be his most intimate friends. Along with their trust, they also endowed him, apparently, with all their sensitivity and intelligence. Such advantages enabled this much loved son of well-connected German progressives to pursue his own growth with remarkable self-assurance. Always a joyful scholar, Otto endured an uninspiring time in a self-governing school community at Wickersdorf, and at a Berlin *Gymnasium*, before being entrusted to private tutors at his parents' comfortable home in Bavaria. Poetry, music and art, history, politics, the natural sciences, and especially the classics, Otto's deep and varied interests were zealously explored with a keen and creative mind that was further enriched by his summer travels.

"Thou shalt be a Titan!" he writes at the age of eleven as part of a twenty-article creed that reads, surprisingly, without arrogance since his emergent sense of his own genius also demands of him a responsibility to develop his talents as seriously as he might. "Thou shouldst have great passions," he proclaims in another rule for his conduct, "and thou shouldst know how to fight them."

The purity of these adolescent ideals is as awesome to contemplate as are his prodigious capacities. And his belief in the power of the Will, as well as his devotion to the new German State, is almost frightening to consider. But while reading the diaries that Otto Braun kept from the age of seven until two days before his death, any adult will surely recall the high-minded dreams of his or her own adolescence, those urgent times when one yearned for connection with the grand ideas and events beyond one's garden wall. To remember that this aspiring Titan is still just a boy is also a source of amusement, amusement that turns to dismay when, in seeking transcendence, the boy becomes a soldier at seventeen, is wounded, but goes back to the front to be killed by a shell at Marcelcave in northeast France at the age of twenty-one.

1907

13TH JANUARY. . . . Anna ordered me, just as if I were her slave, to "pack everything away neatly, each in its box, for tomorrow I have to clean. What isn't put away I shall sweep up!" That made me feel for the first time that there are ways and ways of giving orders, and ways and ways of obeying them. I had up till now held the point of view of Fortunatus; I had always wanted to achieve big things, but in the way he did. Now I feel that I am not made to follow, I am made to lead. I feel that I shall one day be something great. But proud I never will be, the gods forbid! Dreams particularly make me realise this.

1908

6TH AUGUST. This morning we went to Garmisch to fetch Frau K. and O. Then we drove back in the carriage. I showed O. all my things straight away and we were very happy. But the real holiday mood was gone. No more walks to the Badersee, no more pleasant talks, no more tranquil evenings bathed in the Alpine glow, by which we used so peacefully to wander along the road to the Eibsee. A new and different mood had taken possession of me. But I didn't like it half as much as the earlier one. Sad, and yet happy, I went to bed. It was the first day on which I lost more than I gained.

9TH AUGUST. Today was the fateful day on which I had to say good-bye to mother, to Bavaria, to the mountains, the day on which I had to return to Wickersdorf. I shed but few tears at parting, for when I am really in trouble I suffer in silence and do not show it to the world. In the train I read Selma Lagerlöf's *Antichrist*.

BERLIN, OCTOBER. I have been having a terribly difficult time since September 3, and even before. I am continually home-sick and depressed. I have tried to express these moods in poems.

5TH OCTOBER. Everything is alive. I am once more in the right mood. I have changed from a stay-at-home into a living being. I'm quite astounded at myself, and keep on asking myself whether I am still in that prison-house, Wickersdorf, which deadened all my feelings and weighed down my whole being with an oppressive armour of reason. Now I've shaken off the last vestiges of it, it lies in fragments at my feet, and the gracious gods are approaching. I am free once more, a life-giving, creative human being. All that was dead is shaken off, all that was evil and ugly has been transmuted and spiritualized. I have passed through one stage of my development, the stage full of cobwebs and dust, of rage within, pearls without. Away with the past, let us look into the future! There, not in the past, lies happiness. A new life has begun.

OCTOBER. On our arrival in Berlin I was, mentally, in rather an unsettled state and had to fight a hard battle till I got to the point of being able to write the *Anti-Christendom* and my latest poems. I'm quite certain the first great victory was on October 5. Then followed blow upon blow, it *was* a battle! . . . Wickersdorf has been of great use to me, as has the development I went through there. Now, of course, I have reached quite opposite views. But it was at Wickersdorf that I learnt to work, I had very bitter inner conflicts there (—and later too), and they have helped me most of all.

1909

22ND NOVEMBER. Great men must have terrific passions, and such wills, such self-control, that in a way they need only press a button to keep them back or let them out. Napoleon had that power, and chiefly therein, I expect, lay his great genius. What I said is true of moods, too. If you have always got to wait till nature or God puts you into the right mood, it isn't worth much. Of course, there will always be times when one is so completely swept off one's feet by a subject, that one is especially capable of doing creative work. But you can't count on these moods. Strength of will is everything, nothing can be achieved without it.

1910

20TH JANUARY. It is curious that in the darkness one can see even the tiniest glow, while in broad daylight it is difficult to see the biggest fire; I believe the same is true of human beings.

10TH FEBRUARY. I had a very interesting talk with father this morning. There is so much which leaves me unsatisfied at present. What is the purpose of Man, what is his origin? Where does all Life spring from, where do all things start?,

JULY. I am keeping this diary in order to account to myself, in order to be absolutely honest—toward myself. . . .

14TH SEPTEMBER. I've now read the first chapter of *Zarathustra* slowly over and over again. I'm still under the influence of the book to such an extent that I can say nothing. Just one thing: it is curious that I never heard of the principle of "self-realisation to the uttermost" from Nietzsche, only that of the *highest* fulfillment of duty, but in a different sense from the ordinary, of course. When I'd finished the chapter I took my Latin book and worked like mad, instead of reading another chapter, which I might have done. However, "what is difficulty? Thus asks the willing mind, thus it kneels like the camel wanting to be well-laden." But the parasites of humanity—and there are far too many of them—those who indulge their lusts and their coarse pleasures, their laziness and their decadence under the cloak of Nietzsche, they are his real enemies; the sort of people who do not wish to burden their minds with anything weightier than cigarette smoke, a few Beardsley drawings, and the rather more elaborately and ingeniously vicious novels of the Rococo. Generally speaking, one of the hereditary faults of the Germans seems to be that they are always anxious to find a moral justification for their vulgarities.

19TH NOVEMBER. I wouldn't mind anything now if I only had some real work to do. I relieve my mind by writing this down: as soon as I have finished working at the *History of Literature*, I shall start *Political Economy*. It seems to be the foundation of all politics and of all knowledge—all earthly knowledge. I want to be of this world, quite of this world. But at present I want very much to do some *creative* work. Something within me is urging me to it; there's something in me that must come out and that it will not come out makes me quite unhappy. Every evening I go to sleep with a bad conscience and awake with it in the morning. It's beastly, and I want to get rid of it. Passive study alone doesn't satisfy me. I'm quite sure that nothing could ever completely satisfy me but creative work, no pleasure, no reading, no love, no physical occupation. Nothing at all. . . .

1911

16TH MAY. Home again at last. It was delightful to be with Pa again and in our little house. And I can't measure the good this journey will have done me. I hope that I have got over that awful feeling of want of confidence for the present. I'm overflowing with ideas and ideas in the making. The garden is beautiful beyond conception; an immense roof of oak-leaves and below it lilies of the valley and flowering shrubs.

4TH JUNE. Life cannot exist without devotion to an ideal, which one must have conceived for oneself. For life is struggle, struggle for an object. But this implies devotion to a cause, giving oneself up completely to something.

29TH JULY. I am working tremendously. Before I went to Florence I had the time, but no ideas and no thoughts. Now that I have got the ideas, I have no time. But I prefer this state of affairs. For ideas are within you and can be grasped, even if they are not put into execution immediately. Time, however, lies outside us and so can only be made use of when we have it; it cannot be stored. . . .

7TH OCTOBER. What Lange says (in the second chapter) about the law of the struggle for supremacy is excellent. But his apparent assumption that everybody is equal from birth seems remarkable. If that were the case, then the cry for equality, which he thinks justifiable because of it, would be awful. If everybody obtained the same powers from the same mental nourishment—*ugh*! Zeus protect me from the world! No, it is because all people are unequal, and only because of that, that I want absolute equality of conditions.

1912

FEBRUARY. One of the worst vices of our age is that we are never at rest, we want to be present at everything, we are anxious when we miss anything, in short, we do not carry balance and poise in ourselves nor breast the current of life with complete self-assurance. Men are more varied in their interests without being more self-contained. We have lost the art of solitude which is so necessary to true inspiration. And as I am firmly convinced that the only way of correcting one's own faults is to recognize them and keep them constantly in mind, I will not hide from myself that I have been bitten by this evil too. Therefore, I shall put at the beginning of this volume the bold and defiant phrase: "Be sufficient unto thyself!"

2ND MARCH. I have found out, to my great regret, that I cannot keep to my work properly. I sometimes steal a few hours, but these continual diversions keep me from getting my ideas into shape, and even from thinking them out properly . . . . I do not know what to make of it. At first, of course, I was annoyed, but then I thought that it may be quite good at my age to be forced not to turn out too much, but to absorb instead, so that one can accumulate a store of energy. I am not sure that this is right; at first it was only said as a consolation but now it seems to me fairly convincing. At any rate I am longing for the holidays, when I can at least get something done. Of course, the things that interrupt me give me great pleasure too. Today I read eight pages of Homer. How divinely beautiful is that Sixth Song. It shines like white-armed Nausicaa in Ulysses' wonderful Introduction. Then Plato.

1913

1ST FEBRUARY. In the morning I read an article of Maeterlinck's in the *Neue Rundschau*, on psychical research and the phenomena connected with it. I learned one thing from it; it is a subject that I may not take up. I have a strong sense of duty and I know that neither am I now, nor shall I ever be, entitled to do just what I like or what pleases me. I do not know whether other people feel the same, but there is no doubt about it for me. And there is no doubt in my mind that I am watched over by a *Daimon,* as powerful as Socrates'— an infallible star which, while it leaves me undisputed responsibility in the choice of things, guides me in everything which does not depend on my personal decision; and which, above all, enables me to make up my own mind. I do not know whither I am going, but I do know that if I keep in mind what I have just said, I shall certainly go in the right direction. . . .

26TH JUNE. Glancing over this year of my life, the second half was unusually beautiful. The gradual development in me of the idea of God seems particularly important. My ardour for all things grows more intense, my soul is growing stronger and purer. I have grown out of that lack of concentration which troubled me last year. So I look into the future with hopeful expectancy, and am ardently longing for its beauty and its richness.

1914

2ND AUGUST. I enrolled as a volunteer. They advised me not to at the military H.Q. of the District Council; they told me that volunteers would hardly be accepted. If only I were already called to the colours!

4TH AUGUST. In the morning to Berlin in one of the few trains that were still running . . . . Now is the time when all elemental emotions are brought into the foreground, pain, brotherliness, readiness to help, manliness. Everyone is thinking of his rightful duties and tasks. All are united in one mighty aim, all trivial things vanish. . . . Then we went to the Reichstag. One of the greatest days one could live through, for, however it may end, this 4th of August is immortal.

The Chancellor's face was almost tragic.

18TH AUGUST. Had a long talk with Pa about my joining the Army. I believe this war has come to our time and to every individual as a fiery test to make men of us all, men prepared for the terrific events in the years to come.

17TH SEPTEMBER *Before leaving for his regiment.* So I will end this book. All my longing and all my desire I poured out to the gods yesterday, in a prayer prouder and humbler than any before. I am setting out in great joy and expectation, not in search of adventure and the spurious excitement of unknown experiences, but in the firm belief and hope that I shall become manly and firm, fully developed, broad-minded, full of power and strength, in readiness for the great life which will be waiting for me later on.

That on my return from battle and victory, honourably endured, I may find my parents with many hopes fulfilled and happy in new work, that I may find myself again, well and strong and ready for anything the world may offer, that I may find my country again, grown prouder and yet more modest, stronger and more courageous, pregnant with the rising form of the new era—in spite of the conflicts and the raging storms of the yet unredeemed future; that I may play my part in helping to create this new era in the spirit of the still sleeping godhead; this, oh ye ruling powers, I hope for, I implore, nay I demand, of you.

Chapter Six

Alan Seeger
1888-1916

THERE ARE TWO SIDES to every war. For his own high-minded motives, the young American poet Alan Seeger also went off to do battle while living in Paris at the start of World War I, immediately joining the French Foreign Legion as part of the American Volunteer Corps. One might wish that Seeger had questioned more closely the nature of men's penchant for violence, what of warfare is socially induced, what is innate, what concepts of masculinity are thought at stake. But Seeger's passions are those of the idealist—the dedication to the greater cause—and the glories of the sacrifice. From all the war diaries consulted, it is with deliberate irony that I chose to include here the one of a romantic young man who had to bide his impatient time digging trenches, cutting wood, carrying up ammunition, and standing watch for many miserable months of trench life before finally being allowed his own "testing ground for valor," which gave him the glory he craved and then killed him.

No swashbuckling adventurer, Alan Seeger had always been far more innocent and chivalric in his vision. And at the front he found a focus for his ideals, as well as the discipline that his desultory bohemian life in New York and Paris had lacked, and the brotherhood of men in a group facing "a common danger to be shared and overcome, not shunned."

Who can say how important a poet he might have become? But warfare certainly deepened his poetic impulse as it did his descriptive powers as a correspondent for the New York *Sun* and *New Republic*. "I have a rendezvous with Death," Seeger writes in his most famous and prophetic poem. He met it at Belloy-en-Santerre on July 4, 1916 while running forward, bayonet fixed, to fall among his comrades-in-arms who were dropping in rows under heavy German machine gun fire. His body was buried in a mass grave—not a tomb "on some green slope of the Vosges" as he had envisioned—and in a later barrage even this common grave was completely obliterated.

1914

Cuiry-les-Chaudardes, Aisne, OCTOBER 28. . . . I was given sentry duty immediately on arriving and remained in front of the wagons until midnight. During this time an attack by one side or the other took place on the lines only a few kilometers from our encampment. For twenty minutes or so the rifle and *mitrailleuse* fire was continuous, broken every few seconds by the booming of the artillery, while magnesium lights were shot off from the trenches to light up the battle field. Very impressive in the darkness. Only a few hours before, a soldier of the 127*me* had been telling me at Fismes how his regiment had made such a charge a couple of days ago and had been practically wiped out, leaving 700 dead on the field. At midnight I lay down on the wet ground and managed to get some sleep before three, when we got up again and continued the march 10 or 12 kilometers to this wretched village, where we are lodged for the day in a dirty stable. Here we are just behind the lines. We are resting and go into the trenches tonight. At last we shall be under fire.

NOVEMBER 10. Fifth day of our second period in the trenches. Five days and nights of pure misery. We came up here Thursday evening, a foggy, moonlit night, bright enough to show the fields through which we ascended, spattered with shell-holes as thick as mole-hills, and the pine woods full of shattered trunks and broken branches. The Germans had been trying to destroy the Château des Blancs Sablons, below which our kitchens are situated, but by some miracle it has escaped. It is here that the *état-major* is lodged. Our position this time has been a claypit on a high summit above the château. Owing to its exposed and dangerous character very formidable bombproofs have been built at this point of the line. To those we have been confined for five days from morning to night. A big hole here in the pit, a few yards from our door, marks the place where three men of Batallion D were killed by a shell only a few days before our arrival. We expected a heavy bombardment, but five days of continuous fog have made the firing very infrequent, though we have heard heavy cannonading at other points of the line. A *brancardier* was killed a few days ago and there have been a few wounded. It is a miserable life to be condemned to, shivering in these wretched holes, in the cold and the dirt and semidarkness. It is impossible to cross the open spaces in daylight, so that we can only get food by going to the kitchens before dawn and after sundown. The increasing cold will make this kind of existence almost insupportable, with its accompaniments of vermin and dysentery. Could we only attack or be attacked! I would hear the order with delight. The real courage of the soldier is not in facing the balls, but the fatigue and discomfort and misery. Tonight we are to be relieved, but whether we are going back to Cuiry or just to the last line of trenches down by the château I don't know. What a winter's prospect if our campaigning is only going to alternate between these two phases of inaction and discomfort!

DECEMBER 22. Returned to Cuiry after five days in trenches. Will be here, it seems, until Christmas. Great things seem to be brewing. Rumors of a general advance in preparation. Last night a violent cannonade and rifle fire all along the line, the first about eight o'clock, the second at midnight, just after I had come in from guard. Hope this means business.

Went to a farm nearby today and, waiting for coffee to be heated, missed *rassemblement* of company at noon. May get into trouble for this later but it has given me at least a free afternoon. An afternoon of memorable beauty; mild, sunny weather and loveliest blue skies. Sitting enjoying it on a pile of *betteraves* in the field behind Cuiry. It is so seldom one can get off by oneself to have a little solitude and time for uninterrupted reflection. I shall never forget the beauty of this winter landscape, the delicate skies, the little villages under their smoking roofs. Am feeling perfectly happy and contented. This life agrees with me; there will be war for many years to come in Europe and I shall continue to be a soldier as long as there is war.

1915

JUNE 15. . . . That we have been eight months on the front without having once attacked or been attacked need not cause any surprise, for a great part of the troops now in the trenches are in the same position. It seems to have been pure hazard that an easy sector fell to us, just as it was good luck that our battalion and battalion D had the low sector at Craonnelle, whereas F and G, who were on the crest of Ouldres, suffered almost daily losses during the winter from bombardment. The winter in the trenches was certainly hard, but it is already far enough away for the miseries to fade out of the picture, and for the rest to become tinged with the iridescence of romance. What is Virgil's line about the pleasure it will be sometime to recall having once done these things? I have known that all along, through no matter what fatigue and monotony. Never have I regretted doing what I am doing nor would I at this moment be anywhere else than where I am. I pity the poor civilians who shall never have seen or known the things that we have seen and known. Great as are the pleasures that they are continuing to enjoy and that we have renounced, the sense of being the instrument of Destiny is to me a source of greater satisfaction.

Nothing but good can befall the soldier, so he plays his part well. Come out of the ordeal safe and sound, he has had an experience in the light of which all life thereafter will be three times richer and more beautiful; wounded, he will have the esteem and admiration of all men and the approbation of his own conscience; killed, more than any other man, he can face the unknown without misgiving—that is, so long as Death comes upon him in a moment of courage and enthusiasm, not of faltering or of fear; and that this may, if necessary, be the case, I shall strain all my will the day that it comes round to our turn to go into the furnace. I have a feeling that that day is near at hand.

La Neuvillette, JULY 8. Our last six days in the trenches were broken by the most memorable, extraordinary, and happy event since we enlisted. On the evening of July 3rd the sergeant came quite unexpectedly to get the names of all Americans wanting permission of 48 hours in Paris! We could hardly believe such good fortune possible. But it seems the American journalists in Paris had made up a petition to get us a Fourth of July holiday, and the Minister of War had accorded it. We fairly danced for joy.

Notable absence of men in Paris; many women in mourning. A great many wounded soldiers on *congé de convalescence*, almost all wearing the old dark blue capote and red trousers. A little *malaise* and discouragement among the Parisians, probably at the absence of good news from Arras, the certain prospect of another winter's campaign, and the great weariness of the war, which it is difficult for them to realize so far from the front.

The visit did me good, on the whole, for with all its bringing home the greatness of the sacrifice I am making, it showed me clearly that I was doing the right thing, and that I would not really be so happy anywhere else than where I am. The universal admiration for the soldier from the front was more than any pleasure. It was a matter of pride, too, to salute the officers in the street, especially the wounded, and feel the fellowship with those who are doing the noblest and most heroic thing that is given to men to do. . . .

JULY 31. . . . Today comes the news I have been expecting, that the Russians are to evacuate Warsaw. The Germans then will enter probably on the anniversary of the declaration of war, and a wave of enthusiasm will pass over the country, which will drown all memory of past reverses and all discontent at the unlooked-for prolongation of the conflict. The great question now is whether the Russians started their retirement in time, and whether they will be able to extricate their central army from the difficult position in which it is placed. If they do not, it will mean disaster. Perhaps historic fatality has decreed that Germany shall come out of this struggle triumphant and that the German people shall dominate in the twentieth century as French, English, Spanish, and Italian have in preceding centuries. To me the matter of supreme importance is not to be on the winning side, but on the side where my sympathies lie. Feeling no greater dignity possible for a man than that of one who makes himself the instrument of Destiny in these tremendous moments, I naturally range myself on the side to which I owed the greatest obligation. But let it always be understood that I never took arms out of any hatred against Germany or the Germans, but purely out of love for France. The German contribution to civilization is too large, and German ideals too generally in accord with my own, to allow me to join in the chorus of hate against a people whom I frankly admire. It was only that the France, and especially the Paris, that I love should not cease to be the glory and the beauty that they are that I engaged. For that cause I am willing to stick to the end. But I am ready to accept the verdict of History in this case as I do, and everyone does, in the old cases between Athens and Sparta, or between Greece and Rome. Might is right and you cannot get away from it however the ephemeridae buzz. "*Victrix causa diis placuit, sed victa Catoni.*" It may have to be the epitaph on my tomb. I can see it on some green slope of the Vosges, looking toward the East.

AUGUST 7. Coming into the Cheval Blanc this morning I found cloth labels lying out to dry on a table, addressed in indelible pencil to the son of the house, who was made prisoner at Lassigny in the first weeks of the war, and who is now in a concentration camp at Cassel, in Germany. They send him bundles of bread and good things to eat every week through the Croix Rouge of Genève, and these *envois* seem to arrive regularly. I remarked to the good woman that her son was really happier as a prisoner than he would be in the trenches, and that she especially ought to consider herself happier than so many other mothers, who must worry all the time and remain in continual uncertainty, but her eyes showed that she had been crying, and she was unable to speak.

It is in these villages behind the lines that one gets an idea how the country is suffering. There is more than one young man back here without a leg or an arm. . . . But the most tragic seems to me that of a mother whose only son appeared early in the list of the missing. After months of uncertainty she read his name one day in a list of prisoners in Germany. Full of joy she wrote him and began sending packages. But one day, after several weeks had passed, she received a letter from the soldier she had written to, saying that he had received the letters and packages, that his name was indeed identical with that of the person to whom she addressed them, but that he came from quite a different locality, and was not the son that she sought! And she has never heard anything more. . . .

SEPTEMBER 1. Great and unexpected news this morning at report. All American volunteers in the Legion are to be given the privilege of entering a French regiment. I have always been loyal to the Legion, notwithstanding the many obvious drawbacks, feeling that the origin of most of the friction within the regiment was in the fact that we had never been in action, and had consequently never established the bond of common dangers shared, common sufferings borne, common glories achieved, which knits men together in real comradeship. It was a great mistake, it seems to me, not to have put the regiment into action immediately when we came on the front last year, when the regiment was strong and the morale good, instead of keeping us in the trenches in comparatively quiet sectors and in a state of inactivity, which was just the condition for all kinds of discontent to fester in. Of course discontent is the natural state of mind of the soldier, and I, who am accustomed to look beneath the surface, always have realized this, but it must be admitted that here discontent has more than the usual to feed upon, where a majority of men who engaged voluntarily were thrown in a regiment made up almost entirely of the dregs of society, refugees from justice and roughs, commanded by *sous-officiers* who treated us all without distinction in the same manner that they were habituated to treat their unruly brood in Africa. I put up with this for a year without complaint, swallowing my pride many a time and thinking only of the day of trial, shutting my eyes to the disadvantages I was under because I thought that on that day the regiment, which I have always believed to be of good fighting stock, would do well and cover us with glory.

Our chance, now that we are in with the Moroccan division, of seeing great things is better than ever. This has almost induced me, in fact, to turn down the offer and stay where I am, since perhaps the greatest glory will be here, and it is for glory alone that I engaged. But, on the other hand, after a year of what I have been through, I feel more and more the need of being among Frenchmen, where the patriotic and military tradition is strong, where my good will may have some recognition, and where the demands of a sentimental and romantic nature like my own may be gratified. I think there is no doubt that I will be happier and find an experience more remunerative in a French regiment, without necessarily forfeiting the chance for great action which is so good here now. Among the regiments of the 7th Army, from which we were allowed to choose, are three of the *active,* who it seems are in the Meuse in exciting sectors. I have chosen the *133e de ligne,* whose dépôt is at Belley, and will leave the rest to Fate.

SEPTEMBER 19. Went up and worked again last night. Beautiful starry night; bright moonlight. A pleasure walking up, but the work was tiring and the road long. A violent artillery duel. Our advance batteries of heavy guns fired continually. The Germans replied less frequently, but when their heavy shells fell by twos and fours the explosions were terrific beyond anything I have heard before on the front. They covered the lines with smoke, through which the *fusées* glimmered, blurred and reddened. The smell of powder was heavy in the air. It was daybreak when we returned. . . .

Today at *rapport* the captain read the order from Joffre announcing to the troops the great general attack. The company drew close around him, and he spoke to us of our reasons for confidence in success and a victory that would drive the enemy definitely out of France. The German positions are to be overwhelmed with a hurricane of artillery fire and then great assaults will be delivered all along the line. The chances for success are good. It will be a battle without precedent in history.

SEPTEMBER 21. About twenty heavy shells fell yesterday evening around the Suippes station, which is right near the park where we are bivouacking. Went out to watch them burst; no serious damage. Went up to work after supper. The dead and wounded were being carried in litters through the streets of Suippes, which had been bombarded, too. The fine weather is continuing, and it was a beautiful moonlit night, but frosty. Hard work until two o'clock digging communication ditches. Officers went down to the trenches to reconnoitre the *terrain*. The captain spoke to us again at *rapport* today, and gave us his impressions of this visit. The Colonials apparently are to lead the attack; we ought to come in the third or fourth wave. Our objective is the Ferme de Navarin, about 3½ kilometers behind the German lines. Here we will halt to reform, while the entire 8th Corps, including numerous cavalry, will pass through the breach we have made. These will be sublime moments; there are good chances of success and even of success without serious losses.

SEPTEMBER 24. We are to attack tomorrow morning. Gave in our blankets this morning; they are to be carried on the wagons. Also made bundles, in order to lighten the sack of all unnecessary articles, including the second pair of shoes. We are admirably equipped, and if we do not succeed it will not be the fault of those responsible for supplying us. A terrific cannonade has been going on all night and is continuing. It will grow in violence until the attack is launched, when we ought to find at least the first enemy line completely demolished. What have they got up their sleeves for us? Where shall we find the strongest resistance? I am very confident and sanguine about the result and expect to march right up to the Aisne, borne on in an irresistible *élan*. I have been waiting for this moment for more than a year. It will be the greatest moment in my life. I shall take good care to live up to it.

Chapter Seven

Alfred Hassler

BEFORE THE UNITED STATES entered World War II, Alfred Hassler, a member of the Fellowship of Reconciliation, registered himself as a conscientious objector, expecting to be sent to a Civilian Public Service camp when called to the draft. Reports of the "make work" nature of these camps, however, made him decide that his resistance to the war must also include "resistance to conscription as part of the system of modern war." Indicted in the spring of 1944 for his refusal to enter a C.P.S. camp, he pleaded guilty as charged, and at the age of thirty-four was sentenced to three years in prison.

Although he served less than a year of this sentence before being paroled to work as a hospital aide, the journal he kept, first at "West Street," New York City's Federal Detention Headquarters, then at the U.S. Northeastern Penitentiary in Lewisburg, Pennsylvania, not only reflects the rigors of his ordeal, but the power of an idealist's sustaining convictions, for unlike most of his fellow prisoners, Hassler had the advantage of serving his time to serve his strong principles.

With similar zeal he continued to counsel the hopeless, the outraged, the toughened, while also attempting to evaluate the damaging effects of life behind bars. His conclusions are those of many prison reformers, but as Hassler labors in the penitentiary kitchens, library, and parole office, suffers the long separation from his wife, Dot, and feels the anxiety, boredom, and menace of prison, he learns as much about himself as he does about the system he so despises. Whether or not one agrees with his position as pacifist, at its best Hassler's reconstructed journal, *Diary of a Self-Made Convict,* illustrates the conversion of a rather self-righteous young missionary into a man of more unassuming compassion.

SATURDAY, JULY 8. I am beginning to regret never having gone in seriously for contemplation, or Yogi-ism, or something. What a place this would be for someone who really wanted to meditate at length! The same thing has happened today as yesterday, only more of it. The only chance one has to talk is at meals and during stockade, and the meals have to go so quickly that it's dangerous to spend much time talking. Aside from the likelihood of having to go back to your cell hungry, there is some unspecified but horrid punishment promised to anyone who does not eat everything on his tray. Probably he gets sent to bed without his supper. . . .

MONDAY, JULY 10. More of the same, though broken by the arrival of a couple of letters from Dot, which I have practically committed to memory. If anyone ever reads this and has anything to say about my preoccupation with time, I shall invite him to try sitting all day, while in good health, with nothing to do, in a room six by ten feet furnished with a cot, a tin desk (empty), a tin chair, and a toilet. Then he should repeat that for a couple of days more, trying at the same time to imagine that he is facing in his thoughts some years of much the same thing.

We were hauled out for a medical examination, education test, and general "briefing" today, but all three took no more than a couple of hours. The only thing of significance was the briefing, where the guard—the inmates refer to them as "hacks" or "screws"—urged us solemnly to "do our own time," by which he meant that we should not try to share the worries or unhappiness of our fellows. That way, he warned, trouble lies, but failed to be any more explicit than that. Obviously an adaptation of the "divide-and-conquer" technique. He warned us not to gamble, too—said some inmates who had lost and were unable to pay up had been the victims of mysterious accidents with very unpleasant consequences. I shall have to keep my loaded dice hidden, I guess.

THURSDAY, JULY 13. . . . Of course, as is always the case if one looks, there are compensations. My cell is on the third floor, and through my window I can see over the wall to the rolling peaceful countryside beyond. In the early evening I have stood for an hour or more, watching the dusk settle imperceptibly over the hills, while a herd of cattle moves slowly out to pasture for the night, a train whistles mournfully in the distance, and the lights wink on one by one in the few houses that are visible. A couple of times I have sung quietly to myself—which has not the same connotations as talking to oneself in prison—and felt as though I were having my own private vespers. There is green grass below me, too, and white clouds floating puffily in a deep blue sky today. For two days I have watched a baby rabbit play on the lawn outside, protected from predatory animals by the very walls that confine me, and three times today a little English sparrow has perched on my windowsill for minutes at a time and peered curiously in at me. The world is wonderfully rich in good things when we take the time to see them. . . .

SATURDAY, JULY 15. . . . Yesterday I got moved out of my cell and into the quarantine dormitory, a room about sixty feet long by twenty wide, presently occupied by eleven other men and myself. The change evidently is supposed to be a boon, since only men expected not to start riots or fights get the chance to live in the dormitory, but they can have it back for my money.

I never met such a bunch in my life, and I don't *think* I have led an especially sheltered life. The largest bloc are Army prisoners with sentences of from ten to forty years; the second largest group are draft dodgers; and besides these there are a white slaver, an absconder, and I. Most of the Army men come from the Southern mountains, and the rest of the men are mostly slum-raised, virtually illiterate characters. . . .

Some of the time they brag about their criminal exploits in the past, and these are childishly naive and lead one to wonder how they ever managed to stay out of jail at all, but most of the time the talk is of sex, which they explore over and over, painstakingly and in incredible detail, and on a level I have never heard or imagined before. . . .

I have not changed my feeling about going to prison when that is the one way open to protest effectively something one feels to be wrong. But to believe that such an experience will "deepen one's spiritual life," or something of the sort, seems to me as unreasonable as to believe that a man can be strengthened physically by being denied all nourishing food. . . .

MONDAY, JULY 24. . . . I think I am over the worst hump. I have decided to apply for parole at the earliest possible moment, but I feel reasonably confident now that I can do the whole three years if I must. I am beginning to recognize, too, how lucky I am compared with these poor devils with me. My closest associates these days are a bootlegger, an embezzler, a forger, a deserter, and two draft dodgers. I have come to realize that the bravado, the obscenity and all the rest that hit me so hard when I first came in here are all manifestations of their fear and insecurity, and attempts to get some slight measure of status by becoming part of the "gang." Actually, I am humbled to discover how little essential difference there is between us—or, rather, how large a part chance has played in making what differences there are.

SUNDAY, AUGUST 6. It seems almost incredible that I have been in prison less than two months! It seems much longer since I stood in that New York courtroom.

I had a measure of how quickly a man becomes totally engrossed with the life in prison when Dot first visited me in West Street, only four days after I had gone in. Today, after a month of not having seen her or anyone else from the outside world, she brought the same kind of reminder she did then that an outside world does exist—and I need it as much.

Sometimes I get discouraged with myself about this. There is a terrible war going on. Hundreds of thousands of young men must endure much more dreadful experiences than this, including the danger of death or wounds. Millions of non-combatants never know from one day to the next when the bombers will roar out of nowhere and drop their deadly loads.

I know all this, yet in here it is not only easy to forget it, but actually hard to remember! I suspect it is because one never has any escape from the problems here. Unhappiness saturates the place, and saturates it for twenty-four hours a day, seven days a week. The rough jokes, the horseplay, the fights and the braggadocio—all are parts of a many-faceted camouflage for the misery and fright beneath.

My own reactions, as I noted in Quarantine, are not what I would like them to be. I find myself thinking over much of release, months before even the most optimistic possibilities of parole would let me out. It is an infectious thing, of course—there *are* only two general subjects of conversation in here: release and sex. It would take a stronger character than I to banish either one from one's thoughts! . . .

TUESDAY, AUGUST 15. I am finding prison a curious combination of unrelenting tension and acute boredom. The boredom comes from the lack of stimulating things to do, of course; the tension rises out of the collective tension of more than a thousand convicts. On the surface, life here appears to run almost placidly, but one needs to go only a very little beneath the surface to find the whirlpools and eddies of anger and frustration. The muttering of discontent and rebellion goes on constantly: the *sotto voce* sneer whenever we pass an official or a guard, the glare carefully calculated to express contempt without arousing overt retaliation, the tempers that rise so swiftly to the breaking point. . . .

68

MONDAY, AUGUST 21. Wild weekend in H-2. Saturday night, after everyone was presumably asleep, somebody tried to "rape" somebody else's "girl friend" in the latrine room. The resulting fight was quickly broken up by some guards who happened to be nearby. All three participants are reportedly now in the hole. When they come out they will be distributed around among different cell-blocks and dormitories—the administration's optimistic method of "handling" homosexuality.

After a while a man tends to get somewhat self-centered in here, I am afraid. My first reaction when the racket broke out was, "For Pete's sake, awake again!". . .

WEDNESDAY, SEPTEMBER 6. . . . And with this I know, so often these days, the background of a friend's behavior, dug out of the surreptitious looks at his file that I manage in the parole office. Here is a youth deprived of everything: raised in a family dominated by a brutal, drunken father, with no toys, no friends, no love, sent out to steal before he was ten, beaten savagely when he failed to bring home all that his father thought he should. How can it be surprising that he should have turned to crime and wound up in a federal prison at the age of twenty-two? And what will prison do for him, or for society, in the ten years he has to serve? When he is released, six or seven years from now, how will he have been improved, and how will the phenomenon of crime have been dealt with?

It is this that lacerates the spirit of the onlooking friend. Punishment and retaliation will not help. He has known them all his life, and they have driven him deeper and deeper into ruin. It is mercy he needs now, and it is only mercy and compassion that will do either him or society any good. He needs to know that men are not all his enemies, and that forgiveness and love exist, and can be extended to him. And so it is that a score of "over-sensitive" conscientious objectors keep filling their three letters a week and their one visit a month with pleas that somehow, somebody arrange to extend some mercy and compassion to Bill or Joe or Smitty or Bob. It does no good, most of the time. Society is not geared to the expression of compassion. But we go on pleading because we have to, because we could not live with ourselves if we did not.

SUNDAY, SEPTEMBER 10. . . . The doors have double locks on them, so that they can be locked either singly or *en masse*. Generally only the mass-locking procedure is used, with the guard throwing the lock for all the doors on one side by pulling a lever at the end of the corridor. This arrangement resulted in an amusing little contretemps Friday morning.

Thursday evening I had gone both to the library and to choir practice, the latter followed by the "vespers" service in the chapel. Evidently when I returned to my cell I did not pull the door quite shut, and the locking mechanism failed to engage when the hack later pulled his lever, though neither he nor I noticed it. The result was that Friday morning, as he was marching along busy with his count, I leaned negligently against the door, which promptly swung open, leaving me standing face to face with a very startled guard. A moment's thought evidently reassured him that I would not be the likely spearhead of an escape attempt, but the panic that showed itself on his face in the first instant revealed the kind of tension these men live under all the time, too.

SUNDAY, SEPTEMBER 17. . . . Prison involves a whole sequence of petty humiliations: uniformity in clothing and cells, censorship of the mail and reading matter of all kinds, locks and keys and passes and the whole impedimenta of inferiority. The irritation is constant and cumulative. . . .

For me, as for many others I have talked to, the simple irritation of being addressed always by name, without the prefix "Mister," while being expected always to attach the prefix when addressing any member of the staff, from warden to guard, seems to focus all my own resentment. It is a simple thing, as all these things are simple, but it is also unmistakably significant of a sort of second-class citizenship that is a fact, and so it loses its simplicity. . . .

To get back to the civilian clerks—we have had some interesting chats together in the past month and a half, in the course of which I have tried to show them what prison is like from the inmate's point of view, and to persuade them to get out before they could become corrupted by it. . . .

Today I had the satisfaction of learning that at least one Hassler project had borne fruit. Both of them told me, in confidence, that they were leaving. . . . Both said they had thought very seriously of what could happen to them as part of a system that cages men like animals in a zoo, and had decided that the "security" of a government job was not worth the price.

I suppose a good many people would have a hard time understanding why I should want to persuade two of the kindlier persons on the staff to leave, taking the chance that someone much less desirable, from the point of view of the inmates, might take their places. It is not too easy to make a completely convincing case, because it springs from the personal conviction of the pervasiveness of evil and futility in the prison system, and its ability to corrupt, to bring out the least humane drives in the people who make up the staff.

. . . This hardening and coarsening of human sensitivity is not something that begins at eight in the morning and can be sloughed off at four-thirty in the afternoon. It will extend into a man's whole life. It will affect all his relationships. You cannot learn to despise a whole category of human beings without losing a big share of your respect for humanity in general, including yourself. These two young men had not yet come to that point and so, for their own sakes and for the sake of a society that needs as many sensitive spirits as it can get, I encouraged them to leave.

THURSDAY, SEPTEMBER 21. . . . A favorite occupation among the "regulars" is the construction of elaborate "writs" of various sorts, designed to demonstrate some compelling reason for immediate release.

I am no exception. During the first few weeks in the newness of the experience, I felt that I would accept almost anything to avoid three years of this. As I settled down, getting out quickly became less important, but it remains a highly desirable end to be achieved without unnecessary delays. By this time I know that I can "take it" for the full three years if I have to. I would be depressed at the necessity. I am more positive now than ever that a long stay in prison is a deteriorating experience. I have constantly to combat the evidence of that in myself. . . .

The experience is emotionally and spiritually frustrating, too, and in time is sure to develop a spiritual callousness. I can feel that developing in me, too. At first one is struck by the magnitude of the tragedy being enacted in here. All one's impulse is to combat and alleviate it in some way. It seems intolerable merely to sit and witness such things.

One seeks various channels through which to express this concern. Some of the COs have tried direct action against the prison on one or another pretext: strikes against censorship, against segregation, against parole provisions. Others, like myself, doubtful of the wisdom of that course, try to work with individuals, both inmates and staff, but particularly with inmates. But there, too, one can go just so far before running up against a blank wall.

You talk to a man about a different approach to life; over a period of weeks or months you win his interest and perhaps his whole-hearted commitment. And then what? The next step should be some practical step to help him get started on his new life. But what practical step? To all intents and purposes, here is a new man, ready to take his place as a responsible member of society. But the law is inflexible. He must serve out his sentence. If he has detainers against him, as many have, he must serve them, too. And when he does get out, society will make it difficult or impossible for him to live according to his new views.

As these facts are borne in on him, his enthusiasm becomes overlaid with a cynicism and disillusionment more bitter than before. And for the CO, faced with that sort of galling frustration, the alternatives increasingly become hysteria or callousness. The latter is what develops, of course: to a large extent he forces himself to ignore the tragedy, adopts the protective shell of the other prisoners, gradually becomes coarsened in speech and sensibilities, and perhaps suffers a major disillusionment in the power of his own beliefs.

It is this kind of reasoning that has led me to the decision to get parole soon, if I can. . . .

MONDAY, OCTOBER 23. . . . Last night some wild geese passed overhead, flying low. Their honking was quite clear as they flew south, and for just a moment I caught a glimpse of the "V" of their flight silhouetted against the patch of sky visible from my cubicle. At the very moment of their passage, from some other near-by cell I could barely hear the deep, almost silent sobs of one of my fellow convicts. It is no longer a novel sound, but it wrenches my whole spirit with wretchedness whenever I hear it. During the day, the men maintain the cloak of bravado in which they wrap their self-respect; at night, alone in the darkness, their grief and fright sometimes become too much for them to bear.

Chapter Eight

Arthur Bremer

WHAT HAPPENS to a young man's urge toward some greater and more meaningful identification with his society when that society serves up contradictory ideals—and with all the hard sell of the media that inform him? *An Assassin's Diary* by Arthur Bremer causes such conjectures. In a nation where notoriety is often rewarded with celebrity, where purchasing power is considered a virtue from which the poorer consumer feels exempt, where the spirit of cooperation is propounded in highly competitive classrooms, where wrongful wars are prolonged in order to prove its warleaders right, where concerned citizens have turned cynical—the confused aspirations of an Arthur Bremer might well be understood.

After his assassination attempt on Governor George Wallace of Alabama on May 15, 1972, a part of Arthur Bremer's handwritten diary was found in his car, the first part having already been hidden away in the hope that it might eventually prove negotiable for money or fame—those symbols of self-esteem that this unemployed busboy of twenty-two deeply craved throughout a lifetime of failure. How he orchestrates much of that failure himself as he calculates his daily finances, visits a New York massage parlor, and travels to Ottawa to try to slay Richard Nixon before turning to stalk George Wallace in Maryland, is central to the odd poignancy of his·diary. Certainly his dismal spelling and grammar lead to speculations about the quality of his education, as do all the pop clichés that pass for his wisdom, the fragmented messages recalling the lessons of Marshall MacLuhan about our "post-literate society" with lettering that reads like newspaper ads or echoes the sound of a TV sales pitch.

Before being sentenced to prison in Maryland, Bremer remarked, "Looking back on my life, I would have liked it if society had protected me from myself." One might rejoin with Bremer's own helpless phrase, "Irony abounds."

1972

APRIL 21, FRIDAY. The funnyest thing happened to me when I arrived in N.Y. just after I got off the plane. I forgot my guns! I was in a washroom when I heard my name over the loud speaker. WOW! The captain of the plane smiled & nodded as he gave me them. In the wash room, I didn't quiet hear the announcement & asked a fella next to me if he heard what was said. He didn't. "Well they mentioned my name." I thought a couple seconds & said, "Oh yeah, now I know!" Irony abounds. . . .

APRIL 22 [in Ottawa]. I drove round the place a few times befor & the day of his arrival. . . . The T.V. & papers had said, were saying, & continued to say that Nixon was getting the heaviest surcurity coverage of any President to visit Canada. . . .

I tryed to conceal the gun in my rubber boot, it was raining & the puddels were bad in places. I drove to the International Airport & took a couple aspirin & adjusted the bulge in my right boot. I couldn't make it look as flat as the left one. And wouldn't it look funny me bending over & grabbing my boot as the President spoak? I left the boots on & put the gun in my pocket. Fuck it. With *the tightest* security *ever* I felt for sure a metal detector would be used on everyone. I thought the rubber of my boot would fool it, I don't know why. Dressed in my vested conservative bussiness suit & overcoat with gun & a tie that was just rediculus for anyone my age. . . .

. . . Pulling up from a side street I asked a fat cop in orange traffic control vest where a good place was to watch the President. He pointed to a empty gas station at the corner. I thanked him & pulled in. . . .

. . . Stayed out of the car 10 minutes, fingers got nume. . . .

Come out & went inside again. Longjohn weather. I was conscience of my hands. Didn't want to keep them inside of my pockets & get searched. Didn't want to keep them out & nume them too much. Some folks there kept their hands in their pockets almost all the time, they weren't questioned & either was I. But I wanted to be careful, didn't know if a stop & frisk law existensed or what my rights were as an American here. Felt added confidence with my suit on & short hair & shave.

Didn't recognize my self clean shaven at first. My head hair came in nice & thick.

People jumped from their cars. Would the assassin get a good view? Everyone moved in close (about 20 people). We were the only people other than cops for a few blocks.

He went by before I knew it. Like a snap of the fingers. A dark shillowet, waving, rushed by in the large dark car. "All over," someone said to no one in particular. . . . I walked back to my car. I had missed him that day. The best day to make the attempt was over, I thought. . . .

The news the next day said there were very sparse unwaving crowds. Said the rain stopped some demonstrators from showing up to protest his arrival. All along the fucking Ottawa visit I cursed the damn "demonstrators." Sercurity was beefed up—overly beefed up—because of these stupid dirty runts. To this day I blame them for partial responsibility in failing my attempt. . . .

. . . Out of the Gallery I walked down Sparks Street, shopping area were cars are prohibited. A woman, middle age gave me an antiwar/anti-Nixon leaflet. I glanced it over & handed it back to her, politely. What could I say to her? You stupid bitch stop this useless accomplish-nothing form of protest, let the sercurity slacken & I'll show you something really evective? Tons of leaflets have been handed out all over the world for years & what did they get done? Wipe your ass with this you radical commie? I support the President?

She was dressed decently. The hipie-types also tryed to give me this stuff, I looked away & walked on. Wonder what they would of done or thought of me if they could read my mind?

Were the cops really afraid of these people?! Was Nixon afraid, really scared, of *them*?!

They're nothing. They're the new establishment. To be a rebel today you have to keep a job, wear a suit & stay apolitical. Now **THAT'S REBELLION!**

APRIL 23. I walked from Sparks St. right on to the main drag with the American Embassy on one side & Pariliment on the other. . . . SHOCK! SHOCK! I saw what I took to be the President's car parked directly in front of the Embassy! Was he inside? Wasn't scheualed to be & WHY would he be in there?

I went immediately home, ran part of the way. . . . I stupidly took time to, I'm now ashamed & embaressed to say, brush my teeth, take 2 asperin & think change from a salt & pepper knit suit into my black bussiness one. It was about 2:30 either when I left my room or when I arrived at the Embassy.

Car gone.

I had planned to get him as he entered the car. . . . I took my time in the hotel room because he had made me wait so long for him on Riverside Road. I didn't want to attrack too much attention standing near the barracade for so long waiting for Nixon. And I was concerned, overly concerned with my appearance & composure after the bang bangs. I wanted to shock the shit out of the SS men with my clamness. A little something to be remmered by. All these things seemed important to me, were important to me, in my room.

I will give very little if ANY thought to these things on any future attempts.

After all does the world remember if Sirhan's tie was on straight? SHIT, I was stupid!!

APRIL 24, TUESDAY. Shit! I am thruorly pissed off. About a million things. Was pissed off befor I couldn't find a pen to write this down. This will be one of the most closely read pages since the Scrolls in those caves. And I couldn't find a pen for 40 seconds & went mad. My fuse is about burnt. There's gona be an explosion soon. I had it. I want something to happen. I was sopposed to be Dead a week & a day ago. Or at least infamous. FUCKING tens-of-1,000's of people & tens-of-millions of $. I'd just like to take some of them with me & Nixy.

ALL   MY

      EFFORTS

           &

               NOTHING

                 C
                H
                A
                 N
                  G
                   E
                  D

Just another   god Damn

        failure

Oh man, I a werewolf now changed into a wild thing. I could give it to the fucking mayor really fuck his little machine. Burn all these papers & what I buried & no one would ever know ½ of it.

But I want em all to know. I want a big shot & not a little fat noise. I want that god damn
    tired of writting about it.
    about what I was gonna do.

about what I failed to do.

about what I failed to do again & again.

Had bad pain in my left temple & just in front & about it. Kept me awake for a—seemed a long time last night. Remember I had at least 2 night mares last night. Bad frieghtening dreams—that's a night mare ain't it? I allmost never dream & now when I did it was terrible. Didn't want to remember them long enought to write them down either then—was I ½ awake?—or at a later time. Forgot 'em pretty well now.

Everything drags on . . . drags on . . . and on . . .

It was supposed to be all over now. Don't think I have enought money to pay the rent on the 15th next month & eat that month too. I gota get him. I'm tired, I'm pissed, I'm crasy. Was gona get drunk last night—WOW—what a personality change. Decided against it—just wanted to pick a fight with the bartender some where or someone. Get arrested & then where am I. I got something to do—something big befor I ever get arested again.

I'm back to writting.

MAY 4, THURSDAY.   . . . I had to get away from my thoughts for a while. I went to the zoo, the lake front, saw "Clockwork Orange" & thought about getting Wallace all thru the picture—fantasing my self as the Alek on the screen come to real life—but without "my brothers" & without any "in and out." Just "a little of the old ultra violence."

I've decided Wallace will have the honor of—what would you call it?

Like a novelist who knows not how his book will end—I have written this journal—what a shocking surprise that my inner character shall steal the climax and destroy the author and save the anti-hero from assisination!! It may sound exciting & fasinating to readers 100 years from now—as the Booth conspricy seems to us today; but to this man it seems only another failure. And I stopped tolerating failure weeks ago.

As I said befor, I Am A Hamlet.

It seems I would of done better for myself to kill the old G-man Hoover. In death, he lays with Presidents. Who the hell ever got buried in 'Bama for being great? He certainly won't be buryed with the snobs in Washington.

SHIT! I won't even rate a T.V. enteroption in Russia or Europe when the news breaks—they never heard of Wallace. If something big in Nam flares up I'll end up at the bottom of the 1st page in America. The editors will say—"Wallace dead? Who cares." He won't get more than 3 minutes on network T.V. news. I don't expect anybody to get a big thobbing erection from the news. You know, a storm in some country we never heard of kills 10,000 people—big deal—pass the beer and what's on T.V. tonight.

I hope my death makes more sense than my life.

MAY 8, SATURDAY.   Yesterday got books about Sirhan Sirhan, "*R.F.K. Must Die!*" a Warren Commission like report by Robert Blair Kaiser & an unread as yet dumpy looking "Sirhan," by Aziz Shihab. I think he's a fake & a phony.

Gotta leave soon.

I'll stay here long enought to eat all the food up.

Still don't know weather its trail & prison for me or—bye bye brains. I'll just have to decide that at the last few seconds. Must secceed. Gota.

As late as yesterday I had thoughts of burying this whole paper & reading it decided later after I had gone to Hollywood (I **KNOW IT SOUNDS INSANE, SO DON'T THINK IT**)

. . . Passed the last week or so fasinated with storys in the papers discussing murder, suicide & the death penalty. Disapointed that Michigan doesn't have the death penalty. But I remember from High School that a man can drownd on one drop of water. I think I could do it if I held my head back & jaw open & quickly dropped an ounce of water down my throat without swallowing. Right into the windpipe—bypassing the food tube. I have other more realistic plans for that kind of stuff. I won't write this down.

Hey world! Come here! I wanna talk to ya!

If I don't kill—if I don't kill myself I want you to pay thru the nose, ears, & belly button for the beginning of this manuscript. The 1st pages are hidden & will preserve a long time. If you don't pay me for them, I got no reason to turn 'em over—understand punk!?

One of my reasons for this action is money and you the American (is there another culture in the free world?) public will pay me. The silent majority will be my benifactor in the biggest hijack ever!

It was kidnapping in the early part of this century. Then hijack became popular with sky diving a often time extra added attraction.

I'm gonna start the next crime binge! HA. HA. And the silent majority will back me all the way!

Irony!!

Irony!!

SUNDAY, MAY 7. There's les than a hundred pages in my "un-hidden" journal. I was about right—60 to 70 pages ago was to be one of those days "which will live in infamy" & all that. Yesterday I even considered McGovern as a target. If I go to prison as an assissin (solitary forever & guards in my cell, etc.) or get killed or suicided what difference to me? Ask me why I did it & I'd say "I don't know," or "Nothing else to do," or "Why not?" or "I have to kill somebody."

That's how far gone I am.

Often I've thought of just turning this whole manuscript over to a welfare (can I spell it?) pyscologist & asking for his opinion.

NURSE! GET THE JACKET!

If you think you need a doctor I guess you're

. . . A short drive from Jackson. I stayed at a hotel overlooking the Kalamazoo National Guard Armory where he'd talk. Watched it carefully. Wanted everything perfect. Paper said 10% chance of rain Sat., today, afternoon. I'm checked out of my room & sitting in my car now & writing & its raining like a son-of-a-bitch. Will this spoil everything

. . . He drew 4–6,000 in '68 at a near by city Park. Read the paper in the beautiful mall area of town. Listened to rock music, in a park. A small ineffective protest is planned today.

Wanted to be the 1st in line. Thought I saw people standing in front of the place at 9 this morning. They moved on. Rain is letting up slowly now. It's about 1:30. He isn't in Warren yet. But I'll soon be on the front steps of the Kalamazoo Armory to welcome him. Got a sign from campaing headquarters here. To shield the go for the gun.

Is there any thing else to say?

My cry upon firing will be, "A penny for your thoughts."

Chapter Nine

John
L'Heureux

WHILE JOHN L'HEUREUX was in attendance at Holy Cross College in Massachusetts, his devotion to his religion began to take priority over his interests in literature, the theater, and campus life. In 1954 he entered the Society of Jesus as a novice. After twelve years of study, reflection, and practical work under the rigorous disciplines of the Jesuit seminary, he was ordained a priest in 1966. Remaining true to his love of poetry, he also wrote and published two volumes of his own poems, *Quick as Dandelions* and *Rubrics for a Revolution*, while still working toward ordination. The problem of serving an exacting muse while serving a church more exacting is often explored in the witty and moving journal John L'Heureux kept during the three years preceding his priesthood.

The following excerpts from *Picnic in Babylon*, however, deal with deeper conflicts between the idealist and his calling—his difficulties with prayer and obedience, those dark nights of doubt that seem always to follow his bright days of faith and lead to his discovery that if this imperfect servant of God is to be of any use to his Master, he must begin to forgive himself for being human.

Eventually John L'Heureux left the Society of Jesus. He has since married, continues to publish extensively—poetry, novels, short stories—and directs the Creative Writing Center at Stanford University.

1964

SUNDAY, 14 JUNE. Priests today. All those men who earlier this morning were just other Jesuit Scholastics are now fulfilled in a way which makes coherence stutter. The ordination ceremony is beautiful anyway, but because I daily get closer to my own ordination in both time and desire, I found today's surpassingly beautiful. The parents of the new priests shook me up a little with their white unbreakable joy and with their selflessness, which somehow seemed particularly in evidence as they stood about with their new priest-sons. And I found myself wishing terribly, wishing with a great ache in my stomach, to be ordained soon; partly because of the great happiness ordination brings to everybody who has helped raise and teach and train the priest, but mostly because I want to belong completely and irrevocably to Christ Jesus. Forever.

FRIDAY, 3 JULY. . . . Reading Merton's first little meditation in *Thoughts in Solitude*, I felt inclined to assess my spiritual status; that old temptation still skulks about my darker recesses. From an analysis of the spiritual status—always an appalling ordeal—we proceed directly to discouragement, and after a period of feeling grim and grimy, we move on to distraction and disinterest: the attempt to forget what appears to be guilt, to escape from accusations leveled by nobody but the self. The Puritan is in my blood, taking pleasure in acknowledging the clean sweep of the burnt village, in admitting that no progress is possible. God, what a tortured psyche we create for ourselves. What explains it, I wonder? Novitiate emphasis on personal faults, the old negative concentration on spiritual truancy and the ponderous peccadillo? Whatever explains it, nothing excuses it. But I will escape it—this Puritan syndrome—even if I have to live the rest of my life half suspecting I am damned. And today I begin my escape by refusing to give in to morbid speculation on how bad I am because I do not pray enough. . . .

WEDNESDAY, 2 SEPTEMBER. I don't understand what happens to me. We're on the second day of retreat and I'm suddenly wondering *why* I want to live a life of blind obedience in the Society of Jesus. Now, don't misunderstand. I'm not saying that I find myself tempted to leave the Society; I just wonder why, after ten years a Jesuit, I feel I must be one. . . .

. . . A priest, yes, but why be a Jesuit surrounded by inflexible rules and attitudes and this incomprehensible medieval concept of obedience? My only answer is that this is part of the mystery of fact, I am a Jesuit—for me, irrevocably a Jesuit—and I must be a saint this way, crazily, with all the difficulties the Society has already thrown up and all the future ones it can and will throw up against me and topple down on me and maybe crush me, out of concern for me, not out of spite. . . . I suppose it sounds funny for me to answer myself with recourse to mystery. Yet isn't that what fact always leads to? The soul's relation to itself is wombed in mystery. I love God and I love the Society. I am tempted to pray that the former protect me from the good intentions of the latter. . . .

MONDAY, 7 SEPTEMBER. I must content myself with prayer that is not arid so much as blank, negative, nonbeing. I must not expect—I do not *want*—those superficial and dangerous consolations of prayer: peace that borders precipitously on complacency, satisfaction at having "put in my time," ease of conscience at being comfortably saved. They are too easy, too delusive. My salvation, my hobbling sanctity, will consist, it seems, in learning to live with myself on Christ's terms—accepting my gross failures and my dissatisfaction and my restlessness in prayer as that which God intends for me, being careful to keep in touch, however, with the Holy Spirit. The prayer of quiet too easily tapers off into one long snooze.

TUESDAY, 22 SEPTEMBER. . . . I had a fine talk with a young priest after dinner tonight. . . . We talked about being happy in Christ's service and we agreed that few of us really are. But happiness is not the point. We so often think that happiness in God's service is somehow equivalent to some sort of success, that it's God's imprimatur on the evidence of our lives. And it isn't. Christ never called men to follow him and be happy on this earth as far as I remember from my imperfect acquaintance with Scripture. He spoke about yokes and burdens and all that. Talking with this priest makes me glad I'm not especially happy. Though I'm not *un*happy either. I'm just restless. With a holy restlessness . . . I hope.

SUNDAY, 27 SEPTEMBER. It occurred to me at lunch today that half the people in religion are desperately trying to find out who they are and the other half are just as desperately fleeing that same knowledge.

1965

SATURDAY, 9 JANUARY. . . . The spiritual difficulty is something I don't really understand. I'm lonely, but that's nothing unusual. I feel lost and unloved and unloving, but that's not particularly unusual either. I have an occasional temptation against faith, an occasional longing for a wife and family to care about and to have care about me, but again there's nothing unusual in that. A failure. I feel somehow a failure (no, not that silly canon law [examination]; aside from that; indeed, despite it). Rootless. Useless. A conviction of my total inadequacy hounds me and along with it a terrible longing that is at last, after a month or two, driving me to prayer; a blind and almost helpless prayer, repeated requests that God will help me to appreciate (if not to understand) that this anguish and this longing is for him, to be with him, to love him. In somebody else, this trial would be a step to a degree of holiness. In me it's just a necessary roadblock, which, causing me to exert myself a bit in the attempt to get over it, keeps me at least from total backsliding—like the terrain in *Alice* where you have to run to stay where you are and run twice as fast if you expect to get anywhere. . . .

SUNDAY, 21 MARCH. This weekend has been for me the most profound spiritual experience of my Jesuit life. It would be absolute folly to try to put it in words; naturally I'll try, but not now.

MONDAY, 29 MARCH. A strange thing happened to me Saturday night. One of my closest friends here suddenly told me, so far as I could see with no provocation, that he found my overly strong personality a threat to his liberty, my visits to his room too frequent, my way of trying to find the summation of our whole relationship in even our most passing conversation at the least distressing. . . .

A kick in the belly is still a kick in the belly even when you offer it to Christ. And this has been a kick and a half—be a sport, call it two kicks. And it isn't easy to find Christ in a rejection that involves me so intimately, right down to the core of my personality. It isn't easy because all that I see is myself, my eyes put out. But this new situation is really just an extension of the incredible graces of last weekend. Christ loves me. Now he wants me to love him, just a bit more honestly, a bit more emphatically than I did before. I once wrote that I must find Christ in the cross because only there would I be sure it was really Christ I had found. I wrote more truly than I knew.

FRIDAY, 23 APRIL. . . . I am in a horrible black depression. I am tired to death of obeying, of doing what I have to do rather than what I want to do, of sitting at this damned desk with these boring notes. I would like to throw everything off, tear up the notes, pitch out the books, have done with the whole sick business of study. Surely God doesn't take all this nonsense as seriously as we take it. He couldn't and be God. But I don't pitch out the books. I sit here blackly and do what I ought. Three cheers for me? Don't be a damfool.

SUNDAY, 18 JULY. I suddenly feel that my spiritual life has gone to hell. I'm praying less, am distracted, seem always to be doing something frivolous. And I haven't read a spiritual book in far too long a time. The one thing that matters is that in less than a year I am going to be a priest: ergo it's high time I started living like one. I don't want to spend the last few months of preparation for the priesthood agonizing over whether I can in conscience go through with it. I've seen too many men do that and it's a tragic thing to watch. And so unnecessary. God doesn't call men to his service to torture them but to fill them so full they overflow with his goodness and drench everybody within splashing distance. But you've got to *let* him fill you, and that means you've got to keep open to him, you've got to be receptive, responsive to the subtlest workings of grace. Which means you've got to pray, chum, and you've got to maintain an interior silence even in the midst of hurricane social activity and all that cavorting you engage in.

SATURDAY, 4 SEPTEMBER. Why should the attempt to love God give me headaches? I guess because I worry about *me* loving God instead of me loving *God*. I can't quite believe God has called me to his service with the intention of seeing how miserable he can make me.

Later. Terrible depression. I am a dilettante at everything I've ever undertaken: painting, criticism, poetry, the spiritual life. And I'll always be this way. Never an expert at anything; all superficial gloss, and in the end even the gloss will go.

SATURDAY, 25 SEPTEMBER. Jesus Christ was a *man* as well. A real one—not God dressed up in flesh for a thirty-three-year charade—but a real man. He had gas pains and he wept real tears over Lazarus and he loved Mary Magdalen, a poor type. Furthermore he encouraged her to love him, even though the neighbors must have been horrified and though he surely must have sensed the risk he took of breaking her heart. And what do I risk?

FRIDAY, 5 NOVEMBER.   Tonight I was walking outside, praying, thinking of being alone. I imagined myself standing on a low hill of asphalt . . . with the whole world with all reality sloping away from me. I felt nothing; just hollow and alone. And I thought that I have nothing but God, nothing, because love seemed incomprehensible and because nothing else matters but love. So I thought how I *do* have God and how I'll be ordained in June. And then I thought of the death of God theologians and I wondered if I really do believe in God. Immediately of course all the defenses rushed in, the fears and insecurities, but I pushed them back and looked as honestly as I could at the problem. Conscience kept getting in the way but I think I succeeded in looking beyond that to the possibility that maybe there is no God, that maybe I've projected him out of my deepest need. At least I faced that possibility. I decided that God does exist and moreover loves me and I spent some time then praying for an increase of faith and love. It was a grace-filled experience for me, I think. Perhaps it is unwise to flirt with temptations against faith; I do think it *is* really; I also think at some time in your life you have to challenge yourself on what matters most to you. The year of my ordination is making me a bit hyperconscious, I think, of my state before God.

1966

THURSDAY, 24 FEBRUARY.   Vows ask much more of a man than may appear. The vow of chastity, for instance, asks not only that a man abstain from sexual activity, which is perfectly legitimate for other men (married men, perhaps even bachelors), but also that in his deepest self he surrender to Christ all hope of ever possessing or being possessed. That most natural desire of every man to give himself to another, to one other whom he can hold through a long and terrible dark night, must be quietly put down again and again and again. Thus one risks with a vow of chastity the danger of never becoming a man, a real one.

The whole core of the person depends for its flowering upon being able to give and be given to in love. And though for a religious, giving and being given to always remain possible within certain confined areas, one must keep in mind that those areas are indeed confined—circumscribed by prudence and necessity. Loving God is not the same as loving another human person; with God the physical remains unsatisfied. Constantly to force back physical demonstrations of affection is to risk killing emotion and response, to risk the glacial heart and the hard unfeeling stare. Only Christ; no other. And sometimes the emptiness within the circle of my arms is almost more than I can bear.

MONDAY, 14 MARCH. As my twelve years of waiting and preparing are at last coming to an end, I'm somewhat preoccupied with the mystery of vocation. And about time. Thinking about the priesthood so much myself, I look around and wonder if everybody else is doing the same thing. I'm not wondering if I want to be a priest; I do. I'm wondering if I ought to be one in view of the history of my failures. However, I'm getting ahead of myself.

Let me conjure up the extreme case. Suppose I'm being ordained as an act of rejection. Perhaps I was not loved enough in my childhood; perhaps I was jealous of my brother, who was always so competent in everything, and so I have turned from my family and the world as a gesture; sort of this—you have rejected me, now I reject you, formally, ritually, and I bind myself to this action of mine by perpetual vows. Even this hypothesis, the most appalling I can conceive . . . is possible grounds for vocation. God *uses* our neuroses, our clouded vision, to call us to himself. His love after all is more powerful than our convoluted motivations.

Now to exonerate my family: they did love me; my brother's success didn't intimidate me. Still, in looking into your vocation you must test all the possibilities, you must question even the most unlikely and disheartening hypotheses. And so, unwilling to be a priest for the wrong reason, I question all my reasons and check the possibility of reasons I've not suspected. . . .

SUNDAY, 17 APRIL. Thinking about ordination as I do all the time, I find only one thing disturbs me and I don't know how to formulate it so that it doesn't sound like the old "I'm not worthy" plea. (Of course you're not worthy; it would be impertinent of you to wonder if you were.) I have no doubts that I want to be a priest, no uncertainty as to why. But it pains and embarrasses me more than I can say that what I will bring to that altar for ordination is this nauseating sack of guts: selfish, small, lecherous; a mind like a whorehouse; a tongue like a longshoreman's; a soft mousy body that seeks always its own comforts; a will deluded by hyperactive desires. Poor wreck that I am. Can I give over to God's service only so little, and *that* so badly damaged, so in and out of sin and desire? I shall have to let my grotesqueness testify to his mercy. God help me.

Later. Today's liturgy texts are about the peace of the risen Christ. For the first time in a long while, I don't feel anything except a ghastly abandoned ache in the pit of my stomach.

MONDAY, 16 MAY. . . . I just returned from my Mass exam. It went rather well, with only two negligible omissions. Both uglies went unnoticed by the examiner, who spent an embarrassing half hour heaping praise on me for the way I read the Latin and my manner at the altar and (God help us) the sense of sincere dedication I conveyed. I was so nervous I didn't realize where I was half the time. Another exam over. My name is John L'Heureux and I am thirty-one years old and I am in the twenty-sixth grade and when I grow up I hope to retire.

FRIDAY, 10 JUNE. Tomorrow at this time I shall be a priest. And, except that I will be able to give Christ to others in a visible and sometimes dramatic form, I shall be exactly the same: worried and selfish and loving and wanting only to love properly. So this morning

I meditate on God's mercy and humor in choosing me. He *has* chosen me and therefore I rejoice. This is what he makes of the mystery of whatever I am: his instrument, his servant, his other Christ. I am the only Christ some men will ever know. He will have to make me the Christ he wants; the one bit of wisdom I possess is that all my willing has never won me a trace of virtue. God, come; set your tent within me and build a fire. And let them warm their hands at it.

Part Three

Lovers, Husbands, Fathers

Chapter Ten

Edward
Weston
1886-1958

"WHAT IS LOVE!" the renowned American photographer, Edward Weston, asks his *Daybooks* in 1928. "Can it not last a lifetime? Will it never be for me?" Are these the questions of a young romantic or of a seasoned lover? At the age of forty-two, Weston appears to be much of both, as he is throughout most of the intimate journals he kept for more than a quarter of a century. Though already separated from his wife Flora after the birth of their four sons—Chandler, Brett, Neil, and Cole—and having also concluded long affairs with, among others, another photographer Margrethe Mather (M.), and Tina Modotti (T.), a model with whom he lived in Mexico, Weston continues to raise those enigmas that confront any man still both delighted and disrupted by love. How do women differ from men in their expectations of love? Must passion always be undone by time? Why does the *idea* of love often seem more satisfactory than its reality? What does a man owe himself while giving himself to a woman? And how, even in the interests of comfort, can a man give up the thrills of pursuing and loving anew?

If the following passages from Weston's *Daybooks, Volume II— California*, read a bit like the scenario of a bedroom farce, the hazards of excerption and the purposes of this anthology are accountable. Weston's love life thickly threads his journals, but also woven into the rich tapestry of his writing are his relations with his friends and family, the esthetics of his photography, accounts of his extensive travels and his homes and studio life. And everywhere are his observations, served by his strong emotions. For Weston the journal was "My way of exploding . . . the safety valve I need in this day when pistols and poisons are taboo."

At the end of this selection, we find Weston still enjoying a period of domestic peace that apparently has mollified this need to explode on paper. But that old fairy tale ending, "And so they lived happily ever after," is always a lie. Lives, like Weston's many loves, are bound to time, and time will also end his marriage to Charis, who will go on to marry a man more her own age and to raise a family of her own. Edward will eventually begin to feel the crippling effects of Parkinson's disease, which will severely limit his work with the camera and plague him all his remaining years.

1927

(UNDATED). . . . This is a turn unexpected, but too beautiful to be disregarded. When an experienced girl, though she be young, writes, "I love you," one can no longer remain untouched—Love is too rare and precious for flippancy. Her love has changed the incidental attitude I held. Now I would give her all that I can spare.

APRIL 24. What have I, that brings these many women to offer themselves to me? I do not go out of my way seeking them—I am not a stalwart virile male, exuding sex, nor am I the romantic, mooning poet type some love, nor the dashing Don Juan bent on conquest. But it is B.

MAY 31. C. came: I admire and care for her so much that I wish I could respond to her love side more fully. My mental and physical regard for a woman rarely accord: an approximation was attained with M. and T. Now, I am most completely satisfied, physically, by K. or E. To be sure K. has a good mind for a young girl, but E. has nothing for me but an exciting body! A strange twist of life has found one of my loves working for another: E. is now B.'s maid—and neither know! . . .

1928

MONDAY, SEPTEMBER 10. Margrethe Mather here to buy antiques for a holiday shop. She spent Sunday with us. . . . I warmed Margrethe's soul with a bottle of gin. Five years ago, madly in love with her, what an exciting experience this would have been—together in S.F.—far away from local discords. Now, light gossip, bantering, but not a thrill. What is love! Can it not last a lifetime? Will it never for me? Do I only fool myself, thinking I am in love, and really never have been?

And these girls, all friendly after—corresponding, meeting. Does it indicate the affair was not so deep: otherwise might not the end come with an explosion, and a parting forever? . . .

SEPTEMBER 19. . . . It has been a long time since I have had the delights of love! Letters full of tender thoughts have come from K., B., and C. But one cannot live on such vicarious love. Twice I have noted indications of desire in rather interesting girls, but I have "manfully" resisted. Too busy, preoccupied, or indifferent—the indifference may be a result of the former condition.

NOVEMBER 5. . . . A. told Lula, M. is sore at her "because she wanted an affair with me." I had not sensed this, because it had not occurred to me, not seriously.

I have no illusions about the women who fall in love with me. I am in the same boat with the man of wealth. He attracts with gold, I with the glamor which surrounds me, much as the torero or champion pugilist or matinee idol fascinates. Women are hero worshippers. I suppose it has a biological reason, an unconscious selection of the finest type—according to their light—as a father.

I would like to be loved for myself: which means I would like to be a highly sexual animal. But would I? We can't have everything! I am a poor lover, in that I have no time nor desire for sustained interest. I make a grand beginning, then lose out through indifference. The idea means more to me than the actuality. . . .

My ego is gratified by all these easy conquests over the cream of the crop—many of them I know to be girls not easily persuaded. I "kid" myself, and yet I don't. If anything should give me honest satisfaction, it is the friendship and regard these women feel for me after all passion is over.

NOVEMBER 14. The weekend of A. and Edward is now a memory, a rare and perfect one. Hours of exquisite delight for me—and I am sure for A. too—seeing, feeling, her response.

I have had women, burning with passion, women stirred with romance, sensual women: but no one who has quivered in my arms so sensuously responsive to my caresses as this slip of a girl.

So—my own approach being sensuous rather than passionate, the union was well-nigh perfect. . . .

MONDAY, NOVEMBER 26. . . . I am having another reaction, from my statement that I could go through life with one woman! Ridiculous thought! Imagine never again having the thrill of courting— the conquest, new lips to find, new bodies to caress. It would be analogous to making my last print, nailing it to the wall forever, seeing it there, until I would despise it or no longer notice it was there. No! let me stay free! . . .

DECEMBER 8. . . . I awakened with thoughts of A. She is coming this afternoon—and I know beforehand what for: to tell me that we should part. She has been avoiding me with various excuses, too obvious excuses. Real desire overcomes all obstacles. She claims deep melancholy, megalomania, and I know she is subject to depression. But if I had even temporarily "inspired" her, she would be buoyed up and happy. Somehow I have failed—why, I shall try to find out for my own education!

Am I sad with the thought of parting? No, though I wish the affair could have lasted longer. Now, unless the aspect of our association changes, I want it definitely over.

I need someone to be gay with, not one who needs continual cheering. I "kid" myself better than most of my friends. I have my work to fall back on. . . .

Thinking over A. again, maybe I am all wrong as to why she wants to come today. Maybe my thoughts are prompted by *my* desire . . . . Maybe I am the one who wants to end it all and she receives my wish. . . .

DECEMBER 20. . . . Who would have guessed that Weston would be identified with the "Art Colony"—Carmel!

. . . I would like some girl to come with me, to share the interest and growth of this adventure. But who? I shall not go in search of one, I am not that desperate. I am glad now that A. and I parted. She would not have been the right one. Too weak to pioneer, physically, mentally. She has a good mind, but it lacks the directness of purpose to carry through. My momentary enthusiasm got the better of my judgment. C. would come in a moment, but alas dear girl, I could not have you around me long. Yet no finer, truer person ever breathed. K., I would be willing to take a chance. Whether she is strong enough to face the disapproval of her family—and it certainly would cause an eruption— I am not sure. An opportunity for someone willing to gamble with me on a sure thing!

1929

FEBRUARY 21. . . . And letters have come from . . . nine old loves who reach a higher significance through continued interest. All these women—what do they mean in my life—and I in theirs? More

than physical relief—one woman would be sufficient for that . . . .
Actually it means an exchange, giving and taking, growth from contact
with an opposite, more to be learned than could be possible from a close
friend of my own sex, chosen maybe because of similar tastes and ideas.
Such a friendship is stimulating only through a bolstering up of our
own egos, a sympathetic assurance that we are not alone in thought
and desire. But the opposite sex provokes, excites growth, and most
important, affords an opportunity to give. We cannot give to a man of
our own pattern—only accentuate what they already have or clarify
their thoughts—and to give freely, to withhold nothing from one or
many who come with desire, seeking the answer to their riddles—this
is the very meaning of life and the way of personal growth. The spoken
word need not enter in to an exchange: only to be near another, to
read their eyes may be sufficient. Of course this is all idealistic. How
can one *give* when continually worried about the actualities of life—I
mean eating and a corner to sleep in. Coming generations must work
out a better plan.

My one way to give is through my work, for which I find so little
time apart from earning my salt. Somehow, somehow there must come
a solution. I have not had a period of real concentrated work for nearly
a year. I believe I am ready, ripe to begin once more, and the way will
be clear.

TUESDAY, MARCH 12. . . . K. will not come to me for two
years, having decided she must pay off her educational debt to her
parents. Does this mean she will never come? What will she mean to
me in two years? Where will I be? But I do know this—despite all my
protests—and actions—to the contrary: I need some one woman to go
through life with, to build up something not based on an erection of
the moment. . . .

UNDATED. Time: 3:30 a.m. Place: The white sands of Carmel
shore—the moon setting over the ocean. Characters: Sonya (Nosko-
wiak) and Edward.

Edward: "Sonya!"
Sonya: "Edward!"
—and then the first embrace—the first kiss.

Literally they were not the first. I have to thank wine and dancing at a party I gave for A. last Saturday for the prelude.

I danced many times with Sonya, there was an immediate, mutual response. I kissed her cheek and neck and ears as we danced—she did not resist. Then she invited me to supper Tuesday night. We talked, played many records, and she sang until way past midnight: but I made no attempt to renew familiarities. I was sober—she was sober—and I am always backward, afraid to make a false gesture. Perhaps, I thought, the other night her yielding was only due to wine. . . .

How stupid I was! But I put on my coat. She did too!

How wise these women! How subtle was Sonya.

I took the cue and walked with her toward the moonlit water and what I knew was inevitable. . . .

She resisted just long enough. Wise little Sonya—

No sleep that night—no desire to. Tender, lovely, passionate Sonya! . . .

MAY 28. I was showing to Sonya and Brett a portfolio of photographs I had made of some twelve old loves—one fell out and was found on the floor later, one of M. I walked home with Sonya—the first night she has slept at home for a week—on the way stopping at P.O. I had one letter—from M., the first in months. She has been in a mood similar to mine. "I am sick of temporary relations, of making beginnings that are endings. I want a relationship that has some stability, some mutual foundation of companionship, and as you say, building."

M. would be a fine person to consider as permanent. But what of Sonya? Yes—she has already become very close to me, and I can easily imagine a lasting association. And K., whom I asked to come here, with whom I have a sort of agreement? She attracts me physically, she apparently loves me—but I wonder would it last—

Sonya is young—maybe not ready to settle down—

1931

FEBRUARY 21. . . . I have escaped—but a day ago—from a madhouse! A week spent near Flora when she is nursing is nothing less—They sent for me to come—Cole very sick with diphtheria. . . . Poor little Cole—terrible disease—I am glad that I went to him. He might have pulled through without me, but I'm sure I gave him confidence, calmed his own fears. He has inherited or acquired—probably the latter—Flora's appalling terror. . . . Flora right in her element, for if ever she "feels her oats," asserts her ego, rises to supernal heights, it is when nursing: and she is the world's worst nurse. Efficient, yes— so damned efficient that the patient, nor anyone near, is allowed no moment of calm. We all went around like jumping jacks with Flora pulling the wires, issuing the orders, commanding, nagging, countermanding—anything that popped into her poor old rattlebrained pate. When anyone relaxed—high treason—she would find another job—to be done at once!—a spot wiped off the sink—a can taken to the garbage: and when the order was ignored—children become deaf, inert, impervious under continued nagging—then would come over her that look of self-pity, and indignation—toward me—that I would not back up her hysteria. . . .

I called Flora efficient, and that is misleading: I meant to indicate that she is a hard worker, a slave, one who would die for the children, extravagantly generous, but with qualities which lead to utter confusion. The order she so much desires, and could have with half the effort, is dissipated through her most disorderly mind. . . .

All my past has been revived by this experience, and I am satisfied that I did the only possible thing—leave forever. . . .

OCTOBER 14. Sonya is away, visiting her parents. Do I miss her? Yes and no. I miss her as much as I would anyone: but though my friends mean very much to me, I have grown away from any need of their presence—indeed to be alone is a condition I welcome, greatly desire. To know that my friends love me and I them, to see them at rare intervals, is enough. More and more I am absorbed in my life's work. I have set a goal: when the boys are finally started in life, I retire. This means that I will find me an isolated spot as far away from the general public as possible, a place where only those who have a great desire can reach me, and there I will work undisturbed, sending my prints to city markets. . . .

Returning to Sonya: She is industrious, thoughtful, sensitive, and loves me, I'm sure . . . . Since the other family left . . . the house is more at peace—the tension I felt has gone, except when the boys nag or fight. But we four get along quite well together. Praises be that Sonya is a quiet little mouse. . . .

1932

JUNE 26. . . . Sonya is my problem. I love her now as a *best* friend, a true one, never was there truer. But would she accept this change? She has given me the most peaceful "married" life I have ever had, three years of it. She has stood by me, worked for me, saved for me. We are companionable, physically and mentally. Why then this desire to change, to go from a comfortable arrangement, a reasonable adjustment, into the unknown! Or should I say unknown? Do not L. and I know each other, even though our days have been few together? Yes!

I have been "untrue to Sonya once before: the first year. But I knew the adventure for what it was, a passing excitement . . . . But recently, before meeting L., on the way to a party at the Highlands, I sat in the back seat of a car with P. She snuggled close, dropped her head on my shoulder, and I, almost too astonished, caressed her hair. I had known P. for three years, with never the slightest hint of this. But I was willing—no great desire—more curiosity . . . . A psychically different person, P. Admitting she likes to make the conquest—wanting my assurance that I would do anything without being shocked—explaining that she loved to sleep with a man without doing anything—that she liked women, too—in fact I don't think she was sure what she wanted. And I was not interested enough to press "my" suit. Lately she has shown renewed desire. It's too late. I am too filled with L. I will be true to her "in my fashion."

1933

JANUARY 18. Pouring today; much needed, this rain. The south is pathetically dry. I returned from there Friday. Now Sonya has gone, returned with Merle for a week's stay. Just Neil and I left. It is well. I like to be alone; it has connotations of adventure! And this rain augments the feeling I have of something pending. Maybe Sonya is having the adventure. I hope so; then my conscience might be eased. But am I not expressing that thing one is *supposed* to have—a conscience? Actually, I have never felt guilt over my philandering; only a desire not to be discovered for *her* sake; not yet at least. And I could feel quite as guilty toward L., from whose arms I went to H. in L.A. To be sure it was unpremeditated, and we had both reached a delightful intoxication but that does not absolve me from the guilt I should feel— and don't! Yes, and before going south I made love to both S. and X.! Am I then so weak that I fall for every petticoat? Am I so oversexed that I cannot restrain myself? Neither question can be dismissed with a "yes." First, I can go long periods with no desire, no need; then I see the light in a woman's eyes which calls me, and can find no good reason—if I like her—not to respond. I have never deliberately gone out of my way to make a conquest, to merely satisfy sex needs. It amounts to this; that I was meant to fill a need in many a woman's life, as in turn each one stimulates me, fertilizes my work. And I love them all in turn, at least it's more than lust I feel, for the months, weeks, or days we are together. Maybe I flatter myself, but so I feel. So what will you answer to this, Sonya?—and L? L. is my most difficult problem; for I am in a position which amounts to saving her sanity, if not her life. I am not conceited in this; it is all too true. She lives for the day when we can be together. And if it can become possible and I cannot remain true to her—from past records it would seem improbable—what then? I love her, yes, but so have I loved others; and they all pass, not the love, but the emotion, the flame. I love Sonya, but only with tenderness, the calm affection of a friend. And that is not enough for most women, not even the emancipated; they are basically conservative no matter how intellectually radical.

1934

APRIL 20. The busier I am, the more vital and interesting my life, the less time I find to write down my experiences, naturally. Since Jan. so much has happened. Perhaps most important, from the effect it will have upon my future, is the step I took to regain my personal freedom and its achievement. First L. wrote me, a sadly beautiful note, telling me that she realized that we could not go on, that we must start on another basis. She must have sensed this from our last contact. When I have nothing more to give, I do not easily simulate. My reply must have been too unemotional, showing all too ready acceptance (I had made up my own mind months past), because her answer showed that I had caused her a great hurt. Oh, these difficult relations which involve the tragic—because misunderstood—differences between man and woman. . . .

This step toward my freedom, though I did not literally take it, I actually did. She sensed that I held out no hope; this plus my lack of ability to act a part unfelt, caused her to take the initiative. But I did take the first step with Sonya. On our fifth anniversary, April 17, just passed, I wrote her frankly that I must have my freedom, that I could no longer live a lie; of course granting her the same. She rose to the occasion in fine spirit, better by far than I had expected, considering her jealous nature. Perhaps she too had already realized, and become partially reconciled to the fact that she would always have to share me. I told Sonya, and mean it, that I had no desire to live with any other woman, that she was an ideal companion; but that others in my life were as inevitable as the tides, that I rebelled against being tied, that if her jealousy stood in my way, we would have to part. . . .

DECEMBER 9. I have not opened this book for almost 8 months, and with good reason; I have been too busy, busy living. . . . On 4-22 a new love came into my life, a most beautiful one, one which will, I believe, stand the test of time.

I met C. (Charis Wilson)—a short time before going South . . . saw her at a concert, was immediately attracted, and asked to be introduced. I certainly had no conscious designs in mind at the time, but I am not in the habit of asking for introductions to anyone, which means that the attraction was stronger then than I realized. I saw this tall, beautiful girl, with finely proportioned body, intelligent face well-freckled, blue eyes, golden brown hair to shoulders, and had to meet. . . .

I left for the south before our paths crossed again. While there a letter from S. said she had a new model for me, one with a beautiful body. It was C.—Poor S.—How ironical. But what happened was inevitable.

The first nudes of C. were easily amongst the finest I had done, perhaps the finest. I was definitely interested now, and knew that she knew I was. I felt a response. But I am slow, even when I feel sure, especially if I am deeply moved. . . .

After eight months we are closer together than ever. Perhaps C. will be remembered as the great love of my life. Already I have achieved certain heights reached with no other love. . . .

1944

APRIL 22—*Carmel.* Ten years ago today on a Sunday afternoon was the beginning; now Charis and I are married, have been for five years. This is the first entry in my once-well-kept daybook since 1934. I laughingly blame Ch. for cramping my style as a writer—and there may be some truth in this charge—but the fact is that I have not had much time, nor necessary aloneness for keeping an intimate journal. . . .

Chapter Eleven

Ned Rorem

L EFT, RATHER THAN LEAVING, what is an abandoned lover to do? Shoot down the faithless as a demonstration of rage? Turn anger inward and shoot himself in ironic revenge? Or go dead other ways—by anesthetizing the feelings through one of the many escape routes available in our modern age? Men of feeling, of course, continue to feel: their fears, their angers, their griefs. Easier said than done—to stay with so much emotion, to experience the loss of oneself through the loss of another, current suffering calling up so much suffering already assumed laid to rest.

Through the following selection we see a man facing the struggles of one left behind. Attempts at escape and denial prove futile when the strongest truth for this individual resides in his feelings. And the process he undergoes during the months of recovery from his lover's betrayal is classic. From bafflement and self-pity—filled with vain pleas and vainer resolves—the self-condemning defenses begin to disintegrate, bringing him closer to his fear and his grief, which allows him eventually to experience a belated rage that leads to the reaffirmation of his own worth. At last he is able to take responsibility for these feelings, to accept these assaults to his ego without unduly blaming either himself or his former lover, until further distance from the event has him also sense that the gains and losses of love have taken their essential place in the rhythms of a whole lifetime.

Along with his candid series of published diaries, the American composer, Ned Rorem, continues to write critical essays on music and theater while he goes on with his own creative production. Born in Indiana in 1923, educated at Northwestern University and Juilliard, Rorem has had his musical career take him into the heart of the cultural life of New York and Paris, both scenes acutely observed in his diaries. Just as acutely observed is himself, as will be seen in this excerpt from his *New York Diary*, written while in his thirties. Here, in part, Rorem also employs a method familiar to many diarists: the unsent letter, through which one speaks to oneself by addressing another—in this case, Claude, a past lover whose defection served as the catalyst for Rorem's agony, insight, and reconciliation.

Letter to Claude:

New York and Paris
March-May 1957

Cher Claude,
    You've come and gone.
    I write to you now in my journal because I no longer dare speak. You've imposed a straitjacket, though if I could get out I'd be more useless than before: suffering only seems unreasonable to those who cause it. . . .
    And I'm writing in French, because when I think of you it's in that language and I think of you always. To hear it now hurts the heart. I've tried to rid my room of your traces, but go into the city

only to find you there again in fifty souvenirs. I can't stop shaking. Every morning at the mailbox, knowing there'll be no letter, fearing what you might or might not write . . . . I reread new meanings into everything, from your first impotence of last October to your indifference of last month. Was it that in having, you no longer wanted? You said you'd loved me in secret four years before we met, for *my* indifference, but wasn't the result more conquest than affection? It's harder to investigate the shadows of one's own soul than of someone else's, but we've got to try, or we'll never know each other (though must people know each other?). . . .

Once you wrote that I belonged to you. That meant ownership, not affection. To be jilted unexpectedly is rough. It's crazy what two people will do bad to each other, as though the world weren't going to anyway. Flay each other without anesthetic. I've never been left before. Yes, my vanity's touched: why not? Happiness is made mostly of pride. But I'm sad by what will have been errors in judgment, in having selected someone unable to get over the shock of clay feet, the vague conception of what virility is supposed to be in anyone. Thank God I'll have learned it soon enough to be able to find a taste for life again— though not soon enough to have had heart bruised or ideas altered about what used to be called human relations. Now you lower your eyes before the deluge you've provoked.

I tell you all that, but do I believe it? Inscribing mad solutions to enigmas too close to be seen. What's clear is that I love you and could die of it—maybe all the stronger in that I'm no longer anything to you. *Tu m'obsèdes.* The mind reels. Let me see you again once, twice, or seven, or twelve times, no more, please, normally, if only to be rid of your phantom. We were both too terribly impatient. My mistake's always been in committing suicide on the eve of a revelation. Certainly there's an antidote against the poison you write of; could it be friendship? Could it? Could I learn to loathe you?

You used to miss me when I went to the bathroom. I'd based my life on such myths of charm. Now it's sickening to watch weeks go by without the relief of change. A month ago I stopped living. One word from you (which will never come) and I'd start all over. It's not your fault if you no longer love: it's the one thing we don't regulate. Yes,

yes, from the beginning you glimpsed unnatural lights, why did you lead me on, slaughtering? Why did you lose faith? Oh, such holding back when I make these reproaches: you too must have unanswered questions. The irony is that so recently I was saying: "Finally, happiness, I've got it!" No sooner said than gone. . . .

On the phone across the ocean you advised patience. Patience, my God! Obviously there's a difference between a little patience and the paranoid hell of waiting, waiting. I swear, that phone call will be my last abject action. No, it's dumb to swear such things. But I'll make a monstrous daily effort because I want your esteem as much as your love. As proof of goodwill, I've already stopped drinking. Almost. I'd say even it's . . . well . . . licked, and I'm a little scared, because not drinking is like not masturbating: explosion lurks. (Can explosions lurk?)

It's the first morning of spring and I wish I were dead. Got up at noon to see a sticky sky and one season leaking into the next as though the earth had stopped in its tracks, as though the hate and veneration which ooze into love were an eternal repetition of those tears which won't stop flowing, not to purify, but to insult the mud. Oh, I'll get over it! Meanwhile nights are sleepless or if I drop off it's to a recurrent dream in which you take me back, and I'm filled with joy, and wake up to the hard truth that everything's over and done, done, done, and the day's started hopelessly like yesterday, like last week and the week before. Sexual tension's been horrible: there may be pleasure with others, but they don't exist when I think of what I liked from you, and you in me, and I catch fire and can't put it out. . . .

The lover renounced because a bore because he no longer functions as human. With the death rattle of any affair, they say, there's always one hurt more than the other. I love you, joylessly . . . . I'd so love to have the word which would inspire me to go buy a ticket for Paris, a word saying: let's at least try to mend this mess enough for the remembrance to be nostalgic and not sordid, enough for us to see each other as friends and not monsters. . . .

. . . In *Other Voices, Other Rooms* there's a character in love who no longer knows where his lover is. He writes the world over, care of General Delivery— to Oran, Frisco, Shanghai, Frankfurt, in vain. He hadn't got it through his head that the incident was one-sided, that it was finished, that his friend no longer cared. Today I'm that character, nor do I know where you are, nor have I got it through my head that you don't care, but continue to hope against hope and pray on my knees for all soon to be better between us. The worst moment of a life is when you look in the mirror and say (knowing it to be true): "No one wants you anymore."

I think more about you in not having you than when I did, my cloud, my steed, javelin, sapphire. I've never loved anyone but you— the others were . . . . And I'll love you always . . . . We endow our poor lovers with godly traits, then destroy them for being mortal. Make one repugnant gesture that would permit me to despise you, a release from this tender anguish which I stalk, stroking the brief past with its thorns and afternoons at the Pont Mirabeau or the Buttes Rouges, and the first evening when I sang you my songs, which you pretended to like. Love with its soggy crust and petulance must come before the music it's now hard to hear because I ruminate too much, too much on you until there's melting in tears six times a day. . . .

. . . Was it conflict of careers or a jealous disdain of my hamminess that got on your nerves? But I don't want your slavery—except to my body from time to time.

Why on earth write all this? Nothing but an insignificant wind, a sentimental breath which sounded feebly in an immense Sahara, heard by no one, by nothing except a heart that drips, loves, bleeds, snaps, wants still to give itself away. You sought yourself in me but found nothing.

Today's your birthday. Is it possible to dwell on you more intensely than I've done for the third of a year? Not a minute goes without wondering where you are and who you're seeing. It's classic—the banal fixations of leftover people. . . .

You left America a month ago, and since then there's been not one gentle word from you. If you could have foreseen the aftermath, would you have tempered your revenge? No. By accusing me of irony do you clear a bad conscience? But letting myself destroy myself is a sin. Was I too weak or too strong for you? Could you tolerate such fishwifely questions? . . .

. . . I show my foliage too much, heart, ruses, I shouldn't: I'm the mountain who goes to Mohammed. But no one changes anyone. Since no one has anyone, how do other people pass the time? Love is impossible. But when it becomes possible it's no longer love. . . .

Your systematic and somewhat inhuman way of seeing everything could end up exasperating me, making me so ill with jealousy I'd roll in your old sheets, bury my head in that drawer of soiled clothes like a bee in gray roses eager to retrieve your crotch and underarms, needing to possess your yesterday's sweat. An envy of shoes for being closer than I to you. An itch to crawl under the sleeping eyelids so that no dream could waft you where I was uninvited. Now I cannot think of any of those others without crying, and I think of them always. But this time I'm not going to cry, not this time, oh no! . . .

Nobody, even if he's fed up, has the right to do to another what you've done, in changing without warning, condemning without trial. Yet haven't I done it myself so many times? You claim you're the least complex of beings, and it's true for you who've never tried to know yourself as I have tried to know you. . . .

Love is mutual respect; I'd forgotten that you existed too. And love is always a game. And an invention. And what we learned in the last affair trains us what to unlearn in the next; yet when the next's over we realize that what we now refrained from was just what should have been done.

You helped me look into myself, so I love you, to know how to live this little life, and also curiously because you didn't encourage me to love you. I love you for what you are not, with a constructive ego, the best way: one can't healthily love without faith in oneself; and though I haven't it anymore, it will be back.

. . . Today, if by chance you were to come across these pages, you'd hate me in not finding yourself because you don't see yourself as I do yet you think you see yourself entirely. Never again will I believe what were nevertheless the dearest words I've ever heard—those murmured by you in discovering yourself *grâce à moi*. . . .

. . . How boring are loving couples to their friends! bereft of elegance or dignity! Whenever a friend gets married we lose him. How stupid the happy lover! and how stupid the rejected one! Fickle as fairies who break each other's hearts more easily than peasants twist geese necks . . . . You must never learn how indispensable, irreplaceable you've become, how I seek you in nightmares, and by day pitifully in the features of others, in wet places, bars somber and stuffed, or rainy streets or public baths, bottles of gin, or slimy mouths offered risibly. You resent what I've been able to keep of you in me, the you of yesterday who is no more and whom you've forgotten. . . .

We failed thanks to the twentieth century. Because one flies over seas. Because one's in a hurry. Because so many of us see love as being loved (and we're right) that few are left over. Because of the difference between falling and staying in love, because we confuse relief-from-loneliness with infatuation. Loneliness is hard work, infatuation is laziness. Not just anyone can be unhappy . . . . Laziness takes us away from the *practice* of love like practice of music or dentistry. We're certain of only the past and death. *Et encore!* We're ashamed of love though it's the cheapest remedy for solitude. . . .

Having read and drunk everything, what's left but you? Still, we threw ourselves into a disintegrated fusion where, once bars were down, we were quickly without the miracle of astonishment at those discoveries which must constantly renew ourselves, that two become one yet stay two. Is love the act of giving without sacrifice? Even in receiving one gives in sex they say. Bromides of responsibility, respect, love is the offspring of liberty, the do-it-yourself banalities of Erich Fromm, who has recipes for every kind of love except the unrequited. (My self-love is unrequited!) But respect is hard without knowledge, and we're unknowable even to ourselves. I had desired, Claude, that you relinquish your secret in making you suffer rather than in liking you.

. . . I'm less deceived by your attitudes about love than by your ignorance of friendship, your blind good conscience, by the risks you run without running risks. For instance, our last morning in Holland you said: "Well, tonight we go back. The pain if you said what a nice outing, and now *adieu!*" Tables turn. You speak in formulas as you act. I'd not understood that "others" meant yourself. Not understood that, like 90% you existed through habit by surrounding with halos all passing excitements. But to have humiliated me! I've thought too much about you lately to have anything left to say when next we're face to face.

. . . I've said I love you to I don't know how many, each time was the first, and each sincere. For the "always" of lovers is a time set apart and out of daily usage. One has time for everything if one wants:

being busy's a pallid excuse. You'll see when you grow up. When I grow up I'll have lost curiosity. Anger begins to replace languor, it's health, are you glad or not? There remains simply the question of faith. . . .

It's you who were mistaken, I remain consistent in still adoring you. It's up to you—the reparation gesture. . . . You were the flop of my life, meaning: my own flop—as though you said "I was the flop in Ned's life." Ironically I no longer remember the names or faces of so many whose hearts withered through me. There's our justice!

Paris, chez Marie Laure.

Well!! We've met again. Last evening. *Nous avons même fait l'amour.* And though it didn't work too brilliantly (as you say) it was not so much from my shyness as your casualness. Yet I think we both were moved, that you were even lonely and would start up again (on quite another foot, of course—we're no longer the same people, etc.). Maybe I'm wrong. You know, I rather despised you later? All the same, in the taxi home there was sorrow caused by the strange-familiar streets of your far part of town, your slaughter-houses of La Villette, the heavenly prison of blue Paris again. I'd sworn never to confront you with injustices, nor will I . . . since vengeance is not a strong point. But neither will I ever tell you my true feelings. But will tell you this because you want to know: yes, I still love you (what a dull word now) but with a love denuded of gentleness, one doesn't feel gentle toward the heel of a shoe. So much was, and will remain, unsaid. No doubt best. I only ask to see you amicably, painlessly from time to time. But yes, I detest you somewhat. . . .

I've no more time to lose with those who don't pay me court. It was myself who made me suffer, not you; myself who was able to endure the purge, not you. Anyone else could have been an indirect cause. Not you.

One doesn't torture another almost to death only to be later merely vexed that the "victim" misunderstood. You pushed to the utmost limits, cat and mouse, exasperated. From self-protection here's the definitive break. I've had you again and am not interested. Therefore

I dump you—*je te plaque*. As conquest I cost you plenty. It's always a mistake to show one's love too much. You bastard.

These are the calmest, the least mean words with which to end this letter addressed to a misunderstanding. How changed a person I've become only someone else will tell. But I would rather have as remembrance the smell of those arms in a Chicago park tightened sharp around me nineteen years ago again tonight in the heat of France. *Salaud! Espèce de maquereau!* You pig, you real pig! You bad damn son-of-a-bitch, you prick. You shit!

Summer-Autumn 1957

Paris, Italy, Hyères, Paris, New York

I've been back in France four weeks. Still not back, etc. But *l'episode Claude* is over and closed with the ugliest finish imaginable. I have no more force to note the details (thought when I spit in his face a molar fell out!), nor does it make any difference. Yet I think often of it with a heavy heart, and still feel lonely. I'm lonely because I know too many people, and pacify myself by writing letters, it's my habit: the literature of separation. Drinking too much. No sex (nor feel the need, though feel I should feel it.) I grow confounded by the intimacy of such acts where two bodies strive tragically to be one, and the empty-stranger post-orgasm abyss. It happened last night: the frenzied pathetic joy of a child before his birthday cake, followed by the tears of abandonment when the last guest is gone. I'm ready for the calm assurance of a single person, the thatched hut, a cabbage patch.

Looking back—now three seasons have come and gone—at that endless letter to Claude (and it was only one of the many not sent), I feel both embarrassment and impatience. I now see myself as a self-indulgent nag, in view of what I've since learned (do we learn?). True, that suffering was close to unendurable, though in viewing it now (but one doesn't "view it now"—such things freeze) my anxiety was less from love or even privation than from insult, an insult spewing a blank year of recovering from two months of bliss. Still, is time lost in mourning time lost? . . .

1959-60

New York, Saratoga, Buffalo

I've never let myself go all the way—in loving, suffering, drinking, composing. Each is reined to prevent its infringing on the others. So they all diminish.

To feel, one must think. Yet to think—at least for me—precludes feeling. Seldom have I loved for the sake of loving, to have loved and lost, that is, been lost in love—in the *act* of love. Though surely I've been lost in the *thought* of love. I think I feel.

1960-61

Saratoga, New York, Buffalo, New York

I am in love again for the first time. Need to giggle, to jump up and down. Our planet, bulging with joy, seems too small, etc.

Did I write that! Are nearly two thousand days gone since the fall of 1956 when I met Claude? How utterly remote, the agonies of love when they're over, while those of work remain as irksome (to put it mildly) as Damocles' sword! The comings and goings, risings and fallings, the *breathings* of this diary appear, with the overall scope of hindsight, more steady than a sleeper's. . . .

Chapter Twelve

W. N. P. Barbellion 1889-1919

UNLIKE WESTON AND ROREM, love comes just once to W. N. P. Barbellion, but is profound enough to transform the man and the substance of his "disappointed" life. Plagued from childhood by severe ill-health, handicapped by his family's economic setbacks, this largely self-educated English zoologist was an enthusiastic but soliatry naturalist. Brilliance in his profession earned him only small recognition, and at last a hard-won assistantship at London's Natural History Museum, a position which soon had to be relinquished to endure a lingering death by sclerosis at the age of thirty. But while still unaware of the gravity of this degenerative disease, he married and was miraculously rewarded with a wife whose love and devotion illuminated the darkness that surrounded their union.

Barbellion, the pen name of Bruce Frederick Cummings, kept diaries from the age of thirteen until near death. His *Journal of a Disappointed Man*, published the year before he died, often reads like a George Gissing novel—the fateful history of yet another bright but poorly placed young Englishman who is as doomed by his lack of privilege as by his own constitution. But what redeems this sad life from bathos is Barbellion's unwavering zeal for his work, the honest exploration of his feelings, the wit within the rage as he weakens with paralysis, and most especially his moving love story—that evolution from doubting suitor to ecstatic husband whose wife soon frets him with the birth of a daughter he is too ill to support well. A traditional love story, in which the idealized woman of a young man's dream—despite her "lamentable thumbs"—descends from the heavens to be helpmate to her hero, it is, finally, a tragic story, as the agonized but loving invalid writes: "I am only twenty-eight, but I have telescoped into those few years a tolerably long life: I have loved and married, and have a family; I have wept and enjoyed; struggled and overcome, and when the hour comes I shall be content to die."

1912

NOVEMBER 11. Met her this evening in Kensington Road. "I timed this well," said she, "I thought I should meet you." Good Heavens, I am getting embroiled. Returned to the flat with her and after supper called her "The Lady of Shalott."

"I don't think you know what you're talking about."

"Perhaps not," I answered. "I leave it to you."

"Oh! but it rests with you," she said.

Am I in love? God knows—but I don't suppose God cares.

1913

FEBRUARY 15. Tried to kiss her in a taxi-cab on the way home from the Savoy—the taxi-cab danger is very present with us—but she rejected me quietly, sombrely. I apologised on the steps of the Flats and said I feared I had greatly annoyed her. "I'm not annoyed," she said, "only surprised"—in a thoughtful, chilly voice.

We had had supper in Soho, and I took some wine, and she looked so bewitching it sent me in a fever, thrumming my fingers on the seat of the cab while she sat beside me impassive. Her shoulders are exquisitely modelled and a beautiful head is carried poised on a tiny neck.

AUGUST 9. . . . In the evening went over to see her. She was wearing a black silk gown and looked handsome. . . . She is always the same sombre, fascinating, lissom, soft-voiced She! She herself never changes . . . . What am I to do? I cannot give her up and yet I do not altogether wish to take her to my heart. It distresses me to know how to proceed. I am a wily fish.

AUGUST 14. I tried my best, I've sought every loophole of escape, but I am quite unable to avoid the melancholy fact that her thumbs are—lamentable. I am genuinely upset about it for I like her. No one more than I would be more delighted if they were otherwise. . . . Poor dear! how I love her! That's why I'm so concerned about her thumbs.

1914

NOVEMBER 9. In the evening asked her to be my wife. She refused. Once perhaps . . . but now. . . .

I don't think I have any moral right to propose to any woman seeing the state of my health and I did not actually intend or wish to. . . . It was just to get it off my mind—a plain statement. . . . If I don't really and truly love her it was a perfectly heartless comedy. But I have good reason to believe I do. With me, moments of headstrong passion alternate with moods of perfectly immobile self-introspection. It is a relief to have spoken.

NOVEMBER 14. Before going over to-night bought *London Opinion* deliberately in order to find a joke or better still some cynicism about women to fire off at her. Rehearsed one joke, one witticism from Oscar Wilde, and one personal anecdote (the latter for the most part false), none of which came off, tho' I succeeded in carrying off a nonchalant or even jaunty bearing.

"Don't you ever swear?" I asked. "It's a good thing you know, swearing is like pimples, better to come out, cleanses the moral system. The person who controls himself must have lots of terrible oaths circulating in his blood."

"Swearing is not the only remedy."

"I suppose you prefer the gilded pill of a curate's sermon: I prefer pimples to pills."

Is it a wonder she does not love me?

NOVEMBER 29. This evening she promised to be my wife after a long silent ramble together thro' dark London squares and streets! I am beside myself!

DECEMBER 9. . . . I shook her angrily by the shoulders to-night and said, "Why do I love you?—Tell me," but she only smiled gently and said, "I cannot tell. . . ." I ought not to love her, I know—every omen is against it. . . .

Then I am fickle, passionate, polygamous. . . . I am haunted by the memory of how I have sloughed off one enthusiasm after another. I used to dissect snails in a pie-dish in the kitchen while Mother baked the cakes—the unravelling of the internal economy of a *Helix* caused as great an emotional storm as to-day the Unfinished Symphony does! . . .

All this evidence of my temperamental instability alarms and distresses me on reflection and makes the soul weary. I wish I loved more steadily. I am always sidetracking myself. The title of "husband" scares me.

1915

MAY 29. . . ."It's funny," she said, "but I thought your letters were cold. Letters are so horrid."

The incident shews how impossible is intellectual honesty between lovers. Truth is at times a hound which must to kennel.

"Write as you would speak," said I, "you know I'm not one to carp about a spelling mistake!"

The latter remark astonished me. Was it indeed I who was speaking? All the week I had been fuming over this. Yet I was honest: the Sun and E's presence were dispelling my ill-humours and crochets. We sealed our conversation with a kiss and swore never to doubt each other again. E's spell was beginning to act. It is always the same. I cannot resist the actual presence of this woman. Out of her sight, I can in cold blood plan a brutal rupture. I can pay her a visit when the first kiss is a duty and the embrace a formality. But after 5 minutes I am passionate and devoted as before. It is always thus. After leaving her, I am angry to think that once more I have succumbed.

In the evening we went out into a field and sat together in the grass. It is beautiful. We lay flat on our backs and gazed up at the sky.

AUGUST 1. Am getting married . . . on September 15th. It is impossible to set down here all the labyrinthine ambages of my will and feelings in regard to this event. Such incredible vacillations, doubts, fears. I have been living at a great rate below surface recently. "If you enjoy only twelve months' happiness," the Doctor said to me, "it is worth while." But he makes a recommendation. . . . At his suggestion E— went to see him and from his own mouth learnt all the truth about the state of my health, to prevent possible mutual recrimination in the future. To marry an introspective dyspeptic—what a prospect for her!

. . . I exercise my microscopic analysis on her now as well as on myself.
. . . This power in me is growing daily more automatic and more
repugnant. It is a nasty morbid unhealthy growth that I want to hide
if I cannot destroy. It amounts to being able at will to switch myself in
and out of all my most cherished emotions; it is like the case in Sir
Michael Foster's *Physiology* of a man who, by pressing a tumour in
his neck could stop or at any rate control the action of his heart.

AUGUST 6. . . . Most married men are furtive creatures, and
married women too. But I have a Gregers Werle-like passion for life to
be lived on a foundation of truth in every intercourse. I would have my
wife know all about me and if I cannot be loved for what I surely am,
I do not want to be loved for what I am not. If I continue to write
therefore she shall read what I have written. . . .

1916

MAY 5. Hulloa, old friend: how are you? I mean my Diary. I
haven't written to you for ever so long, and my silence as usual indicates
happiness. I have been passing thro' an unbroken succession of calm
happy days, walking in the woods with my darling, or doing a little
gentle gardening on coming home in the evening—and the War has
been centuries away. . . .

The only troubles have been a chimney which smokes and a neighbor's dog which barks at night. So to be sure, I have made port after
storm at last—and none too soon. To-day my cheerfulness has been
rising in a crescendo till to-night it broke in such a handsome crest of
pure delight that I cannot think of going to bed without recording it.

MAY 20. Spent a quiet day. Sat at my escritoire in the Studio
this morning writing an Essay, with a large 4-fold window on my left,

looking on to woods and fields, with Linnets, Greenfinches, Cuckoos calling. This afternoon while E rested awhile I sat on the veranda in the sun and read *Antony and Cleopatra* . . . . Yes, I'm in harbour at last. I'd be the last to deny it but I cannot believe it will last. It's too good to last and it's all too good to be even true. E is too good to be true, the home is too good to be true, and this quiet restful existence is too wonderful to last in the middle of a great war. It's just a little deceitful April sunshine, that's all. . . .

JULY 20. The cradle came a few days ago but I had not seen it until this morning when I unlocked the cupboard door, looked in and shuddered.

"That's the skeleton in our cupboard," I said in coming down to breakfast. She laughed, but I really meant it.

E keeps a blue bowl replenished with flaming Poppies in our room. The cottage is plagued with Earwigs which fly in at night and get among the clothes and bedlinen. This morning, dressing, she held up her chemise to the light saying: "I always do this—you can see their little heathen bodies then against the light. . . ." Isn't she charming?

SEPTEMBER 26. The numbness in my right hand is getting very trying . . . . The Baby puts the lid on it all. Can't you see the sordid picture? I can and it haunts me. To be paralyzed with a wife and child and no money—ugh!

Retribution proceeds with an almost mathematical accuracy of measure . . . . There is no mercy in Cause and Effect. It is inhuman clockwork. Every single act expended brings one its precise equivalent in return. . . .

OCTOBER 5. Home again with my darling. She is the most wonderful darling woman. Our love is for always. The Baby is a monster.

OCTOBER 27. Still awaiting a reprieve. I hate alarming the Doctor—he's such a cheerful man so I conceal my symptoms, quite a collection by now.

The prospect of breaking the news to her makes me miserable. I hide away as much as possible lest she should see. I *must* speak when she is well again.

NOVEMBER 6. She has known *all* from the beginning! M— warned her *not* to marry me. How brave and loyal of her! What an ass I have been. I am overwhelmed with feelings of shame and self-contempt and sorrow for her. She is quite cheerful and an enormous help.

NOVEMBER 17. E— has been telling me some of her emotions during and after her fateful visit to my Doctor just before our marriage. He did not spare her and even estimated the length of my life after I had once taken to my bed—about 12 months . . . . Poor darling woman—if only I had known! My instinct was right—I felt in my bones it was wrong to marry, yet here was M— urging me on . . . . I know her now for all she is worth—her loyalty and devotion, her courage and strength. If only I had something to give her in return! Something more than the dregs of a life and a constitutional pessimism. I greatly desire to make some sacrifice, but I am so poor these days, so very much a pauper on her charity, there is no sacrifice I can make. Even my life would scarcely be a sacrifice in the circumstances—it is hard not to be able to give when one *wants* to give.

DECEMBER 4. The Baby touch is the most harrowing of all. If we were childless we should be merely unfortunate, but an infant. . . .

1917

JANUARY 20. I am over 6 feet high and as thin as a skeleton; every bone in my body, even the neck vertebrae, creak at odd intervals when I move. So that I am not only a skeleton but a badly articulated one to boot. If to this is coupled the fact of the creeping paralysis, you have the complete horror. Even as I sit and write, millions of bacteria are gnawing away my precious spinal cord, and if you put your ear to my back the sound of the gnawing I dare say could be heard. The other day a man came and set up a post in the garden for the clothes' line. As soon as I saw the post I said "gibbet"—it looks exactly like one, and I, for sure, must be the malefactor. Last night while E– was nursing the baby I most delightfully remarked: "What a little parasite—why you are Cleopatra affixing the aspic—'Tarry good lady, the bright day is done, and we are for the dark.'"

The fact that such images arise spontaneously in my mind, show how rotten to the core I am.

. . . The advent of the Baby was my *coup de grâce*. The little creature seems to focus under one head all my personal disasters and more than once a senseless rage has clutched me at the thought of a baby in exchange for my ambition, a nursery for the study. Yet, on the whole, I find it a good and satisfying thing to see her, healthy, new, intact on the threshold: I grow tired of my own dismal life just as one does a suit of dirty clothes. My life and person are patched and greasy; hers is new and without a single blemish or misfortune . . . . Moreover, she makes her mother happy and consoles her grandmother too.

JUNE 1. We discuss post mortem affairs quite genially and without restraint. It is the contempt bred of familiarity I suppose. E– says widows' weeds have been so vulgarised by the war widows that she won't go into deep mourning. "But you'll wear just one weed or two for me?" I plead, and then we laugh. She has promised me that should a suitable chance arise, she will marry again. Personally, I wish I could place my hand on the young fellow at once, so as to put him thro' his paces—shew him where the water main runs and where the gas meter is, and so on.

You will observe what a relish I have for my own *macabre,* and how keenly I appreciate the present situation. Nobody can say I am not making the best of it. One might call it pulling the hangman's beard. Yet I ought, I fancy, to be bewailing my poor wife and fatherless child.

JULY 25. I don't believe in the twin-soul theory of marriage. There are plenty of men any one of whom she might have married and lived with happily, and simpler men than I am. Methinks there are large tracts could be sliced off my character and she would scarcely feel the want of them. To think that she of all women, with a past such as hers, should be swept into my vicious orbit! Yet she seems to bear Destiny no resentment, so I bear it for her and enough for two. . . .

JULY 26. . . . I get out of bed about ten, wash and sit by the window in my blue striped pyjama suit. It is so hot I need no additional clothing. E– comes in, brushes my hair, sprinkles me with lavender water, lights my cigarette, and gives me my book-rest and books. She forgets nothing. . . .

AUGUST 31. My darling sweetheart, you ask me why I love you. I do not know. All I know is that I *do* love you, and beyond measure. Why do *you* love me—surely a more inscrutable problem. You do not know. No one ever knows. "The heart has its reasons which the reason knows not of." We love in obedience to a powerful gravitation of our beings, and then try to explain it by recapitulating one another's characters just as man forms his opinions first and then thinks out reasons in support.

What delights me is to recall that our love has *evolved*. It did not suddenly spring into existence like some beautiful sprite. It developed slowly to perfection—it was forged in the white heat of our experience. That is why it will always remain.

SEPTEMBER 1. Your love, darling, impregnates my heart, touches it into calm, strongly beating life so that when I am with you, I forget I am a dying man. It is too difficult to believe that when we die true love like ours disappears with our bodies. My own experience makes me feel that human love is the earnest after-death of a great reunion of souls in God who is love. When as a boy I was bending the knee to Haeckel, the saying, "God is Love," scarcely interested me. I am wiser now. . . .

SEPTEMBER 2. But am I dying? I have no presentiments—no conviction—like the people you read of in books. Am I, after all, in love? "I dote yet doubt; suspect yet strongly love." It is all a matter of degree. Beside Abélard and Hélöise, our love may be just glassy affection. It is a great and difficult question to decide. I love no one else but E– that, at least, is a certainty, and I have never loved anyone more.

SEPTEMBER 30. Last night, E– sitting on the bed with me, burst into tears. It was my fault. "I can stand a good deal but there must come a breaking point." Poor, poor girl, my heart aches for you.

I wept too, and it relieved us to cry. We blew our noses. "People who cry in novels," E– observed with detachment, "never blow their noses. They just weep." . . . But the thunder clouds soon come up again.

Chapter Thirteen

Peter Marin

For W. N. P. Barbellion the blunt fact of death caused him to find in his marriage to E– a brief but astounding blessing. For Peter Marin, the social critic and poet, that intricate bonding with his wife Rachel proves more problematic. In a difficult season during their marriage, Marin had to leave their Santa Barbara home several times for his work as an educational consultant and administrator in San Francisco and the Santa Cruz Mountains. The journal he kept that long summer of 1972 was eventually published under the title *In a Man's Time*.

Very much a man of his time and place, Marin uses his understanding of humanistic psychology to help him describe the anatomy of his marriage and his unorthodox lifestyle. As he feels his complicated way into the heart of his relationship with Rachel, and with the other significant women and men who also have a place in their open living arrangements, feminists might be appalled by some of his observations, men perhaps even more disturbed by the implications. With a wife no longer content with the traditional role of housewife, and a husband who could never be a mere householder, we are made to wonder what value remains for them in such a marriage. In pursuit of his own answer, Marin recognizes the impossible burden our society still often expects a marriage to carry, and illuminates the paradoxical nature of much of human desire—that need to struggle free of ties that bind too tightly while needing the comfort that only such binding secures.

1972

JULY 12. Strange, what goes on these days with Rachel. Sometimes I think longingly of home, filled with tenderness for her and the children. But when I talk to her on the phone, as I did this morning, the feeling vanishes almost instantly. I don't know why that happens, whether it is something she does or something I do or something that merely happens between us. But something goes dead in me, closes itself off, and by the time we have finished talking I feel emptied, exhausted. Beneath everything we say to one another there is always anger, and though Rachel claims to be unaware of hers it is there nonetheless: a need to get even, to clothe in her words the angry words she is reluctant to speak more openly. I enter our conversations aching for a kind word, a touch of generosity, and I emerge from them still aching, somehow humiliated by Rachel's dark stubbornness, something almost miserly in her which refuses these days to open or give. . . . I have a perpetual sense of deprivation, hopelessness, entrapment. . . .

Ah, I might have told Rachel I have been missing her. I might have told her how important she is to me. I might have said, I might have said. . . . But instead my words are empty and flat. Despite my good intentions something in me turns sour and small, and I think: *She is doing it, she means to do it.* And something rises up in me to defend itself, I step back, I close off; in the distances between us I turn away still more, and whatever is between us thins, worsens and continues.

JULY 15. . . . Now, back together after a few weeks apart, we are thrown almost instantly into the same confusions between us as before. I am as puzzled as ever by what happens to Rachel in my presence. I do not know what it is, save that I am never what she hopes me to be, and that raw fact throws her back into darkness, into her worries about her life and where it is taking her, and what she must do with it. . . . But that is wrong, for the truth is that I do not often reach out to try to touch her, but am content instead to steer clear of her darkness, and that, of course, is what disappoints her: the distance which envelops us both when we are together. I am so anxious to keep from promising anything that my later deeds will betray that I fail to assuage the sense of betrayal already there. So we wheel in endless and absurd circles, and Rachel says to me unhappily, "All my plans turn to dreams."

I do not know what to say in return. I am caught between contrary desires, feeling myself more alive when away and yet more at home when here, feeling always in my chest the awful magnetism of the household and my children, an attraction there as strong as any impulse to pull away. Watching Rachel watching me, I fill with a sense of her pain mixing with mine. Sometimes when I am talking about my plans for the fall I say something careless, and I can see her face change and blur with tears. It is then that I feel within myself the vertigo she must feel when considering her own life, her feeling of senselessness, emptiness. It is sometimes more difficult to suffer that feeling—her sorrow—than my own. What I experience becomes a combination of the two of them, my own fear of separation and my projected sense of Rachel's grief. They knit themselves together into a body inside me, and just as I feel my friends to be a web, a shield within my breast, so too I hold the household at the center of my life, and its projected absence leaves a space inside me into which I fall.

AUGUST 1. . . . It is late at night, my first night back. We are lying together and talking in the loft of Rachel's room.

I say, "When I'm away I think of you with tenderness. I want to be with you again. We have been together a long time, and there is no one else I would want to live with."

130

And suddenly Rachel is crying, is down at the end of the bed, doubled up, is saying back over her shoulder, "But that isn't enough, not enough for me as a woman. I feel that my life as a woman is over. I want something more. . . ."

She sits, sobbing, her feet dangling over the loft's edge, back bent. I lie stiff and silent, diminished to speechlessness, impotent, unequal to her. We are by this time halfway to the center of our confusion, drawn there against our wills, for an hour before, at midnight, we had lain down together. Gently, carefully we had begun to make love. Soft, soft, we had moved with hands and mouths over one another's flesh, touching, licking, had come together—and then, suddenly, something had gone wrong. I do not know, even now, what it was. Rachel seemed to me to pull back and away, to close herself up. I pushed harder into and against her, hoping somehow to bring her up to and alive to me, to see myself somehow in her eyes. But she was gone beneath me, there was no connection between our rhythms, I felt her legs stretched stiff, thigh muscles tightened as if to close, to close me out. I stiffened and stopped and she opened her eyes and then we were looking at one another, our faces close: strangers, ages apart, a kind of horror passing between us, a raw shock. Then we were into it, caught and falling: the past made its way into our mouths and hands, our energies turned into rage, and the storm broke around and inside of us. We seethed with it, it broke us open, we closed against it and against one another; there was no will, no choice, it was something we did but did not do, something we could not stop, for the thrust of the past carried us along, there was too much demanding to be spoken and re-spoken, and every word both relieved the pressure and increased it, brought us closer to the end of the process, drove us father apart.

. . . Now, a day later, working in a sunny room at this machine, slowly, almost automatically, typing one letter after another, emptied of feeling, the whole thing seems to me exhaustive, inescapable, impossible. I feel as if I had been enveloped by the sea and spun round and round and then disgorged, so that I float now on the surface, still dripping, and remember it all vaguely, like a dream. Rachel is vacuuming now in the other room. I go in there to make a phone call, get some iced coffee. I put my arms around her from behind. She turns her head back to me and kisses me, her lips soft. I say, "Are you alright?" and she nods, humming to herself.

But earlier this morning we were screaming at one another, were inside one another clawing to get out. I woke, surly and vicious, late in the morning, I felt crowded into a corner, into myself, felt weak, old, thin and furious. I came up storming at the house's filth, and at Rachel, and then we were at it, tooth and nail and hammer and words, and I broke again and again upon Rachel's hard surface, and she turned her hard, grudging face toward me and her self away, and she told me to leave, to go away, and I broke, threw the phone in my hand against the floor, shouting, "No, no this is also *my* house,". . .

. . . I leaned against Rachel's table, trying to find a combination of words that would not only explain what I meant but also undo the whole mess, somehow spring us free: "I always come home meaning to be different. I've been with enough people to have felt myself often as a whole person, to feel my real size, and this isn't it, this isn't me, I don't know how to explain it, but now I shrink, I . . ."

And I had shrunk, I was complaining again, and Rachel was quick to hear it, and retreat, and she said, "You see, there you go again, picking at me, telling me what I do to you, well, if that's what I do, why don't you go away, go and leave us all alone? All I hear is how we injure you and how much better you feel elsewhere, and . . ."

And we were at it again, and I had done it and she had done it, and how can we turn to one another when every turning and every pain is a judgment about and attack on the other?

I said again, trying again, "Alright. I do it all wrong. I know. But I come here needing something. I don't know how to live without it. I *won't* live without it!"

And Rachel said, "And me? What about me. I too am what I am. You say you won't change, and why should I? This is my life, why should I change it for you?"

So, always, we reach an impasse, and the impasse opens beneath us and swallows us, and so we move today, in the sunlight, still in the darkness of this morning and last night. . . .

AUGUST 4. Late in the afternoon Jim and I go out for a drink.

. . . Jim reads some pages from my journal, then says, "I don't know why you stay with her."

What can I say to that? . . . It is a wedding that occurs in the flesh, a kind of twinning—that is all I know. Even separation occurs always *in relation* to the other; one is never really alone, is merely apart, away. Though I turn determinedly from Rachel toward the world, Rachel is still there, is still part of the I who turn; we seem a complicated constellation moving from one dimension to another. . . .

I say to Jim, "I don't know. I suppose because she is real."

But what do I mean by that? Rachel is dark, enduring, sensual, *rich*. There is in her a generosity of life even when she stubbornly clings to her darkness. Other women usually seem to me thin and opaque, too narrow, exciting on the surface but underneath merely sensational, shrill. They seem to crumple, shrivel.

I say, "I've never seen a long marriage among my friends any different from my own. None of us want what is best for us, but merely what seems most solid, most real."

How many friends, after all, do I know who are truly married? For those who are, it is always a contest, a struggle. Whenever I step away from it I feel light, light-footed, I float free, grow larger. There are baseball players who practice all winter with a ball slightly heavier than the one used in games; then, in the spring, it feels lighter, easier to throw. That is precisely how I feel whenever I leave Rachel. I expand, I soar. But behind me I always need that other, that struggle, that meeting in which the dark implacability of the world shapes itself into Rachel and through her makes its earthy demands on me. . . .

But Rachel, as she moves now in my mind, is large, fleshed, serious, real. What confronts me as I turn to her is a world I cannot fathom, perhaps cannot survive. I no longer know whether it is her hardness or her softness that frightens me away and draws me back, but I feel still part of my own destiny there, hidden, if not in her, then in the landscape that we create between us, in which I become a child again, and fight for my life, and learn—slowly, slowly—how to survive, how at times to dance and sing. If I have a muse, it is this dark, demanding, sometimes generous and grudging one: this black moon. It is this I cannot and have not learned to live with or without, must find a way to live with. The rest is a vacation, a schoolboy's holiday.

Where Rachel and I struggle is a place so private, so deep, that words disappear. I emerge from it bloodied, disordered, and with no way to say to others, to Jim, what I have been doing there, or why I return to it.

AUGUST 22. "Listen," I say. "It is my house too. I need it now. I want time and space, some kind of order, a place to work, a *place*. I'm going to come back *now*."

Even as I say that I understand how it sounds to Rachel, as if I want to sweep her life away and out of the house, as if I am brutal, thoughtless. But I do not know how else to make my need felt, for she deflects it in order to protect her own, or perhaps to punish me, or simply because it is just. Her own life, when I am gone, is busy, tangled. Though she tells me always that she does not like it, at least the house comes alive for her, and she comes alive too, her own vitality asserts itself, she brightens and laughs, senses in herself something new, and then is forced to fight for it, to literally hold it against me when I come along, as I do now, saying into the phone:

"I know it is your life. But it is my house too, and it no longer feels to me like a home, and if it doesn't, why then I will have to make a home for myself somewhere else."

And of course Rachel hears that as a threat, an ultimatum, and she stiffens, fights back. "Where," she says, her voice hard-edged, "am *I* in all of this?"

I stand dumb with the phone in my hand. Where, indeed, is she? How to explain this raw tangle of confusion, this thin affection, this bewildered bond?

She says insistently, "Yes, how *do* you see me? What am I doing while you're in the house? Why do you want me? *Do* you want me?

"Yes," I say, "I do, I want some kind of warmth, some kind of . . ."

But even as I put this down I see its absurdity. What I want may not be Rachel at all, it is not Rachel as she is; or rather, it is not *only* Rachel, it is a way of living, a whole life, and she is part of it but not all of it, and that makes her right; there are indeed things I will not give up for her. That is precisely what humiliates her and seems to her to make us unequal, for she believes that she has given up all things for me—though of course she has not, and she rightfully clings to her needs. So we end as always: I cry out *me, me, me,* and she shouts back *me, me, me,* and I have no answer, I know no solution, I know only that I want my house back and so I end by feeling like a tyrant, a prick. I am not in fact those things; or, rather, I am more than those. But these days I become them entirely, I am left raging and sorry and with a sense of Rachel as victimized, betrayed and *right*—but also brutal to me in some way. . . .

AUGUST 25. . . . Now, writing about all this, I think . . . also about the pressure last night not only on Vincent but also on Michael to enact for Joan and Rachel their dreams of drama and disaster. The two of them are at once like little girls egging boys on and mothers sending their sons off to war. One thinks of Kali: beckoning and beheading, ruling and rewarding. Perhaps it is merely the desire for a strong and potent male, a queenly demand for a king's company; perhaps it is the womb crying out for revenge and homage. But whatever the case, men are often asked to act out and, in the woman's dream of violence and power, to become a part of her myth of herself. There is a disdain in many women for those who will not cooperate, a kind of frustrated unspoken judgment. They want *heroes,* those strong enough to fight with and for them—but only those who play their roles out *nicely,* like obedient boys. That is the tangled need always there, the curious confusion: the wish for male strength and the need to keep the male a child, the insistence that manhood be expressed through power and force, and the wish to quell that force, to diminish and control it.

AUGUST 27. Women! How we want and suffer them, caught in their wombs, pulling away, trapped inside, kept out, wanting in, acting out, at their expense, our own dramas, acting out, at our own expense, theirs. I have never known whether this life I have chosen is my destiny or whether my fate is elsewhere, unlived, kept from me by all of this. Like a house with one door that is three out of four days turned elsewhere, Rachel is waiting to be entered, impossible to enter, impossible to leave, waiting to be left. Yet at times, for a moment, the door opens between us, one sees, inside, the blazing garden of the gods, slips past the guards, the beckoning hand, the sword, and is there, at home, the heart rising up and also at rest.

At times, of course, it becomes a war—not so much with one another as with the presence in ourselves of dreams and needs no one can satisfy. We struggle to wrest from one another what we cannot fully give, what is not fully ours to give. What we need and demand from one another is what ought to be found elsewhere: in comrades and brothers, work or community, vision and the gods. But these shred and vanish and we are left alone or in one another's arms. We turn to the root and source of love and look there for a door, a way home, though the way and the home have vanished, and there is no place for us other than where we are. What is between us cannot bear the weight of what is between us. The age itself is written into our bodies and marriages, and in struggling with one another we struggle with the world, and what we learn—the fragile tenderness, the varied forms of love—becomes, as we live them out, the nature of the age.

SEPTEMBER 1. The house is quiet, empty—like a boat at anchor. Rachel is relaxed and open, patient with me, generous. I begin to settle in and to get a sense of myself here, to feel as if it is my home. I clear out the back bedroom, put away the cartons, set my typewriter and papers out on the desk, begin to work. It goes slowly and without success. Every few minutes I get up restlessly from my desk and wander [through] the rest of the house, where I find Rachel watching television or drinking coffee or mixing gazpacho. We have little to say to one another and what we say is still self-conscious and a bit too loud, as if there were an audience or jury watching us. But we seem at the moment to have nothing against one another, and Rachel is more content than I have seen her in months. I am still wary, a bit numb, unexcited, but I feel myself slipping into this life like a crocodile into the mud. If there is something too safe about it, too snug, too much *known*, then I tell myself, too, that those are the conditions of life, the conditions in which work gets done. I tell myself I am spoiled, that I want too much, that this is my proper share. I half believe it too, and, sitting here at night, working, I am not sure whether I want to sigh with domestic satisfaction or with resigned diminution.

Chapter Fourteen

David Steinberg

FOR BETTER OR WORSE, as Barbellion, Weston, and Marin have shown, the commitment to marriage is often made—and with it often come children. Like women, men handle the expanding responsibility of parenthood in ways they have learned from their own parents, or with the wish to unlearn those ways. When fatherhood comes to David Steinberg, he begins his *Fatherjournal*—a record of the first five years of his relationship with his son, Dylan—as part of his antidote to the tradition of fathers "who have been taught to turn away from their children."

Dedicated to exploring alternative approaches to work, marriage, sexuality, and community, David and his wife Susan, two educators who still live with Dylan in Northern California, deliberately set out to share the job of raising their son on more equal terms than most young couples do. Both understand that personality traits deemed masculine or feminine are as culturally determined as is the clothing each sex wears. Both believe in the flexibility of their tasks as parents rather than in some instinctual proclivity.

For Steinberg, this determination to be more than the traditional "provider" for their child demands his also facing up to feelings that traditional fathering too often disallows—his fear, his resentment, his unabashed love—as he continues to probe the contrary effects that Dylan brings to his marriage, his work, his sense of himself as a man. And ultimately, it is this son, coming in touch with the son still inside his father, who provides Steinberg with his deepening awareness of that universal need for the perfect parent none of us ever has.

1971

MAY 2. Tonight I cried for the first time since Dylan was born. All the walls, all the strengths, all the holding tight, came tumbling down and the tears came tumbling out.

I know so little of being a father. It is too much for me.

I was going to be the perfect father; loving, caring, nurturing, soft. I was going to make up for all the men who leave the children to the women, who back away from intimacy with children, who are cold and distant. I was going to do it right.

Tonight I see how scared I am. There is so much to do for this little creature who screams and wriggles and needs and doesn't know what he needs and relies on me to figure it all out. I watch myself run away, leaving the baby to Susan and her woman's intuition and her breasts full of milk. Part of me wants to get as far away from him as I possibly can. Sitting in the armchair while Susan struggles to get him to sleep, I finally admitted how far I am from where I would like to be.

I tried to tell Susan what was going on with me. It was hard to talk. He's only been here a month, and already it's more than I can handle. I cried for a long, long time. It felt good to confess, to break down.

Afterward, I had the beginnings of a new vision: I need to accept my fear, my reluctance, my instinct to flee. I have to start from where I am instead of where the model new-age father would be. Susan encouraged me to let myself run away when I needed to. It helped to hear that from her, since she will be left to take care of Dylan whenever I do.

I am so small compared to what needs to be done.

SEPTEMBER 15 *(notes at six months).* Dylan is napping: chance to unwind and settle into writing. I still find it hard to write in tune to Dylan's schedule. Like now I've just started and he's woken up crying. I have to stop to take care of him.

. . . Having a baby has brought an astounding amount of day-to-day work. A lot gets lost in the shuffle, like having time to sit and relax, time to talk about things that are hard to say, time to sort out feelings and become whole again. There are no more Sunday morning breakfasts in bed.

I wish now that I had prepared myself better for having a baby. I let myself get caught by surprise, and then felt resentful, as if I had been cheated out of something I couldn't quite define.

. . . I'm an only child and I never babysat as a teenager. I knew nothing about babies when Dylan was born. My confidence in myself as a father was very shaky. I could hold myself together as long as everything went smoothly, but when something unusual happened I panicked. I got very depressed at my lack of intuitive baby sense.

Once I admitted all that to myself, and to Susan, I could face my weaknesses and work on them. I began to see that there were times when I was really good with Dylan, when I really did have good intuitive sense about relating to a baby.

I wanted to jump right in, confident and competent, and be a father who thoroughly enjoyed taking care of his baby. I wanted to cut all the American father bullshit out of me in one slice. But overcoming basic cultural habits isn't that easy or dramatic. Now, after six months' work, I can see the transition is happening after all. And that makes me feel that it's been worth all the trauma and tension.

As soon as I get oriented to one of Dylan's patterns, he changes and a whole new pattern begins to evolve. It's like standing up in a roller coaster. I'm finding that the more I accept this constant change, the more I can enjoy the dynamics of it, the constant growing. Dylan is deepening my sense of change as a way of life.

I can't impose my rules on Dylan. All the persuasive skills I use to get other people to do things my way are totally irrelevant to him. I am forced to accept the validity of his rules, and then to learn to integrate that with my real needs. The trick is to become less of a control freak without entirely sacrificing myself to Dylan.

I know I will make major mistakes with Dylan, that I'll cause him a great deal of real grief. I try to keep that in front of me, to accept it when it happens.

. . . It's always a shock when I remember that Dylan is related to me in a more basic way than that I take care of him. To realize that he is of my body, grown from my seed. He is my son. Occasionally that realization hits me from behind. I still don't know what to make of it. I suffer from not having been pregnant. . . .

NOVEMBER 3 *(New York)*. A long-distance excursion, just me and Dylan. We're in New York to visit my parents for a week, while Susan gets a week to be free and alone.

I prepared myself carefully for the five-hour plane ride and was ready to devote all of my energy and attention to doing whatever Dylan needed to have done. Several trips to the "lavatory-vacant," juggling him on the closed toilet seat while changing diapers in the jiggly little space. Walking him up and down the skinny aisle. Watching him play peek-a-boo with the people in the seats behind us. It became a challenge and I felt triumphant. Dylan was happy, slept part of the way stretched out at my feet, was not overly demanding.

The stewardesses didn't know what to make of us. They tended to assume that I needed a lot of their feminine help. I was determined to put the torch to that bullshit, and I pulled it off. Good for me.

Got some nice hints from an older couple who seemed to appreciate that I was by myself taking an infant cross-country. They weren't condescending like the stewardesses, just friendly and appreciative. They probably assumed that I was a single father.

On this trip I'm enjoying the feeling of being fully responsible for Dylan. He is a focus for my energy, a fixed point around which I can orient myself. Having nothing else that I need to do I am free to just be with Dylan. It feels good, and I sense that Dylan likes it too.

1972

APRIL 1. It is a quiet, grey Saturday. Dylan's first birthday. Dylan is being wonderful and adorable. All dressed in his red shirt and yellow overalls he stands here playing with the spiral binding of my notebook and says "Dadadada." From time to time he bobs up and down to Judy Collins' singing and wants my attention, which is only fair. . . .

One minute later and all that peace and good feeling is completely destroyed. How can everything change so quickly? Dylan turns obnoxious. My parents call to say how sick they are, while Dylan cries more. I get off the phone but he won't stop crying, and suddenly I'm going crazy out of my mind again. Finally I take him out for a walk, having exhausted every other thought about what to do, and now he's fine again. But I'm all clenched up and a little nauseous. I want to yell, "Unfair! Unfair!"

APRIL 21. . . . Today I had a fantasy of clipping Dylan under the chin, a pure energy uppercut with my knee. I could see his head snap back and his body topple over and his head hit the floor. The fantasy felt good when it happened. Now retelling it makes me want to cry. Is this what having a child is all about? Is this what working full-time is all about? What do other people do when they have feelings like these?

It seems that whenever I'm really down like this, Susan's response is to get angry. Sorry, David, stop whining, be strong. This morning I yelled at Dylan when he got on my nerves, and then I didn't feel like picking him up to comfort him. Susan thought I must be an ogre to be so inconsiderate of this dear sweet baby. She, on the other hand, keeps all her resentments about Dylan bottled up until she can throw them all off on me.

I want time alone. What keeps me from arranging that? I feel sorry for Susan who's all alone all day taking care of sick Dylan and being bored. I should be willing to help her deal with all that but it's hard to sympathize with her when she just gets mad at me whenever I'm upset.

DECEMBER 13. Tonight just loving Dylan, that's all. Rolling together, taking the time to really *see* him. Me beaming, filling the room with warmth and goodness. And Dylan soaking it up, rich and soft, all the spastic craziness gone, leaving him peaceful, a calm blue water facing an open sky.

. . . So much is possible with Dylan. So much that I can do, that I can be. Tonight I am open, alive, almost trembling with the richness that comes to me from Dylan. . . .

1973

FEBRUARY 22. Dylan and I are so close in temperament. It amazes me sometimes. We seem to resonate, to pick up each other's vibrations, all the time. We even get hungry at the same time, and I always know what he wants to eat. Unfortunately we also get tired and grouchy at the same time.

Today Dylan was as gentle as I felt, singing Genie Joe to his doll, playing with the blackboard we made him for Christmas. Very peaceful.

I should be writing a brochure for the free schools workshop, but I want to savor this good feeling. It is a nice reunion.

AUGUST 27. Tonight while I was getting Dylan ready for bed he said, "I love you, David, when you do that."

I was confused. "When I do what?"

"When you put on my jamies."

Golly gee.

AUGUST 30. This morning, still half asleep, I heard this from Dylan:

"David, get up. Get up, David. 'Cause the light is outside. Because the sun is shining orange. It's time to get up because it's morning." And then he went on: "Get up, David. I want you to get up. Get up. Please get up. I'll help you get up. You're so heavy! You're so heavy! Get up, David. Let me take off your blanket. Now get up. Get up by yourself."

I got up, smiling.

1974

FEBRUARY 15 *(notes at three years).* Differences in me as a father now, compared to when Dylan was six months old: I have more confidence in my inuition about Dylan; I am less threatened by the thought of him taking over my life; I am clearer about the positive effects of Dylan on me; I relate to Dylan in more consistent, stable ways.

I think I finally feel, way down in my gut, that I am a good father. I still do all sorts of things badly. But all in all, when I look at how I am with Dylan, I get a warm, glowing feeling that says that is something I do well.

Sometimes when I'm doing something with Dylan, or just watching him play, I get an overwhelming rush of love for him—pure appreciation of who he is—this incredibly open, honest, alive, present world-explorer who gets such intense joy out of so many little things in his life. I literally get choked up in my throat. Sometimes I cry at the beauty of being so much in love with him, and at the realization that these moments disappear as suddenly as they come, sinking under all the petty resentments and fears and busy-ness of my life.

I feel so vulnerable when I open the door to my deepest love for Dylan, when I let myself see how important he is to me. What if I lose him? What if Susan and I separate someday? Dylan is taking me into a more committed relationship than I have ever allowed before, even with Susan.

. . . I don't get to talk about my feelings as a father with other men very much. Even the fathers I feel closest to seem far away in terms of how they relate to their kids. They are good fathers, emotionally involved with their children, but none are sharing primary day-to-day responsibility for their children as I do.

I have heard other men talk about the joys of fatherhood, about appreciating their children, but not about the doubts and the fears and the uncertainties. It's as if everyone wants to project a positive, confident image. Surely it's not just me that gets depressed at the bad-tasting patterns. Maybe other men don't feel these things as strongly as I do. Maybe their kids are less central to their lives. Maybe I should pull back from being so intimately tied to Dylan. . . .

JUNE 8 *(Berkeley)*. I feel completely vulnerable to little children these days. It used to be just Dylan, but now I notice that I warm to other kids as well, especially to their sadness and disappointments.

I want to spend more time surrendered to Dylan, doing *his* things or things I know he would enjoy. Usually when we're together we do my things. That's ok, but it's different. It says that he's supposed to fit into my life if he wants us to be together. It says that being together is more important to him than it is to me. (We could take a weekend trip together, come up here and go to Tilden Park or to the San Francisco Zoo or to the Lawrence Hall of Science. Or go to the Santa Cruz boardwalk for ice cream and rides, or to a kids' movie. . . .)

Oh, Dylan, why am I only now beginning to let myself enjoy just being with you? Cheap resentment of your infringing on "my space"? I love you so much. I feel so unworthy of your total trust, and depressed to see your trust begin to fade because I'm not always there for you. There is nothing in my life more important than you, and yet I refuse to simply give in to that feeling.

What is it that makes me cry at every corny song, every TV show, every cheap movie about fathers and sons? There is a sadness buried deep inside of me. It's hard to see how I will ever be through with it. Perhaps through Dylan I will work it out.

From my grandfather to my father to me, and now perhaps to Dylan. This yearning for the perfect, warm, giving, loving, present father gets passed from generation to generation.

. . . Would this feeling be as strong if Dylan were a girl? If he were a girl I don't think I'd be reliving so much of my own childhood. And I wouldn't have the responsibility of teaching him what it means to be a male, of being his role model. He takes in all of who I am. No amount of conscious effort changes that. He learns to be distant if I am distant, aggressive if I am aggressive. If I am unreliable, he learns not to trust men. It is a heavy burden, especially when I am aware of how much bullshit male programming I still carry around.

At least he doesn't learn to fuck women over, or to idolize them. And he learns that it's ok for men to be vulnerable, to hurt, to cry. It's not that I'm doing so badly. It's that he deserves more than I can possibly give him. We all deserve more than our fathers or mothers are able to give. That's what's so sad.

This sorrow is not guilt. It is, simply, sorrow. A huge reservoir of sadness. For me to admit how important Dylan is to me I must also admit how deeply I still want to be close to my father. That's a hard one.

Today I bought a card for Father's Day, a plain card on parchment paper that said inside: "For all the times I haven't said it . . . I love you." Simple. Can I say that so simply? Will he hear?

It's not too late to change, not too late to unravel the tangles, not too late to open my eyes, to my father as well as to my son.

That feels better. Now I can get on with the day. This has been time well spent.

Chapter Fifteen

Josh Greenfeld

To be a good father, as David Steinberg proposes, is a difficult job even under the best of conditions. Imagine what the job must be like when the object of concern is a handicapped child. Our next father undergoes such an ordeal. Noah, the brain-damaged son of Josh and Foumi Greenfeld, is the catalyst that calls his parents' entire lives into question: their marriage, their dreams, their reasons for being. Yet, while enduring these tensions, Josh and Foumi do not stop being parents to Noah. They go on trying to seek some proper diagnosis of Noah's difficulties, to find what might pass for proper help, to work out ways to finance it all. While doing so, they gradually learn to live on new terms with Noah and their first-born son Karl, but most especially with themselves.

Josh Greenfeld is an American novelist, playwright, and reviewer. His Japanese-born wife Foumi is a painter and writer. Their painful and instructive story is recorded in Greenfeld's journal, *A Child Called Noah*. In its sequel, *A Place for Noah*, which follows their son's next five years, Greenfeld also continues to raise important considerations about the way language may be used to obscure truth. By having defined Noah as "autistic," Greenfeld feels his son's handicaps were cosmeticized "in an attempt to conquer with language an uncharted province of science." Such a definition served as a way for certain professionals to turn an organic malady into a self-enhancing psychogenetic specialty, and as a further consequence, helped to create parental guilt when no guilt could be assigned. Autism, he concludes, is a glamorous term that allows those concerned to escape from the "realities and stigmas of old words," such as retarded and brain-damaged, and also tends to hold out a false hope for some miracle cure.

Whether we agree or not with this angry appraisal of autism, Greenfeld is nowhere more truthful than when he reveals his intimate feelings regarding the far-reaching effects of parenthood upon himself, his wife, and their two beloved sons.

1966

JULY 1. I'm a father. I'm drunk. I have another son. His name is Noah Jiro. He was born this evening a few minutes after seven and weighed seven pounds, ten ounces. And whereas Karl seemed to look like me at birth, Noah is luckier. He looks like his Japanese mother, Foumi.

I saw Noah Jiro as he passed on the way to the maternity ward. And next I saw Foumi. She was not very sleepy. Though induced at full term, it was supposed to be a natural childbirth, so I guess she had had only a pinch of anesthesia when it came time to sew her up. I followed the caravan. And soon I was standing at the nursery window, noting proudly to the stranger next to me how much hair Noah had.

I think of my dead father now. I think of the living Noah I already love. He seems like the son of my father to me, just as Karl is the son of my mother. I do not know why, but that is so. Of course, they are both the sons of Foumi too. But then nothing so important is ever that simple.

Anyway, I am happier than I ever thought I would be. I wanted a daughter, I know. But I rejoice in having a second son. Noah Jiro— the name is a breath of hope.

JULY 10. We're back at the basic training of baby raising. We sleep when we can in three-hour snatches, we wander about in perpetual states of fatigue. And now we have Karl to present psychological problems: he moans and whines all day long. Noah is comparatively easy— except for his feedings; he seems to have a more phlegmatic personality than Karl had. While Karl looked strong and western and very masculine, Noah looks like a Bunraku puppet or a figure in one of those eighteenth-century woodprints; intensely fragile, extremely delicate. And he is genuinely attractive, a really beautiful baby. Both my sons fill me with kinds of love I never dreamt possible. . . .

JULY 12. Time has altered me remarkably. I grow a beard and I wear sandals, but I am bogged down with diapers and feedings, washing machines and dryers, and beginning next month I face the daily grind of commuting to New York. I've taken a job, ending my precarious free-lance writing existence. I've had to: a family makes a realist out of any man. I can skimp on meals; my two sons can't. I have dreams to sustain me, while they only live ferociously in the present. They must cry boisterously whenever they are denied, while I, of course, can merely shrug wistfully.

1967

MARCH 26. Today we've had a scare, a psychological scare, and we're still affected by it. We took Noah to the pediatrician for his third triple shot. We thought the visit would be routine. While there we told the doctor that we were slightly worried because Noah, now almost nine months, still does not sit up or turn over by himself. We expected the doctor to tell us that we had nothing to worry about, that we were being overanxious parents.

But instead he asked us about Noah's speech—which is negligible. And whether Noah could pass objects from hand to hand—which he can't. He then voiced concern about Noah's motor development, suggesting that if Noah did not start to develop significantly within the next three months, we ought to have a specialist look at him. Afterwards in his office he tried to reassure us, saying that it was "strictly a gut reaction" but he didn't think we had anything really to worry about because everything else about Noah was so healthy. But we came home and began looking at Noah through worried eyes, and it was easy to see a mongoloid idiot lurking in his beautiful Eurasian face. The good doctor having allowed how it might be a good idea to try to coax his motor development along, we exercised Noah almost mercilessly. But then he wouldn't eat at all. Foumi and I kept trying out new diagnoses and prognoses on each other. We both feel so guilty. We've never really given Noah the time and the attention we gave his brother. But we thought that is the way with second children: they simply demand and require less. . . .

APRIL 15. It is almost midnight, and I'm sucking on a nipple, a milk-bottle nipple, trying to break it in for Noah. He doesn't like new hard nipples; he likes them soft and worn with use. So I suck on his nipple, enjoying the parental role reversal and turnabout in a primordial way.

SEPTEMBER 11. I've noticed something about Noah. He requires my attention, my playing with him. He will refuse to grow without my love. I hope to make time to hold him on my lap, to fondle and hug him, to make him feel sure—and secure—in the knowledge that he is wanted wholeheartedly, enthusiastically. I must constantly be aware that he is the younger child whose sensitivities—and problems— are harder to discover than the firstborn's.

1968

FEBRUARY 13. We all seem well now, winter colds and mumps all gone. But still the problems of parent-being and child-rearing. Last night I was playing with Noah and having great fun. And then Karl came barrel-tumbling along. And the joy went out of our play. Noah rarely gets a chance to play with me alone, so I became angry with Karl. And it showed. The poor kid was miserable. To make matters worse, I was so hostile that I even teased him. I must remember not to be cruel with one kid just because he interferes with my love for the other.

SEPTEMBER 8. Let's face it: Noah has temper tantrums, he does not walk by himself, he is unable to talk too coherently. We live in a shadow of doubt and worry about him constantly.

DECEMBER 1. Putting Karl to bed, I argued too vehemently with him. Foumi raises her voice and the children submit. I threaten too easily, cajole too much, play my aces too soon. They know I'm volatile and do not respect me for it. But why should I want and demand respect from them ever—let alone at the ages of two and four? I'm a bloody fool. I still don't know how to exercise authority: I only know how to bemoan against it.

1969

JUNE 9. Today I am less emotional but more aware of the fact that the problem does exist. Noah is a burden, withdrawing in steps; the moments of connection, of entry into the outer world, becoming less and less. Perhaps it is me, my presence at his side, that he needs the most. Perhaps I should not begrudge him a moment of my time from now on.

We both rack our brains trying to figure out just when he began to stop talking. Foumi recalls how Noah fell a few times on our hard playroom floor last autumn. Afterwards he kept saying, "Oh, my head!" And he never said much after that. She thinks those falls might have something to do with his regression. Or perhaps, she thinks, it was the cold weather, the literally cold world, which froze his fragile sensitivities. Meanwhile he cried and had tantrums, making no other effort to communicate when he was unhappy. Fortunately, though, he is usually joyously, vacuously, absently happy. But I do so wish we could reach him.

JUNE 16. . . . Shit! I wish we had not induced him. But all the pieces fit together: born early, a vomiter rejecting external reality, a furtive laugher, delayed motor development. And my vanity. I thought that by marrying outside my race that bad genes—the diabetes on my father's side, the mental illness of cousins on my mother's side—could be eliminated. Instead, I have further scattered bad genes.

Foumi seems to make the adjustment better than I do. I play intellectual games. I try to feel that Noah must have some wondrous perceptions, that in some way he is ahead of us all. But I also do not fool myself. I know deep down that he has a life doomed to grotesque development.

JULY 14. Somehow the rhythm of our lives, the good fortune of our marriage seems to have dissipated. It is hard for Foumi to believe in me and for me to believe in Foumi anymore. Successful monogamy, of course, must be based on a faith in the union if nothing else. And how can we have faith in a marriage that has biologically backfired? Foumi is traditionally so self-protective that the moment she does not protect herself she has no luck. And though she claims the Freudian dialectics do not apply to her, she teems with guilt toward herself and accusations toward me. And I guess I act the same way toward her. In any event, our house of good cards has fallen apart. At first I thought the news of Noah would stabilize and fix and reaffirm our marriage. Now I'm not so sure. . . .

It is ironic though that Foumi and I, who both believe so in beauty and have enjoyed such a rare esthetic experience in Noah, are thus reminded of the absurd mindlessness of it all.

JULY 18. How to treat Noah? How should I behave toward him? I do not think that I should say "No" or "Bad boy" to him. Rather I should encourage him for his good behavior. Because he may be not only retarded but also complicatedly emotionally withdrawn. Perhaps that sensitive little doll of a human being is so afraid of me that he has decided to cut himself off from a world in which I rant and rave so. I'll play with him tonight as gently as I can.

JULY 19. No matter how severe Noah's retardation, I refuse to view his condition as a life-searing tragedy. We will do what we have to do. We will take care of him as best we can until we can no longer take care of him. We will have him in our home and find ways to live in joy with him. And when I cannot enjoy him as much as I would like, I will love him even more.

SEPTEMBER 13. I'm a lousy father. I anger too easily. I get hot with Karl and take on a four-year-old kid. I shout at Noah and further upset an already disturbed one. Perhaps I'm responsible for Noah's problems. Perhaps he would be better off if I were to take off. It may be something worth trying. If I am a failure as a father, then I should face it.

1970

AUGUST 21. A lovely clear blue-skied day, and I decided to take the family to the zoo. I noticed something about Noah. He didn't seem to notice us at all. If we let him out of sight for a moment, he would attach himself to any adult thigh and wander away with it until I retrieved him. It was as if he did need *somebody*, but *anybody* would do. Not a very heart-warming feeling for a parent.

OCTOBER 20. I've been doing some more reading on autistic children. It seems to me there is a gulf between parents of autistic children and most professionals in the field—and that gulf is guilt. We're wary of assigning it; psychologists and psychiatrists and educators are looking to assign it. And I've decided that from now on I'm going to listen only to the consumers in the field, the parents, not the professionals with their own wares to sell. At the same time, I can't get too locked in with other parents. There is also the danger of becoming a member of an elitist club all wrapped up in a single noble cause. One of the results of my life may be a dedication to children like Noah, but it will not be its purpose.

NOVEMBER 29. I've leafed through three books, chronicles by parents of severely disturbed or brain-damaged children. None of them palpitate with truth for me. The parents didn't burn with enough anger; they were all too damned heroic for me. Because one must be angry about all of the technology and all of the science that does not go into researching what the hell is wrong with a Noah. And as the parent of an autistic child, one is more ridiculous than heroic—like a sludging, sloshing infantry soldier in a nuclear age.

Indeed, the more I read about such children, the more I'm convinced, unfortunately, that only money can solve most of the problems of having a child like Noah. That's the damned truth of it. The more money I have, the less of a problem Noah becomes—I can hire out the problem to others. Have a crazy kid and get to understand the gut meaning of society.

1971

JANUARY 11. For the past several days Noah has "self-stimmed" to an unusual degree before going to sleep. The theory behind "self-stimulation" or the repetition of stereotyped behavior, the constant repeating of the same simple action, such as jumping or head-shaking or finger-talking, is that for an organism to stay alive it must be stimulated. And if it doesn't receive stimulation from the outside world, it stimulates itself. And yet by the same destructive token, while it is stimulating itself it cannot receive stimulation from the outside world. It's all a vicious circle a child like Noah can't break out of.

If one has a child like Noah, one needs money. In order to get enough money, one must have the time and the energy to work. But a child like Noah drains away one's energy, takes away one's time. There is simply no way out.

I must confess something: sometimes I hope Noah gets sick and dies painlessly.

JANUARY 27. Foumi and I are still battling, but a bigger event has overtaken us. Noah started his new school in a small California Ginger Bread house. Classrooms forced into the mold of a structure not quite ready to accept them. A big fenced-in yard with swings and playground equipment. His teacher, Mrs. Harris, called this afternoon with the news that Noah urinated standing up. Foumi and I ceased our fighting and embraced each other in celebration. Foumi feels that if not a miracle, at least the sign of a miracle, has occurred. . . .

. . . But on this bad day between me and Foumi—our fights can last a week, as Foumi is slow to anger but, once enraged, impossible to soothe—I began to think that just as an autistic child can be the cause of the breakup of a good marriage . . . perhaps he can also be the reason for the perpetuation of an otherwise bad marriage.

APRIL 26. Karl is in the playroom, drawing with his crayons; Noah sits in his sandbox, and a neighbor's teen-age daughter who has taken the lyrical step from gawkiness to maturity during our absence, shows him how to fill a pail and empty it. The trees are budding, and soon our view of the river will be filled in by clusters of green, and our grass will be growing wildly, the signs of life, even uncontrollable life, rampant. And I remind myself that I must relearn the lesson of patience with Noah. In the last few sessions I've had with him, I've expected too much. I should be satisfied with less, appreciative of the fact that he has to keep moving in order to stand still. And I should rejoice more in seeing him play with toys placed before him. He can turn his music box, pull his xylophonic teddy, push a shape into a puzzle box.

APRIL 28. Each day Foumi and I discharge our therapy chores, our operant-conditioning chores. Foumi tries to teach him to play; to catch a ball, to select an object, to thread plastic beads. I work on speech, at this point concentrating on getting him to repeat the sound of "O," rewarding him with a smidgen of Frito or a sliver of potato chip when he does so, and withdrawing the reward when he fails to do so. Both the play therapy and the speech therapy go slowly.

Yesterday I told Foumi I have little faith in any therapy—vitamin or operant conditioning or anything. She said, "Then why don't we just put him in an institution?" And I couldn't think of an answer. So I pulverized the vitamins more thoroughly and worked that much harder with Noah today.

MAY 13. Noah goes through stages, has his periods. Foumi says he's much easier to take care of these days again. He listens more, he observes more. And they say the same thing in school. Perhaps we'll be able to manage him longer than we had anticipated.

What do I dream of now? Beautiful women? Far-off travel? Exotic friends? Princely wealth? No. None of these things. I simply dream continually of a normal Noah.

And there are hints to feed the dream. Last night, he suddenly sat beside me, on the edge of the couch, and like any father and son—even if briefly—we were watching a TV baseball game together.

Part Four

Working Men

Chapter Sixteen

Fred
Bason
1907-1972

ALAS, IN THIS WORKADAY WORLD, most idealistic young men soon learn they must also earn a living, and often at work less than ideal. Unfortunately, devotion to some greater glory somehow has a way of getting mislaid in the marketplace, too. But that depends upon where a "bloke" sets his sights: The dreams of glory that Fred Bason held dear—to meet a matinee idol, add an autograph to his collection, find a first edition to net him another "fiver"—might seem as second-rate as many of the second-hand books he sold for his salt, but considering that this pint-sized peddler, a born-and-bred Cockney, had to leave school at fourteen, first to work as a "latherer" in a barbershop, later as a "tea-getter" in a builder's yard, his attaining these star-struck ambitions seems only a bit short of extraordinary. What's more, by the time the indomitable Bason had reached middle age, he was a successful book dealer, a friend to the famous, the author of a bibliography on W. Somerset Maugham, as well as books on theater-going, collecting, the repairing of toys, and a thrice-published diarist.

"Always keep a diary, and some day it may keep you," the critic James Agate said to Fred Bason. Perhaps not the best motive for keeping one, for Bason's later entries, more clearly designed for an audience, are self-consciously full of himself. The earlier extracts, however—hastily kept on the backs of envelopes, menus, ledger sheets, exercise books, shorthand pads—show this sympathetic and witty street sparrow at his innocent, enterprising best; even while already rubbing shoulders in Mayfair and his own palms in Walworth, Bason the bookman had the cunning to keep shop all his working life in the Cockney slum he managed to turn to his own best advantage.

1922

It seems to me that one of the few privileges of a bookseller's life is that he is allowed an insight and some knowledge of what men and women are seeking to know. It's amazing the many ways the mind of a man (or woman) will turn. I have to seek books on the stars, not of the stage but of the heavens. This seems to me a proper silly hobby which no good comes from. I like lots better to study the stage stars in their heavens. They change *all* the time! I have been asked for flogging books. That seems disgusting, and although I said, "Yes, I'll see," I won't see at all. If I can't make a living in what's decent, I won't in the indecent. And why should a woman want a book on food of the sixteenth century?

This ends what I may call my first stage of life as a book runner, and all in all it ain't a bad life when the weather is O.K. But it's a stinker when it is wet because me sack, me stock and me all get wet, and that's no good for none of us. I have managed to keep my head above water and pay my mother whenever I was able. I gives her now 25s a week. It's all I can manage and often I have to drop it to a quid. . . .

I am now closing down as the weather is bad. I shall devote next week to replenishing my stock ready for the new year. People don't want second-hand books at Xmas. My capital is 42s in cash and 119 books, of which I think sixty-three are good and the rest all gambles. I have orders for Haggard, Jane Austen, a set of W. Scott and any oddments of R. L. Stevenson.

1924

They teaches us to be peaceful, kind, good and generous, and of course absolutely honest, when we are kids—but Gord, when you grows up you sees it's a hard world, and them what still keep kind, gentle, peaceful, and absolutely honest all seem to get nowhere fast. Them who are smart boys always get the best suits, and here's me with one suit and that's none too tidy. Does honesty really pay? Do I have to say, "That's a lousy book. It's dull and uninteresting and although I ask you 2s for it, 9d would be a much fairer price?" That's honesty— but that way I'd starve. And being hungry ain't nice. . . .

1925

Had a find today. Bought *The Hero* by Somerset Maugham. Red cloth, crown 8vo., first edition. It's a nice clean copy. Honestly worth £5. This my first bit of luck since G. Moore's little book of *Pagan Poems*. And I wasn't looking for a find—no sensible bloke does.

My father won £12 last week on horses. Today he is broke again. All we got out of £12 was some oranges! Betting is the curse of the working classes.

I think as how I should put me on a bonfire because I am proper poorly. Dr. Brown says as how I've been overdoing it and that I should take things more calmly. He says I am a "highly-strung individual." I do not care to be called an individual—it's so blooming *chilly*. I have to rest up a week and must not go out book hunting. He says that my life is on wires that I pull taut-like. I lift too heavy loads. I tell him

books weigh heavy and he says *why* lift heavy loads? One book at £10
or 10 for £1? He's got something there. But where am I to get a book
to sell at £10? I can sell 200 novels at 1s each in the trade, but I have
no millionaire clients to pay a tenner. Oh well, it's no use worrying.
It will all come out in the wash. But I am feeling done up. . . .

1927

Mr. Arnold Bennett did a jolly kind act to me today that shows
him to be a very human man, providing you don't hero-worship him
and providing you can make him laugh or interested. I passed on to
him a jolly good after-dinner story which Percy told me and A. B. let
out his funny cackle and then he took from his pocket a postcard
photograph of Chaliapin the Russian who sings low, and he said, "You'd
like this, wouldn't you, Bason?" Me, I said, "Oh yes, if you don't
really *appreciate* it." And it was autographed: "To Mr Arnold Bennett,
souvenir from Chaliapin," and is genuine, for I have one from him. I
naturally asked him why he didn't want to keep such a very valuable
piece of property, and he said. "I enjoy singing" and would say no
more. Any rate, I have it and shall keep it, from one great man to
another, and then on to me.

I am today exactly twenty. The world is before me and I want to
get on. But so many drawbacks. I open my mouth and seem to put my
foot in it. Yesterday I went to a party given by Stephen Graham, the
author. It was a sort of little tea fight (at four) and there were ten
people there. All, it seemed, were either authors or artists. I was the
only bookseller. I felt very uneasy because books I couldn't talk with
authority, and all they talked on were their own books, and outside Mr
Graham's I'd read none of them or knew the name of any one of them.
I took my autograph album, but on second thoughts did not bring it
out. It was so very kind of Mr Graham to give me this break, but until
I've actually written bound books I do not feel that I am entitled to go
to a literary do.

Here I had my first Russian cigarette and I met a female writer. She has a nice shaped bust and looked ripe for the pluckings but is so obviously Chelsea. And S.W.3 and S.E.17 will never, never mix. . . .

1929

Today I pushed a barrow from Walworth to Bermondsey for the first time to sell books from the gutter. It was not pleasant but was fairly profitable. Since I started bookselling in 1923 I have been building up a stock of rather dull books that I was forced to buy in order to get better ones. . . .

Now got rid of about half my dead stock. Will go there again, but I hate it. It seems like begging to stand and ask people to buy books at 3d a time—that took writers years of brainwork to write. What heart breaks in this here writing game. What heart breaks in the selling of them. But I *shall* do it again from a barrow, for it pays. . . .

1930

I didn't make a New Year resolution. I always break them. But now I think I'll write a line and it's this: without self-advertisement a bloke gets nowhere in this world. In this year, 1930, the absolutely essential element of success is self-advertisement—and it ain't Shaw but me writing it.

I think I can make a living in the shop instead of with a sack on my back or by post or at the stall, and it will give me more time to write. The rent is to be 12s 6d a week—they've let me have it cheaper than to some as they see it's a sheer gamble. I will pay more if I manage to hold out six months.

Later. With help of my father I have moved in. We have bought from Morgan, the grocer, some egg crates and have converted them into bookshelves. They do not look very nice but will do for the time being. Even as we were moving in I sold a book—on Poultry Keeping for 1s. I gave the man a novel by Le Queux as a souvenir for being my first client . . . it's more dignified than the blastic barrow, which I have hated for so long. I am now a member of a dignified profession, a genuine bookseller with a shop. I shall never have a partner or any assistant (unless it be someday a wife to help me by minding my business when I get called out to sales, etc). I do not believe in partnerships in the book trade. They never work out and are source of constant bickering. I am happy!

This ends my first ten days in the shop. I have taken £5 12s 6½d in these ten days. I would say that's roughly £2 15s 0d profit. It's starvation—but I have yet to get established in the shop. I can hold out about eight weeks. After that I've had it. I sell lots of mags and comics at 1d and ½d each, but the profit is small. Oh God, please let a first folio fall my way! I will be so grateful to you! Now I have my ambition of a shop (be it only a little one) it must *not* fail. It *shall* not fail. I'll get what the clients want best. I can. I need *luck*.

The craze for modern first editions expands daily. Is it a fashion of the moment? I am coining money and can't go wrong. They follow like sheep. There seems so little reasoning and logic. First issue with a fly dirt on page 73–£3. No fly dirt—12s 6d! First issue, in red cloth, £25. Same book in *green* cloth, 10s 6d. It's not sane, but it is happening. . . . I get amazingly good prices from the trade—so they must be getting fortunes! Dawson wants *Jane Eyre,* three vols., 1847, and Scott's *Waverley* in three vols, 1814—so do I!

. . . I now wear a buttonhole flower each day and smoke Russian fags—and why not? I see that Lytton's *Eugene Aram* first edition made £990 at Sothebys. Gord's struth, it's a very funny world—and the world of collectors of firsts is funniest.

P. called in tonight and we talked shop. She says *The Old Wives' Tale* is the greatest modern novel. Couldn't agree. *Of Human Bondage* and *The Way of All Flesh* my choice.

Reckon I'm in love with P. Alas, she is an R.C. She won't change; I won't change; so be it. But she's so cool, calm and collected. Pity her eyes are so troublesome. Be a smart-looking girl without them bloody glasses. We had tea, Russian style with lemon bits. It was nice.

1931

The Bibliography of the Writings of W. S. Maugham is published this day and the Press has sent me £5 in cash, advance, and six copies (ordinary limited) and one of the *de luxe*. . . . I have just written Maugham my thanks and have autographed some copies. Such a thrill!

But what was a red letter day in my life was marred with the complete indifference of both mother and father towards my book. They didn't take the slightest notice of it. This made me cry. Am I a man or a sissy to cry at twenty-four? I was so disappointed. I wanted praise. I got none. I do not think I will show them any more of my successes or failures. They are past my age—sixty to my twenty-four. They don't understand me. Because I am the only author in Walworth the neighbours think I am a freak and shy of "real" work. My God! How I've sweated over writing.

Today I broke fresh grounds with a huge gamble. I have paid £11 10s od cash (leaving myself with £2 capital) for *Of Human Bondage,* first edition. I bought it at Hodgson's in Chancery Lane at their book auction. Willy is coming to tea next Friday. If he will autograph this copy I am sure that I can get £20 for it.

This is my highest one-book investment and if I don't pull it off I am on the carpet proper bad. It's a clean copy and it nearly went for £10. I knew it was worth more and I stepped in and put in the final bid with thirty shillings, for that was my limit and I got it.

Later: Willy obliged—but he autographed it *to me.* I can't afford to keep it. It's the most precious thing I possess. Oh, I wish I was rich! But I need stock for a more varied nature and I need a holiday as well.

Later: An American named Schwartz has paid me £21 for it this day. I am a very happy man. But I will never bid again at any book auction.

1934

James Agate reviewed my *Gallery Unreserved* in the *Daily Express*—and didn't know who the anon. writer was. I felt it would not be fair to tell him. I merely sent him one and inscribed it to a fellow

First Nighter. His review ended with these words: "A Galleryite makes no secret of the fact that his daytime occupation is humble, and the chapter entitled 'The Beggars' Theater' is good enough to suggest that he will do better in his next book to tell us less of his evening and more of his daily experience and pluck the heart of that mystery. It is worth doing. He can do it and we shall read him with interest."

Well, it was a pretty good and kind review. And it is rather strange that Agate, who told me to keep a journal, now pretty well tells me (without knowing that it is me) to reveal my journal and pluck the heart of that mystery. But there is surely no mystery in how a slum bookseller tries to make his living. Would the world really be a scrap interested to know that I buy incomplete pages from comics by weight, and then spends hours and hours putting these odd pages together so as to make a complete comic to sell at 1d each? Or that I buy bashed-to-pieces copies of *Trilby* (first illustrated edition) and spends hours and hours taking pages from one and pages from another until sixteen battered ones become four or five bound and tidy copies? Or that I buy newspapers by the hundredweight, cut out all the boxing data, stick those cuttings in albums, and then sell the albums to fight fans with a great deal more money than sense. No, no, Jimmy. My life is my own. No one would care to read it. . . .

1937

The book trade has been nice and kind to me. And my side-line as a greyhound tipster has been O.K. as well, the dogs I tipped almost all winning, so my clients were able to give me 10 per cent of their winnings. The editors of periodicals realising *at last* that although "weird" I do write interesting articles what the public *do* like. All these facts, plus the advantage of being free, has enabled me to have a two weeks' holiday in Paris all by myself, yet never alone or lonely. I went to the Paris Exhibition. The Palais des Livres was of particular interest to me because although I am, at this stage of living, making more money at tipping greyhound winners—yes, *winners,* and making more cash than I've ever before made (certainly more than I've made at bookselling or writing)—I am *still* at heart very, very much a bookseller; and when my luck—if luck it *is*—at dog tips fails, I shall return to bookselling again. . . .

1940

The war has certainly given the book trade the needed flip up and all bookshops seem busy. My A.R.P. duties do not allow me much time to scout around. But I *have* to dabble and keep in touch and sell as much as possible before the bombs get at my stock. They tell me that it is the war which has also made people more attracted to short stories. . . . But it is very sad indeed that it takes a bloody war to make books sell and see writers come into their own. They won't take me in the Army—I wish they would. I'd make at least a good librarian instead of a light infantry man. But as long as I do something, I don't mind. People are also more matey these days. Yesterday the dustman said "Good morning." I was astounded.

1941

Incendiary bombs destroyed my den and thousands of cigarette cards, autographs and invaluable souvenirs.

Heartbreaking to clear the muck out into the garden after the firemen had put their big hoses on my fragile things. I stood and cried. Twenty-five years to collect and twenty-five minutes to absolutely ruin. My leg fractured. Ribs bad. Part of a house fell on me as I was in the next street, whilst my own home blazed. What bloody luck!

Blast Hitler! He won't stop me. I'll start again. Hell to him!

1945

At last I am free! And thank God for it. From April 1944 to May
'45 I worked for the L.C.C. At first I was a clerk and then they saw it
was heartbreaking for me, so they sent me to Stockwell depot where,
upon showing the boss, Mr. Henderson, my published books on toy
making, he put me on the job of devising new toys for children. For
five months it was lovely, and then someone realised that I was graded
as a *clerk* and not as a toy maker, and so, I suppose, thinking I was too
comfortable, put me to repairing the frames of lantern slides with black
tape.

I repaired thousands and thousands. I dreamed of them! I got fed
up. It was a job a boy of fourteen could so easily do, being so simple,
and I was getting stale. I begged for more useful work. No use. I asked
for the sack and now I've got it. Handshakes all round. . . . They
promise never to trouble me again. And I'm sure I'll never trouble
them. If I can't make my humble living at books then I deserve to
starve and die. Two and a half years A.R.P., one and a half years
Ministry of Supply, one year L.C.C., six months seriously ill. Five and
a half years out of one's life, due to a bastard named Hitler! Oh well,
plenty worse off than me. And now to get back—to be Bason the
bookman again!

Chapter Seventeen

Jerry Kramer

FROM THE START OF TRAINING to the end of the football season in 1967, Jerry Kramer, offensive right guard for the Green Bay Packers, kept a taped diary of his experiences with the game. Edited later by Dick Schaap, these transcriptions bring the reader of *Instant Replay* into daily intimate contact with the sense and nonsense of professional football.

Suffering both old and new bruises, conscious of his veteran's age, and concerned as well with his outside business interests, the thirty-one year old Kramer had not only to face up to his grueling challenges on the line all during that championship season but also to a more complex antagonist, his brilliant coach and legendary taskmaster, Vince Lombardi, who once remarked that "winning isn't everything, it's the only thing." No worker ever had a tougher boss. Again and again Kramer found himself asking why he was submitting to another year of this brutal punishment, his ambivalent attitude toward the game always apparent.

But though Kramer came up with no solid reason for going on with it, his diary quite clearly shows where the joy was. Men in groups—at war, at play—find as much pleasure as they do pain in their use of aggression. What else Kramer's diary suggests about male friendship in our society—the misuse of feelings in order to turn a dollar, the contribution of sports to the myths of manhood—is for the reader to decide.

After the football season of 1968, Jerry Kramer retired from his Wisconsin team with an eleven-year professional record of 136 games, sustaining an unbelievable number of injuries and scoring many personal triumphs throughout his impressive career on the gridiron.

1967

JUNE 15. Practice starts a month from today, and I'm dreading it. I don't want to work that hard again. I don't want to take all that punishment again. I really don't know why I'm going to do it.

I must get some enjoyment out of the game, though I can't say what it is. It isn't the body contact. Body contact may be fun for the defensive players, the ones who get to make the tackles, but body contact gives me only cuts and contusions, bruises and abrasions. I suppose I enjoy doing something well. I enjoy springing a back loose, making a good trap block, a good solid trap block, cutting down my man the way I'm supposed to. But I'm not quite as boyish about the whole thing as I used to be. . . .

JULY 10. "OK, it's $27,500," Pat Peppler said today. "Stop by and sign."

I'm going to forget that I ever thought about retiring. I'm going to forget that I've got a lot of money coming in. I'm going to forget that I don't really need football anymore.

I've decided to play. Let's get on with it.

JULY 16. . . . Kostelnik's cocky because he's only twenty-seven. Gregg and Skoronski are thirty-three, Fuzzy's thirty-two, and I'm thirty-one; we've each put at least ten years in pro football. We're certainly not young by football standards; we're practically doddering. But it's impossible to overestimate the value of experience in this sport. . . .

Some people say that we're getting too old, that experience can't compensate for our loss of speed and agility, but I refuse to believe it. Sooner or later we'll have to retire and make room for younger men, but I doubt we've reached that point yet. . . .

JULY 17. We started two-a-day workouts today, and the agony is beyond belief. Grass drills, agility drills, wind sprints, everything. You wonder why you're there, how long you're going to last. The grass drills are exquisite torture. You run in place lifting your knees as high as you can, for ten, twenty, sometimes thirty seconds. When Lombardi yells, "Down," you throw yourself forward on your face, your stomach smacking the ground, and when he yells, "Up," you get up quick and start running in place again. We call the exercises "up-downs," and when Vince is in a good mood, he gives us only three or five minutes of them. If he's upset, he'll keep going till someone's lying on the ground and can't get up, till everyone's on the brink of exhaustion.

You try to block out all the pain, all the gasping breaths, block it all out of your mind and function as an automaton. Just up and down and up and down and move and keep moving and legs up and when you feel like you can't get up, like you can't possibly make it, then you've got to get up. You've got to make it. You've got to think, "Get up." We did seventy up-downs this morning and the only thing that kept me going was that I looked around and saw some of the other guys my age looking worse than me. Then I figured I wasn't going to die. . . .

The only thing that keeps you going is a little relaxation, a few moments of the civilized world. At times, you really wonder about football, if you need it, what makes you drive yourself, what makes you go through all that pain. You look at the people who come out to watch you practice and you see them in their cool summer shirts, their golf slacks and their sunglasses, and you wonder, "Why in the world do I beat my head against a 280-pound lineman for six months every year?"

I don't know, and I guess I never will.

JULY 27. We had our annual intrasquad game tonight, the offense vs. the defense, in front of more than 30,000 people. . . .

I went over to the locker room a little early and went through my ritual. Everyone has his own superstitions. One of mine is that when I tape up my long socks, I've got to use a new roll of tape, and nobody else can use the same roll. I can't take a half-used roll, and once I've used my share, the roll's got to be thrown away. I don't know why. It just has to be that way.

The offense won the game, which wasn't surprising, since the defense never gets the ball, except on punts and interceptions and fumbles. The score was 10-0, but that wasn't quite enough points for Lombardi, and he had a mild hemorrhage after the game. He said the offensive line looked like Maude Frickert and her crew.

My roomie, Don Chandler, missed two field goal attempts, and he felt pretty low. Kicking is a lonely chore; you don't have an opportunity to take out your emotions on anyone else. When I get real upset, real nervous, real emotional, I just hit one of those 280-pound defensive tackles, and all my jitters disappear.

AUGUST 6. . . . Chandler and I are different types, too. Donny's generally quiet, conservative, a brooder sometimes. He keeps an awful lot tied up inside himself. On the other hand, I like to make a little noise. I like to take a chance. I'm more outgoing. I hate to think there might be a party going on somewhere and I'm not at it. Still, we get along fine. There's a sort of mutual respect agreement on the team. Everybody's allowed to have his own feelings, his own preferences, his own way of life, and everybody accepts everybody else's way. Nobody judges anybody else. . . .

AUGUST 9.   Coach Lombardi gave us one of his periodic lectures today on life and football. "Winning is not a sometime thing here," he said. "It is an all-the-time thing. . . ."

He reminded us for maybe the hundredth time that professional football is not a nice game. "Some of our offensive linemen," he said, "are too nice sometimes. This is a violent sport. That's why the crowds love it, that's why people love it, because it's a violent sport, a body-contact sport. We're a little too nice. We've got to get a little meaner."

Then he made his regular speech about outside interests. "I want every minute of your day to be devoted to football," he said, "This is the only thing you're here for." He looked straight at me, with my bow-and-arrow factory and my diving business. . . .

After dinner, Coach was still steaming, and when a few guys got up to leave, he said, "What the hell is going on here? Sit down. Let's have some singing." Everybody was kind of down, kind of beat. Then a couple of us veterans got up and sang, and then we had the rookies sing, and then all the veterans, and then just the veterans over thirty, and Max got up and said, "How 'bout the veterans over thirty-five?"

So Max and Zeke sang by themselves, and then all the coaches sang, and then the trainers, and finally we all sang together, making a horrible racket, and the whole atmosphere changed, the whole mood of depression lifted. We were a team again.

AUGUST 17.   . . . I hate my helmet. I've always hated it, I guess. You'd imagine that a person would have become accustomed to wearing a helmet after eighteen years of football, but I've never really learned to live with it. After every offensive play of every game I play, I immediately undo the chin strap to my helmet. I used to take off my helmet between plays whenever I got really tired. It seemed the only way I could breathe. I'm sure it was all in my head, not in my lungs, but I still take the helmet off at every opportunity, for a time-out or a measurement or anything.

I'm not going to throw away my helmet, though, because it's a good weapon, probably the best weapon I've got. When I get mad at somebody—maybe the defensive tackle's been clubbing me with his forearm—I use my helmet on him. I hit him with the helmet high on his chest, then slide up into his chin. Of course, I'll hit him with a forearm, too, if I think that'll be effective. . . .

SEPTEMBER 2. The Browns were really laying for us tonight, and they jumped out in front by two touchdowns, 14-0. Some people thought we were in trouble, but we knew we were going to win. We go into every game we play knowing we're going to win. And we always do. We never lose a game. Sometimes, of course, the clock runs out while the other team still has more points than us, but we know that the game isn't really over, that if we kept playing we'd end up ahead. From our point of view, we haven't lost a game in years. . . .

SEPTEMBER 10. . . . When I analyze a tackle I'm facing and my first thought is of his strength, and my second thought is also of his strength, then, in a real sense, I'm criticizing him. I'm telling myself that he isn't fast. This doesn't mean that he can't give you trouble. Anybody's going to beat you at least two or three times in a game— even if he doesn't have great quickness—and if he happens to beat you at critical moments, you've wasted the whole game. . . . The strong guys pound, pound, pound. They're ramming their helmets into you all the time, and if they catch you the slightest off-balance, they'll knock you right on your can—and they'll run over you. . . .

By now, of course, my thought process before each play is auto-matic, almost subconscious. First I think about my spacing, how far I should be from the center. I'll vary the distance. If the center has to cut my man off, I'll line up closer to him to make his job easier. But if I'm going to pull to my left, I'll make certain that I don't edge closer to the center because I don't want to tip the direction I'm going. Then I think about my stance. I don't want to vary my stance at all; I don't want to give the tackle any hint of the direction or nature of the play. . . .

SEPTEMBER 17. Before I left the house this morning for the stadium, my oldest child, Tony, who's nine, asked me who my man'd be in the game. I told him Karras. . . .

"I'll watch for him," Tony said.

"It shouldn't be too tough," I said. "You'll probably see a lot of him."

I thought I was just making a little joke, but the joke was on me. I had a bad day. Alex probably figured he had a good day. I don't know yet how many times he got to the passer, how many times he rushed past me, but it seemed like every time I went to the sidelines, Vince screamed at me. . . .

Alex started beating me to the outside, and one time I knew he had me and I was so frustrated I reached out and grabbed a big handful of his jersey and just pulled him to the ground. Nobody saw it, and Alex got up calling me every name he could think of. I'm sure that he's been held by about 90 percent of the guys he plays against, but he didn't expect it from me. I was desperate. . . .

When I came out from the locker room, my insides all torn up, and climbed into my car, my son Tony looked at me and said, "Daddy, do you like Alex Karras? I don't mean as a football player. I mean as a person."

"Shut up," I said.

My right ankle's extremely sore today, all discolored, black and blue and red, bruised, painful, everything. I guess it's going to be all right, unfortunately. For a while I was kind of hoping it was broken. Then this damned season would be over for me.

OCTOBER 3. Coach Lombardi seemed more disturbed than angry during our meeting this morning. He said there's a general lack of enthusiasm on the club, a lack of desire, something he can't quite put his finger on. He said that sometimes he would rather lose and have everybody play a perfect game than win and have everybody look sloppy. My immediate reaction is to say that's crazy, that's ridiculous, he couldn't really mean that, but somehow, I suspect he does, at least in theory. His desire for perfection is immense, and he's been very unhappy with our habit of doing only as much as we have to do to win. . . .

After the movies, we played our regular touch game, and I intercepted four passes, an all-time Tuesday morning record. The guys awarded me the game ball, and I just hope this is an omen of the game to come. There's been a lot of stuff in the papers about Alex Karras and how great he is. I guess it's been a while since the writers could find anything to zing Green Bay, and Alex's been giving them a mouthful. I'd like to give him a mouthful—of my shoe.

OCTOBER 8. Just for a little extra insurance, I made sure that Chandler woke me up this morning in time to go to the devotional service. I figured a few prayers certainly wouldn't hurt me any against Karras. . . .

I think most of the guys on the team are fairly religious. There may be a few atheists, but they keep their feelings quiet, I guess, because Coach Lombardi is so religious. Personally, I enjoy the chance to pray before a game. I have two special prayers of my own: "Don't let me make a fool of myself" and "Don't let anyone get hurt." I rarely pray for victory, but if we're in a big game, I sometimes say, "I don't like to ask You this, Lord, but . . ."

NOVEMBER 19. I started off the day determined to get mean and serious for the game. It's something that can't be done just on Saturday and Sunday. It has to be done starting Monday or Tuesday, has to be done gradually, building up to the game. You work up an anger, then a hatred, and the feeling gets stronger and stronger until, on Sunday, you've got your emotion so high you're ready to explode. But I had a lot of distractions this week—friends, relatives, business deals—and after the big win over Cleveland I had a natural tendency to relax. Anyway, I really tried to get going this morning. I tried to work up a good hate for the 49ers, for Charlie Krueger in particular. I have one little habit: When I want to hate an individual I make it a point not to look at the other team before the game, not to see the man I'm going to face. I feel if I don't see him, I can hate him a little more.

This afternoon, I deliberately didn't look at the 49ers. I didn't look at Charlie Krueger. I convinced myself I hated him. I hated him for trying to make me look bad. I hated him for trying to beat me. I hated him for trying to take money out of my pocket. I hated him for trying to tackle Bart Starr. I worked up my hatred when we did our calisthenics, and I still hated him when we started back to the dressing room to put on our shoulder pads and helmets before the kickoff. I rushed through the tunnel, started up the stairs, concentrating on my hate, concentrating on getting mad, and as I reached the top step, I heard a voice behind me saying, "Is Gerald Kramer thayuh?"

It had to be Charlie. I laughed and turned around, and he stood there laughing too. "How you doin', Jerry?" he said. He completely ruined my train of hate. . . .

NOVEMBER 26. At our devotional service this morning we had a guest speaker, a retired doctor who spends his time traveling around the country talking to athletes about Christ. He gave us copies of his booklet *Athletes in Action,* and I began thinking about people who never make decisions about their own lives.

The other day, I saw a film called *Cool Hand Luke,* and Paul Newman played a wild character who courted disaster all his life. He had no goal, no fear, and toward the end of his life he escaped from prison two or three times. The last time he escaped, he came upon a church and went in and got on his knees and said something like, "Old Man, whadaya got planned for me? What's next, Old Man? Wadaya want me to do? What did you put me on earth for, Old Man?"

I ask the same questions. I often wonder where my life is heading, and what's my purpose here on earth besides playing the silly games I play every Sunday. I feel there's got to be more to life than that. There's got to be some reason to it.

Many people never take control of their lives, never say this is the way it's going to be, and maybe I'm one of them. I didn't come up with any answers this morning. I just thought about it for a while.

DECEMBER 17. . . . Pittsburgh treated us rough. They bruised Donny Anderson and banged up Ben Wilson and Steve Wright cracked a rib. And Allen Brown almost died . . . two broken ribs and a punctured kidney. . . .

It's curious the way the guys react to an injury like Allen's. Most of the guys try to wipe it right out of their minds. You'll see them turn their backs on an injured teammate on the field, sort of to pretend that it didn't happen. They're afraid to think about injuries, afraid to think that it might happen to them. The more you think about it, of course, the more likely you are to get hurt. I'm realistic myself. I don't really realize how brutal the game is until the off-season, when I go out to banquets and watch movies of our games. Then I see guys turned upside-down and backwards and hit from all angles, and I flinch. I'm amazed by how violent the game is, and I wonder about playing it myself. . . .

I didn't play much of a game. I tried to make all my blocks crisp and low, perfect them for the playoffs, but the emotion wasn't there. Without the emotion, you can't play the game. . . .

DECEMBER 23. . . . We could do no wrong, on offense or defense. Travis dove for another touchdown in the final quarter, even though I only gave Merlin half a block, and we won the Western Conference championship, 28-7. The fans carried Travis off the field— he had a fantastic day—and we rushed into the locker room, laughing and shouting and absolutely floating.

"Magnificent," Coach Lombardi said, when we all reached the locker room. "Just magnificent. I've been very proud of you guys all year long. You've overcome a great deal of adversity. You've hung in there, and when the big games came around. . . ." He couldn't finish the sentence. He broke up, and the tears started trickling down his cheek. He just knelt down crying, and led us in the Lord's Prayer. We thanked God that no one had been injured.

Guys walked around the room, hugging each other. Nitschke actually was kissing and hugging everybody. He came up to me and said, "Thank you, Jerry," and then turned to Gregg and said, "Thank you, Forrest," and he thanked all his teammates. . . .

I was misty-eyed myself I felt so good. I felt so proud, proud of myself and proud of my teammates and proud of my coaches. I felt like I was a part of something special. I guess it's the way a group of scientists feel when they make a big breakthrough, though, of course, we aren't that important. It's a feeling of being together, completely together, a singleness of purpose, accomplishing something that is very difficult to accomplish, accomplishing something that a lot of people thought you couldn't accomplish. It sent a beautiful shiver up my back.

Chapter Eighteen

Martin Siegel

A RABBI WHO doesn't believe in God? Rabbi Martin Siegel tries to explain this paradoxical position and more about his understanding of modern Judaism in his 1969 journal, *Amen*. Often at odds with the values held by the members of his wealthy Reform temple on Long Island, Siegel finds himself saying many things that his congregation does not wish to hear. Within his breast an ancient battle seems to be raging—the war between the radical prophet and the conservative priest.

The alliance he tries to make between these two roles raises more difficult questions about his function as rabbi: Where is the man in these robes? What does the congregation truly expect of him, and what does he *assume* they expect? When do the limitations of his position comfortably suit his own limitations? And when does the role that he feels he must play betray all he holds dear?

Originally taped and transcribed simply to document the working life of a typical rabbi, Siegel's diary grew dense with the complications of his own identity as a clergyman, its impact on his relationship with his community, his wife, and himself, and finally evolved to reveal the complexity of the whole man.

DECEMBER 17. The day certainly started on a cosmic note. The phone rang at 9:30 A.M., and the long-distance caller asked me, "What is the Jewish position on immortality?"

The caller was a member of my former congregation in Wheeling, and he told me that he was going to dinner with the present rabbi and that he wanted to be able to discuss the subject of immortality intelligently with him.

I explained that while Judaism allowed a great deal of flexibility on the subject—and that nobody I knew could prove anything one way or the other—the emphasis generally was on doing good deeds in this life and that they might lead to some kind of ultimate destiny. I told him that we don't put much emphasis on the survival of the ego, none on hell and very little on heaven. The caller said that he personally felt there should be some idea of heaven, and I told him that was fine, that was perfectly all right with me. . . .

1968

JANUARY 4. I was asked to play Solomon again today. Two young people who are planning to be married came to me, with their parents, and with a question: Should the wedding be kosher?

The boy's parents said they maintain a kosher home and they would prefer a kosher wedding. The girl's parents said they do not keep a kosher home and they oppose a kosher wedding. Both sides agreed to abide by my momentous decision. . . .

I listened to both sides for two hours, then ruled that the wedding should be kosher, simply because I felt it meant more to the one couple to have it than it did to the other couple not to have it.

The young lady's mother called this evening to inform me that another rabbi would be performing the wedding ceremony.

JANUARY 17. It was unfortunate that so few people attended services this evening because I gave one of my best sermons of the season. I pointed out the incongruity between spiritual Israel, to which I link our Jewish heritage and emotion, and the state of Israel, which I fear is turning into a nationalistic, militaristic society. If there is one sure way to turn off a Jewish congregation, it is to attack Israel, even as affectionately as I did. . . .

"I only want to say one thing," I said. "I'm pleased that Israel has survived. However, I don't think that an Arab mother weeps for her dead son any differently than a Jewish mother does. I simply refuse to take any joy in the killing of Arab children, any more than I would take joy in the killing of Jewish children."

The congregation was stunned, and the Israeli colonel left without speaking to me. . . .

JANUARY 28. Since the fall, I have been teaching a voluntary afternoon class for high-school students at the temple. At the beginning, a dozen students attended more or less regularly, but in recent weeks, fewer and fewer have been showing up. Last week only one student attended. . . .

I think if I meant something to these students, they would be coming to the class, but I'm afraid I am not reaching them. I tend to think in intellectual, abstract and universal terms which they're not prepared to deal with. Our only exciting discussion so far has been about whether one should smoke before the age of sixteen. I'm not sure I really understand them, and they sense this. I find it all very frustrating. . . .

JANUARY 29. A young man in the confirmation class told me today he doubts whether he wants to be Jewish because he doesn't believe in God.

"I don't believe in God, either,"I told him. "But that has nothing to do with being Jewish."

He looked at me rather oddly. "What do you have to believe in?" he asked. "Anything?"

"Judaism is not a system of belief," I said. "Judaism is an effort to try to find some purpose and meaning to your life."

"Yes," he said, "that makes sense. I believe in that."

A true Jew does not believe *in* God. He believes *that* God can be a vital force in the expression of man's life. People without belief think there is nothing more to them but themselves. How can one look at the great adventure called life, having a genuine feeling for it, if he believes that he himself is so important? In light of what I can be, or what I could do, or in light of how little I really know, how can I be arrogant enough to worship myself? The essence of what I call religion is a realization of the inadequacy of man with respect to all that is around him—a sense of wonder, call it what you will.

Worshipping God has nothing to do with believing *in* Him.

After today's discussion, one confirmation student jumped up and said, "Rabbi, for your information, nobody was listening."

Sometimes I think Long Island is nothing but sand and *chutzpah.*

This evening I learned that at least one member of the class was listening. His mother called me and rather bitterly accused me of teaching her child not to believe in God.

FEBRUARY 22. I learned today that a seventy-year-old man who worked one day a week for $15.80 as the custodian of our synagogue has been fired as an economy move. After services this morning, I took Bob Mandel aside and asked him to reinstate the custodian.

"Are you asking me on the basis of charity, mercy or justice?" he asked.

"Charity," I said.

"Well, on that basis, we'll reinstate him."

I usually don't do that well with multiple-choice questions.

MARCH 28. After officiating at a funeral this morning, I came back . . . for a rehearsal for a special service to be conducted tonight by the Men's Club. The tradition is that we always rehearse these things for fear the service will be lacking professionalism. Tomorrow we will have a mother-daughter Sabbath, and we had a rehearsal for that, too.

Imagine: we rehearse to pray.

MARCH 29. The mother-daughter service this morning was a sell-out. Hundreds of people couldn't find a place to sit except the floor. There is a reason for the turnout. It happens every time we have any program involving children. People today have moved away from an external God, yet really aren't satisfied with just worshipping themselves, primarily because they realize they don't stand for anything except their Cadillacs and Puccis. Thus the children, because they provide all the things God used to provide (immortality, love, relationship, etc.), have been moved in to become the center of value, the living idols.

MARCH 31. . . . A funeral is never easy for me. I hate to see people grieved; I hate to see them hurt; I hate to see them confronted with the reality of permanent absence. I always try to comfort those who feel the loss most heavily and are trying to adjust to it. Everything I do—the way I act, what I say—is intended to help sow the seeds of recovery. Sometimes this is a problem, because people want to be assured there is life after death, even though Judaism is not a salvation system. We don't live for death and we don't promise an afterlife, but because there is nothing concrete in the religion precluding it, I usually fudge the point when people who are under stress persist for an answer. . . .

. . . This past weekend was the second anniversary of the death of my father. Even though it's customary to go to the cemetery, I spoke, instead, at a memorial service for Martin Luther King, where I pleaded for black-white understanding.

I think my father would agree that it was more important for me to do something useful for the living than to pay obeisance to an ancestor. He was a very gentle man. I think of him often. . . . He always seemed so shy toward me. The last thing he said to me was, "Martin, we're going to have a long talk someday."

We never did.

APRIL 30. I found the students in my class at the Woodmere Academy relieved today, because the matter of Ivy League college admissions was over. They were eager to talk about what they called their "ultimate values," which to them seemed to mean getting married, being successful, and holding onto Judaism solely as an identification. They felt they occupied a privileged position and that it was therefore no responsibility of theirs to serve mankind or society or anything other than themselves. The session depressed me, because many of the students sounded like elitist snobs ready to go out and take whatever they can get from the world, and also because after an entire year as their teacher, I don't think I've moved them an inch.

To compound the depression, I later had to conduct a rehearsal, the second or third of its kind, for the confirmation services to be held in a few weeks. In many respects, the affair has turned into a big empty pageant—a march with flowers, and speeches, and the various trappings of pomp—so huge that we had to suspend classes for the month prior to the event just to rehearse. The parents expect the confirmation to look like a gala scene from *The Marriage of Figaro.* . . .

After the rehearsal today, one of the more sensitive students asked to speak to me privately. . . .

"I wasn't sure whether you said premarital sex was against the Jewish religion."

"Sex should be a part of an enduring relationship," I said. "It's only one form of emotional expression among many."

"Does this mean you have to be married to have sex?"

"No."

"Well," he said, "if you have sex and you're not married, does Judaism approve?"

"As far as I can see, it doesn't rule it out."

"Well, how can you tell if you're doing the right thing?"

"That's up to you. It should be a level of communication, not just an act of gratification."

"Then that means you don't have to be married to have sex?"

"That means sex doesn't have to be limited to marriage."

"Well," he asked. "How do you feel? Do you condone premarital sex?"

"I understand it."

After this conversation, I felt guilty about being so evasive, and if it were just I, Marty Siegel, talking, I would have answered him differently. But he wasn't asking Marty Siegel. He was asking the Rabbi. And as the Rabbi, I don't consider it my role to sanction or disapprove of whatever he is doing. I didn't think it was as important to answer his questions as it was to listen to them. Besides, if I had been more direct, his mother would be calling me tonight accusing me of encouraging her son to sleep with his girl friend. I've been through it all before.

MAY 4. . . . Today was such a sunny, exhilarating spring day that I spent most of it in the pool splashing around with little Sally. Judith watched for a few minutes, but said she didn't want to come in.

Later in the afternoon, I drove to the barber. On the way, I entered a narrow congested street where traffic was moving very slowly. The man in the car behind me began honking furiously and followed me closely until we reached a red light, where he jumped out of his car, rushed over to my window and screamed some really crude things at me. I ignored him, but when the light changed and I began to drive off, he spit at me.

Times like this really make me understand how protected I am in my position. People usually hold back in the presence of a rabbi. Maybe next year I'll ask the state to send me a license plate with RABBI spelled out on it to protect me from getting too many more insights into what life is really like.

MAY 31. A lady, one of my disciples in the congregation, asked me today if I thought I were a prophet. The question really intrigued me, and although I didn't have any immediate answer I've been thinking about it all day long.

I've always been a loner. I'm not at any university or connected with any formal movement, and therefore I've never had a barometer on my brain. I don't know if other people share my thoughts.

I think that I sometimes have a kind of emotion which, to my understanding, would be associated with prophecy. It is a feeling I get when there are certain things I say. I feel at times that what I'm saying is more than me saying it, that the thoughts in the words are almost unconsciously compulsive. At these times it's never a question of whether it's right or wrong, appropriate or inappropriate, I just say what I have to say, and I don't seem to have much control over it. This doesn't happen often, but sometimes it does.

If what I say at these times can—and I really doubt it will—have any real impact, then I am a prophet. But no man can call himself a prophet, and few prophets are recognized in their lifetime.

JUNE 25. . . . The other day I wanted to buy a pair of bell-bottom trousers. I didn't. Why? Because a congregation does not *expect* its rabbi to wear bell-bottom trousers. I think at heart I'm a swinger, but I will never let myself swing. I can count many occasions when I've wanted to cry, or laugh, or be sarcastic, or be affectionate, or be silly, but I couldn't. It wasn't *expected* of me. So I just repressed what might have been natural and instead did whatever was appropriate.

So all of the insulation and all of the isolation from which I now suffer is as much my doing as anybody else's. Long ago I should have made my stand: *I will be myself. I will not live up to your role expectations. I, like you, am human. Take me for what I am or don't take me at all.* . . .

AUGUST 2. . . . A rabbi is an abstraction, and now, more than ever, I am beginning to feel the awful weight of this abstraction. While I have been able to carry it, I can see that Judith has not. She wants to be human, and people will only allow her to be the wife of an abstraction, an extension of my own unreality.

People tend to make me a symbol. They say they know me, but they don't. They know only my *roles*. To some of them, I am a radical. To some of them, I am the signature on the marriage contract. To some of them I am the man who opposes the indulgence of the psychotic fear of anti-Semitism. People see me only as they care or need to see me.

And poor Judith has to be the wife to all this.

I can't recognize myself in their eyes, so how could she? We both have to live as exhibits in this community. While people are friendly, we have no friends. We have been made into what they want us to be. Everybody seems to care about us, but yet nobody really does.

It seems that I'm endlessly meeting people—strangers—who say, "I've heard about you. You stand for racial harmony." Or: "You stand for progressive religious education." I have become nothing but a public symbol. I am dissected, examined, interpreted and misunderstood. And Judith? She is prisoner to this reflection. She is allowed no self.

I am dynamic. I am aggressive. I am prophetic. I am concerned. I am lonely.

I want to be what I am, not a symbol of what I am.

I don't want Judith to have to be the wife of a symbol. . . .

SEPTEMBER 11. Until about a year ago, I had a deep fear of death. At night sometimes, I would wake up sweating profusely, my heart beating rapidly, filled with a terror of dying.

It was something I knew I had to work out. But only after I could accept the concept of time as a flow did I begin to feel a little more easy with the thought of my own death.

The state of unexistence no longer frightens me, because I now realize that man is only an expression of his moment, and when the moment fades, so must he. Whether I live or die is not important; it's what I do when I'm alive and what I contribute to the flow of time. Having worked this out in my mind, I have gained an inner peace, and it was in this mood I approached the High Holy Days, which began tonight with Rosh Hashanah. This year I am not going to pray for life, but for meaning. I am going to pray for a life that means something. . . .

And here I am, *Rabbi* Martin Siegel, keeping myself alive and earning a living (the phrase strikes me harshly) by preserving an institution in which God has grown meaningless. Yet I know that the life I've had given to me can't be satisfied by working furiously on the fringe of things. I want to be where people live.

I came here to create not to cremate. But I know I am presiding over the last dying flame of a once great institution, offering tidbits of consolation to make the demise all the less painful. But nobody cares. Why do I bother?

If I were to die tomorrow, it could be said that my work was all useless—that Rabbi Martin Siegel turned over in the mausoleum where he worked and went to his death. He was a man who saw the past and saw the future, while he himself fell victim to a rapidly disintegrating present.

It is a very difficult self-inventory I find myself undertaking this Rosh Hashanah.

Chapter Nineteen

Walter Morris

BUT WHAT OF THE wage-earner who suddenly finds himself out of work? Put him in his fifties as well, with a wife and two teenagers still to support, and a life styled by middle-class expectations. What feelings might such a man suffer when he learns—despite his eighteen years as an editor and office manager for a large New York corporation—that the world isn't waiting to rehire a middle-aged man?

During his many bleak months without work, Walter Morris found out. A periodic journal-keeper since adolescence, who had previously published two others, *American In Search of a Way* and *Notebook 2: Black River*, Morris returned to this personal resource while trapped by unemployment, the interview mill, a rough suburban winter, and an increasing awareness of his own mortality.

His *Journal of a Discarded Man* suggests many questions for the reader about the meaning of manhood that is often assumed through the role of provider. For a man in our world, unemployment can quickly imply failure and defeat. No matter the reason for the loss of the job, the loss of status and self-respect may obtain. If identification with his work is the basis of defining the man to himself, his value as a man is easily undermined when the work is gone. And if money and shiny possessions are the best pay-off for the work done, what is there to show the world except the man bereft? Luckily, Walter Morris, though involved in just such quandaries, had inner resources that sustained him during this cold and fallow time. His journal candidly records these assaults on his faith in himself, and his final gains as he began to forge wider choices—choices that eventually resulted in his leaving the nine-to-five work force for a more flexible career as an independent creative projects consultant and later in his home state's Civil Service.

1962

2 DECEMBER, SUNDAY. Last night I dreamt that I was back on the Corporation's payroll, rehired for an especially interesting job. As I walked buoyantly across the office, a mysterious voice in the dream said, "You'd better not start crying for joy, fella. This is just a dream." Then I woke up. It was nice of him to tip me off like that—whoever he was—and I thanked him. I guess he felt that wish-fulfillment had gone too far and he couldn't bear to see the let-down.

But no more of that. I don't want to run the risk of muddying clear water. In spite of the objective situation (or because of it?) the great deep is quiet: sleep is profound, peaceful and seemingly dreamless, waking anxiety minimal, psychosomatic symptoms almost entirely absent. Yet the pressure of the Problem, day in and day out, is indescribable.

4 DECEMBER, TUESDAY. Miss A sends me a referral slip to a Mr. Chairlock. I had an interview with this gentleman last September as a result of his ad in the Sunday paper. It took a rather lengthy interview to bring out the fact that there was, actually, no job open. . . .

I didn't too much mind being kept waiting fifty minutes beyond the appointment time—or waiting while he had a long telephone conversation with a girl who was asking about a housemaid's job—but I did rather resent spending a dollar on transportation in order to make a pitch for a job that wasn't there. Not that Mr. Chairlock was allowed to know how I felt. In the interview situation I am always the very spirit of graciousness, my theory being that even if the case looks hopeless it is smart to leave the interviewer with a good taste in his mouth. It can't do you any harm (can it?) and it might eventually do you some good, but it requires a hell of a lot of self-discipline.

Today makes thirteen months and one week of plunging against a stonewall.

5 DECEMBER, WEDNESDAY. . . . Picked up Léni and Peter at six o'clock. At least these two are working. Peter is fourteen and Léni got him an after-school job as mail clerk. He doesn't know how lucky he is—after-school and Saturday jobs aren't too plentiful—but he does feel the effect of a pay check. You might call it "getting too big for his breeches," but I call it good. The pay check is giving him some self-confidence; it's helping him to grow up. I don't in the least mind being attacked from the rear by this little boy of mine, who is now almost six feet, and being called "a weak old man," but sometimes, of course, I have to show him who's boss still.

11 DECEMBER, TUESDAY. What I want is to *be*, to function, to produce—and still make money. I want to be carried away in this effort, so that time means nothing, so that morning, noon and night, holidays, lunch hours and coffee-breaks mean nothing. They mean nothing because you can take them as you please, not as they come up on a rigid schedule. If it's flowing—and never mind what *it* is—you don't stop just because the time happens to be twelve o'clock noon or five o'clock in the afternoon. You don't stop because today is Columbus Day or Memorial Day or even New Year's Day. You stop when it stops. It may stop at 10:30 on a Thursday morning. There is nothing awkward about that because you don't have to go through the idiotic motions of seeming to be working until Friday at five. . . . Thursday afternoon you take your wife to the movies and have cocktails at a nice spot

afterwards. Friday you sleep until ten and then go down in your workshop and saw wood. *It* may not start up again until Sunday afternoon, and then it pours forth until two o'clock Monday morning. As you can see, these are not regular (read "respectable") working hours. But *it* just doesn't give a damn. Nor do I.

I don't really want a nine-to-five desk job. That's not functioning. But here I am, moving heaven and earth, to get one. So far, nobody wants to give me what I don't want. They pick me over from stem to stern, though, as if they really had something to offer.

20 DECEMBER, THURSDAY. Bright, cold and windy. The postman brings Christmas cards and another premium-due notice from another insurance company.

I should be in New York, knocking around among the agencies. But here I sit, trying to write and smoke my guilt away. It won't work. You can't write it away, you can't smoke it away, and you can't even drink it away (neither with coffee nor gin). I ought to be in New York, though I know the odds indicate overwhelmingly that such action, today, would be a waste of time and money. I can't eve ease it off a little by poring over the help-wanted ads in the *Times*. (The strike is still on.) But I'll go out and get the North Jersey paper, which will be full of all the jobs I either can't fill or don't want. . . . Doing this duty will increase the sense of frustration while not doing a damn thing for the guilt. . . .

21 DECEMBER, FRIDAY. . . . As all the world can see, I am not entirely bereft of virtue. I rise early and drive my wife to work in a warm car. Moreover, at the end of the day (if she is not riding back with one of the girls), I go and pick her up—in a warm car—and then go back later and pick up Peter. Between times, I may have shopped for bread, milk and eggs, balanced the checkbook against the bank's statement, returned books to the library (always overdue), had the car lubricated and the oil changed . . . and I may have cleaned a drain pipe, fixed a faucet, and at least thought about getting the car washed and doing something about the unlatchable garage door.

If this seems but a minor manifestation of virtue, I submit that there *is* a job hunt going on (though not always recorded here in detail), and while I admit that my smoking is scandalous, my drinking is as moderate as ever. . . .

29 DECEMBER, SATURDAY. Five more makes sixty. This thing is moving right along. At twenty-one I thought I was going to be twenty-one forever. ("The feeling of immortality in youth," as old Hazlitt put it.) At thirty, one is taken aback; at forty, startled; at fifty, incredulous and depressed. Midway between fifty and sixty, time's fleet foot seems fully revealed and I see no logical reason for being taken by surprise from now on out—but who's logical? Today is a day for homilies and platitudes, old saws and bitter-sweet droppings. "If I had it all to do over again . . ." "If I knew then what I know now . . ." These pious exercises are all right, though. They take us away from our close work and present a vista, and in this focus Everyman is a philosopher.

All right. If I had it all to do over again, I'd learn a trade (for bread and butter) and for the high, orbital shot I'd concentrate on painting. The pip-squeak world of the white-collar employee I'd avoid like the plague. This is hindsight, pure, fatuous and futile. . . .

1963

4 JANUARY, FRIDAY. Cold and gray the sky and the light in the sky and the snow and the ice. The world is stark. No color, no richness, no growth . . . all is frozen, brittle, bony and seemingly dead.

This gray light reaches an old eye, thousands of layers deep, and it views the scene exactly as it is: no sign of food or fire. Thus the possibility of death by starvation and cold. The old eye also knows that a stronger animal, gnawed by hunger, may be lurking in the shadow or on the invisible side of the frozen hill. Thus, thousands of layers deep, dread is stirred—and I wonder why.

Memories come flowing in, all in the same grey light: fear of the great city (first encounter) at fifteen; the break-up of a high-school love affair; arriving back in Ann Arbor after Christmas vacation without enough money and shrinking from the thought of all the exams that were soon to come up; being stymied by the depression of the 'Thirties; saying goodbye at the pier to an artist friend whose friendship was lost, later, in the bitter hate of world-saving politics; shivering in the field as a soldier; then out of uniform and looking for a job in the cold gray city. . . . But this isn't quite it. The dread in this gray light seems to arise from a source prior to all these memories, an urangst that was there, somehow, from the beginning. . . .

12 JANUARY, SATURDAY. . . . There are two subjects that are guaranteed to embarrass almost any middle-class group on the East Coast: religion (as spiritual experience, not as law) and money (as personal income, not as investment problem). Thus a person would hesitate to be seen toting a copy of a religious classic—unless, of course, he or she has some connection with an ecclesiastical payroll. Then it makes sense. And when a man loses his job he may say to his wife, "Don't tell anybody!" For such information is in the highly classified area of personal income and what is revealed in this case is not how much but that there is *none*. The old boy doesn't want to be a walking embarrassment to himself and to all his friends and acquaintances. (This may be why men recently fired may have night dreams of being seen naked in public.) It is bad enough to have one's income cut off without everybody knowing about it, and the man strives mightily to make a fast reconnection. If he can bring off this feat he will be able to announce a *change* of jobs before anybody can discover the truth. Seeing that the possibility of making a fast reconnection is usually remote, truth will out, eventually, and the man would have been wiser to let it come out in the beginning.

Financial success is *the* goal—and the automatic measure of worth—and that, kiddies, is all there is to it. . . .

23 JANUARY, WEDNESDAY. . . . But I do wish the end-of-the-world dream would stop repeating itself night after night. The sleeping

is very good, though, in spite of this dreamy conviction that the world will come to an end by morning. It isn't a nightmare; just a kind of vague, slumbering dread. I could do without it, but I suppose I ought to be thankful it isn't worse.

I ought to be thankful for a lot of things, as a matter of fact: that Léni is so patient and so courageous, that there are no serious problems (health or otherwise) in the family, that the house is free and clear. My favorite ailment for many years was severe headache . . . and you would think that now would be the time for this curse to reappear in spades, but there have been only a few mild attacks and these were easily remitted with the usual analgesics. For that, I am *very* grateful. As noted elsewhere (and maybe I'd better not say it too often!) the great deep is quiet, or relatively so. The end-of-the-world thing is evidence of turbulence down there, of course, but it's reassuringly mild. . . .

25 JANUARY, FRIDAY (4:15 a.m.). A night of wakefulness and fear. I am a rabbit among wolves and foxes and diving hawks. . . .

Old Father of the Night . . .

Money.

Only money can keep a family alive, for money puts food on the table, commands medical help when needed, provides heat in the winter . . . clothing, transportation, communication, taxes, recreation, education. (I understand that scholarships are usually refused the child of an unemployed man—"especially if he has been out of work for some time." Another cute angle to this thing.)

Money.

What went wrong? And where do we go from here? . . .

5 FEBRUARY, TUESDAY. Completely stymied. Nobody even bothers to answer my letters. There isn't even a *Times* help-wanted section to pore over. . . .

Léni has taken a temporary clerical job. (Another big outfit—a run-away from New York City—seeking housewives for $1.30 an hour and deftly manipulating the hours of work and the terms of employment of each housewife so that the company will not have to pay unemployment insurance). . . . Today I wrote checks to a total of $665.00: routine expenses, city taxes, and insurance premiums.

Like the slum-kid—but forty years too late—I'm beginning to feel the hard grain of truth in the saying: All men are enemies.

2 MARCH, SATURDAY. If money falls out of the trees into one's lap and there is no convenient way to stop this downpour, I can see how a man might drift into a $300,000 estate, a string of expensive cars, a yacht, fine jewelry, servants, mink coats, expensive vacations and all the rest of it. But if the money doesn't come that easily, I can't see the point. I can't see why any man in his right mind would deliberately work for these things. A $25,000 house can be attractive and comfortable. As much as I like fine automobiles, I must admit that I can be perfectly happy with something less than an El Dorado, a Mercedes 300, or a Rolls-Royce; and as much as I like fine wines and whiskies, I can be immensely pleased with a relatively inexpensive martini.

I'd rather have a relatively secure, moderate income—and have time to paint. And time to write. And time to read. And time to saw wood. And time to sit in a chair and talk to somebody. And time to take a walk and talk to the clouds.

As for being unemployed and having no income at all, this knocks everything in the head. It's no damn good and I don't recommend it. Just because I make only moderate demands on material existence, the gods seem to think I make no demands at all. Thus they reward me for my virtue, and thus I tell them I wish now that I had been the most hoggish, aggressive sonuvabitch in the City of New York—if not east of the Mississippi.

8 APRIL, MONDAY. Following Sophie's suggestion, to New York this morning to look up Robert Vanderbilt Harris who runs a photocopy shop. . . .

Result: I am to start on Wednesday and learn enough about the business to be able to go out and sell the service to book publishers. (Commission—and carfare—only). . . .

So things *are* beginning to break! At any rate, this spring looks a hell of a lot brighter than last. . . .

26 JUNE, WEDNESDAY. . . . Work has to be crowned with some kind of reward. With the possible exception of occupational therapy, the most effective and satisfying reward is money. . . . Work, even for a good cause, may not be enough. There's nothing like money to convince you that your work has value, which is another way of saying that *you* have value. It's a great boost to one's self-respect and as gratifying as a good meal. . . . A painter may be convinced he's produced a good picture and tag it at a thousand dollars; and if you walk in his studio and praise the picture, he'll like to hear it, but the most convincing evidence of your appreciation is your personal check in the amount of one thousand cold clams. As for the job-hunter, it's the same thing again. Personnel artists often praise an applicant before giving him the bad news. That's letting the guy down easy. "Your record of achievement is truly outstanding," the interviewer writes— then comes the knife. . . .

Chapter Twenty

Basile Yanovsky

I N OUR HUMAN UNCERTAINTY we often expect our scientists, like our ministers, to be endowed with certain unalterable qualities: compassion, wisdom, impartiality. To read from the logbook of Dr. Basile Yanovsky, *The Dark Fields of Venus*, his record of life in a New York V.D. clinic, is to meet a doctor as human as the people he treats. We might balk at Dr. Yanovsky's puritanical streak, but cannot help but share his rage and revulsion toward the daily exposure to ignorance, ugliness, a dismal system of public service, and the ineradicable round dance of venereal disease. His sympathy, his exasperation, and his keen eye for human behavior, all show a dedicated physican fully involved with his patients and work, never the indifferent dispensing machine. His journal entries might also suggest a new approach for the diarist—each a sharp observation of a single incident, pungently phrased, and fashioned upon a foundation of feeling.

A refugee from the Russian Revolution, Dr. Yanovsky was born in 1906 and took his degree in Medicine in Paris, where he was also a distinguished member of a group of Russian emigré writers. In 1942 he came to the United States, where he continues to write his widely acclaimed novels while also still practicing medicine.

42

The familiar story: her boy friend called to tell her that he has it. He thinks she gave it to him, and he doesn't want to see her any more.

Her first tests were negative.

"We must classify her G 90," said the nurse. That would call for a strong preventive dose of penicillin.

"Suppose this man wants to get rid of her and invented a pretext. Why should we believe him?" I asked the nurse, while the girl followed the discussion with great approval. I decided to let her go. In two weeks, after the results of the culture for gonorrhea were in, we would see our way better.

46

He wanted a smear from his rectum. He started in a foggy fashion and took some time to indicate the place that worried him. I cast a glance there and noticed an abrasion.

"Does it hurt?"

"It did. It's better now."

We dug into this small ulcer for a Dark Field examination and a short while later the bacteriologist showed me two dangerously slim, beautifully slithering *Spirochaetae pallidae* under the microscope. Their fine, silvery, corkscrew silhouettes conveyed a truly ominous impression.

63

I usually work fast and efficiently. ("If you *have* to do it, do it quickly!" goes for doctors as well as for hangmen. I plunge the big needle in without delay or preliminaries, since no speeches can make it smaller or softer. I am through very quickly and the patient, after a painful grimace, sighs with relief. "Is that all?" they ask, and smile, satisfied. But some curse, complain, and threaten to write to the Central Office about my brutality.

I have noticed that if a patient is particularly dirty and smelly or ugly and dumb, I do my job somewhat sloppily. I do it as if I were holding my nose with one hand, which, spiritually, is indeed the case. . . .

Here is a monstrosity: a female who has lost her human appearance, exposed to me in her most intimate and repulsive aspect. It smells bad—I wish I were far away, I wish she were far away. And she (it is usually a she, though it sometimes happens with a male, too), she feels it and "transfers" it. She complains to the Central Office of roughness, brutality, unprofessional behavior. She wants revenge for a metaphysical humiliation of which she is well aware. In short, she wants me, if not to admire her, at least to approve (physically).

68

"You have syphilis," I told him.

He was a small, frail Puerto Rican, pale and undernourished. He took a deep breath, turned around, and dashed to the exit. After a little while he came back, bringing a girl with him: a tiny, emaciated, pretty Latin. As they approached, they exchanged some words and I heard her say, very womanly and tenderly, "You see, I told you."

What could she have possibly told him on their way here? That she has it? Or that he has it? But certainly that she loves him and wants him.

The boy put his arm around her shoulder, gently, protectively, and looked at me as if ready for execution.

"Both of you will be treated," I said. "We'll cure you. But first she, too, has to register."

Crossing the hall later, I noticed them several times while they were still waiting to register her. If for some reason we ever had to send a sample human couple to another planet, to show what such a couple looks like, what it expresses, to demonstrate its indivisibility, I wouldn't mind sending them: they'd do!

95

As a general rule they blame someone for "giving it" to them. He blames her, she blames him. The female often begs me, "Tell him I don't have it, otherwise he won't believe me." In many cases there is a third party involved; the man (it mostly is the man) will call up and say to his girl, "You'd better go see a doctor. I'm sure I've got it." And the woman tells me, "I know who gave it to him."

It seems that no one can be blamed personally, individually. Often three or four or five persons are involved, and it becomes a circle, a vicious circle, of course. Nowhere is the *perpetuum mobile* of evil so evident as here. "Who gave it to whom?" is like the eternal question about the chicken and the egg.

This vicious circle can be broken only by an absolute stop, a radical abstention (besides penicillin), a six-week moratorium for everyone involved. How clear seem to me the scientific and beneficial implications of Lent! And yet a doctor is reluctant to speak about abstention. It sounds *moralistic*.

103

Many patients have become used—at private offices or at clinics with poor technicians—to getting their needle right in the middle of the buttock. I give it in the upper lateral corner, as prescribed. Suspicious of any deviation from the routine and distrustful as they are of the establishment, they resent this: it hurts more and for a longer time, they claim. Often I am too rushed to explain to them that in the center, where they want it, the huge sciatic nerve runs down, and that one must not stick the needle in its vicinity.

So I stick my needle where I choose, and they are sure that I enjoy torturing them. They call me "Bruto," "Butcher," or preferably, "Fucking bastard."

105

Today is my birthday. Of course I haven't mentioned it to anyone around.

A rather arrogant young man comes in.

"Ah, that's the one who collapses," says the nurse. "You have to put him on the table before you give him the shot."

"Yes, yes," the youth affirmed with a smile. "I'm the one who collapses."

That smile of his, his superior air, and the pride he took in collapsing rubbed me the wrong way.

"If you fuck woman you must be able to take a needle," I said.

"That's an offensive remark," he answered promptly. "And besides, I don't fuck women, I fuck men."

"That makes no difference. Anyway, you get your needle like everybody else." I really hated his guts. "At your age I had been in two wars and I wasn't afraid of bullets." (As if that could prove anything.)

"Congratulations," he retorted with a "knowing" smile. "And how many people did you kill?"

"No more than you."

"Oh, leave me alone." He turned away, as if what I had said he had heard a thousand times and it was below his dignity to argue. "What kind of professional ethics is this, anyhow!"

"And what is your profession?" I asked quietly, preparing the syringe. "If it's no indiscretion."

"It *is* an indiscretion," he answered.

"I thought so," I said.

The needle is of steel or some other metal, and regardless of your emotions and whether you like or detest the flesh into which you have to plunge it, it causes pain.

107

A fair, almost transparent adolescent with a positive Dark Field.

"I wanted to ask you . . ." he began. I knew what he wanted: assurance that after his shots of pencillin he would be completely cured.

"Yes," I said, "you'll be all right, and ready to sin again."

He laughed and insisted, "No, I'm serious. Will I be one hundred per cent cured?"

They do not want an ambiguous or jocular answer. They want certainty. But science, medical science, is only approximation. Certainty one should seek elsewhere.

123

The men's toilet is worth mentioning. In short, it's filthy. Filthy, although once a day a man in heavy-duty gloves goes in and cleans it. It can't be kept clean. Especially since there is a trick for flushing: you have to press down hard (best with your foot) and wait for a long moment; only then does it begin to drain. If you don't press long enough, nothing happens.

I have devised a complicated, and I hope, foolproof technique for using this necessary commodity. First, while still in the working room, I wash my hands. Then I take a paper towel, and, protecting my hands with it, I open the door and close it the same way. Then I take a fresh paper towel and approach the toilet (there are no urinals), which is filled with the usual things plus paper and cigarette butts. From the wall directly to the left a huge inscription greets me: WATCH OUT: THIS COULD BE A CLAPTRAP! Underneath, several appropriate commentaries (they change).

After every step in my adventure I reach for a fresh paper towel; walking out, I again use a new one, still protecting myself from the contaminated knobs. Back in my office I wash my hands. I would advise every customer of ours to adopt this routine; it is a pity we have no pamphlet on the subject.

Of course, there is a separate washroom for the doctors and laboratory technicians, with a special key attached to a huge wooden board and kept under lock in a special drawer. But I don't bother. And, after all, why should the knobs in there be less contaminated?

151

Of the four doctors who were supposed to come that afternoon only one showed up: me. And I had a full house: eighty-five patients to see in two and a half hours.

In the middle of my struggle to clear the waiting room (a struggle in many ways reminiscent of driving crosstown from east to west through Manhattan) this little fairy appeared. He felt all right but wanted to be sure. Wasn't it a sound idea to have regular checkups?

"Yes, it's a good idea," I said wearily. "We'll take a blood sample for syphilis."

But the gay young man wasn't satisfied. He also wanted a rectal smear.

"For Christ's sake," I exploded, "don't you see how busy we are today with the doctors away? And you come with your fucking ass for a routine checkup! Can't you postpone it until after Labor Day?"

"No," he said. "You're here to take care of us."

"And you, what do you do? Whom do you take care of?" I asked in a rage.

"I pay taxes," said this little bastard, who was probably on some kind of welfare. "And my father pays taxes. And all my family pays taxes."

I knew he was lying, but I couldn't prove it. And that wasn't the point, anyway.

152

She spread her legs, and in her pinkish skin, where short red hairs sprouted, a strawberry-red fissure came into view.

A woman philosopher and religious teacher of the fourth century, Hypatia of Alexandria, had a striking discussion with her lover. To discourage his earthly temptations, she addressed him, at the most passionate moment of their relations, in the following manner: "See what it is you adore, Archytas, this foul matter, this corruption, with its secretions, its excrements and its infections. . . ."

But the tenacious and passionate Archytas gave her this answer: "It is not matter I love, but form."

How many times, discouraged and depressed in the V.D. clinic, have I repeated these saintly words of Archytas. . . .

156

"Where did you get such a whore?" I asked. He was dripping, actually spraying, pus.

"She was feeling sick . . ." he began, "and approached me. . . ."

"What do you mean, sick? Nauseous?"

"Yes, sick to her stomach." He looked at me, surprised by my denseness.

"And then what?"

"She needed her junk. So I gave her six dollars. . . ."

"And she spread her legs?"

"Well, yes . . . She said, 'If you want to enter me, I don't mind. . . .' You know how it is."

Many times I feel like sticking my head out the window and yelling across the boroughs of New York, "No, I don't 'know how it is'! I don't know, and I don't want to know."

196

He came in with a paperback: Jacobs . . . something about cities, how to make them beautiful.

He was a personable young man in his middle twenties, with a little pimple on his intimate part and a painful gland in the inguinal region. The Dark Field exposed one pale corkscrewlike *Treponema* epileptically twisting under the cruel beam of light.

Everybody came to look into the microscope. It is always a big catch, and people admire it the way fishermen do when a huge bass or salmon is brought in on the line. I felt that I had achieved something that day, and the doctors around congratulated me with a grain of envy.

"We'll treat you, we'll cure you," I encouraged the pleasant, well-built young man who was shivering with fear. At that moment the future of our cities was the least of his concerns.

197

Sometimes they bring along a guitar, encased in its black sepulcher. I don't know how it starts, whether the young, clap-infected minstrels begin on their own to strum and sing or whether they do it at the urging of the other customers, but more than once I have been interrupted in my work by a concert and have gone out into the waiting room to enjoy the performance. The waiting room is still the same—

dark and dingy in spite of all the scrubbing—but the young, hirsute, suddenly inspired faces project a light, a smile, a promise.

Why not have music, poetry, discussions on the meaning of life, love, and art while they are waiting for their smears and blood tests? Perhaps even free coffee? Sort of an agape.

To separate medicine from ethics, philosophy, religion, and art is absurd. We must allow a new form of clinic to come into being, like the new theater, school, or church. But it must come spontaneously. It can't be planned by the Commissioner and his deputies in the Central Office. There must be an openness, a readiness to let it develop, to nurture it wherever it shows itself in the bud.

247

"Will you see the boy again and tell him that he is infected?"

"No, I won't see him."

"How ridiculous, to make love with a person you never want to see again!" I volunteered, and she, instead of brushing me off or calling me a moralistic old fogy from the rotten establishment, agreed.

"Yes, it's disgusting."

She, too, was an art student, and when I asked her whom she liked most among the post-impressionists she answered, "Vuillard."

Bless her soul. None of my previous art students had even heard his name.

255

The waiting room windows look out onto a schoolyard. In the intervals between patients, while the clerk labors over the next chart, calligraphically printing out names and addresses, I sometimes go to the window and watch the children at play.

Most of our clinics adjoin a local school. Someone had the vision of a saintly Health Department branch in the immediate vicinity of a place of learning: one cultural institution promoting and strengthening the other!

But in reality it is ugly, unnatural. Children in brightly colored clothes scream, swing, slide and race, play ball and turn somersaults next to our V.D. purgatory. In fact, climbing up and clinging to the iron fence, they can—and often do—see the bare buttocks of our patients receive the needles, for most V.D. clinics are on the ground floor.

The children look colorful, but the playground is dismally gray, covered with cement like a prison court, and the jungle gyms remind me of instruments of torture. Why is it all covered with cement? Is it supposed to be hygienic, modern, functional?

I watch the playing children with foreboding. I know that among them are my future clients with the wet pants and positive Dark Fields. There they are: future muggers, rapists, junkies, racketeers, highjackers, candidates for the electric chair, and perhaps, a few nominees for the Presidency, Nobel Prize winners, baseball stars, Einsteins.

But usually I think of Sing Sing. The cement, the cages, the dismal lack of greenery, inspire me this way.

258

He was a dishwasher, and he had come with a skin infection on the dorsum of his hands. It was clear he had severe impetigo and did not belong in a V.D. clinic. So everybody wanted to send him away, to the dermatological department of a city hospital. And yet it was Friday afternoon before the long Fourth of July weekend.

"Impetigo is now easily cured by penicillin. Let's give him a shot, and after the holiday he'll go to a skin clinic. Otherwise he'll lose his job or he'll infect the entire neighborhood around his restaurant," I argued.

"We have no right to do that. It's out of the V.D. jurisdiction," the other doctor, a man with a record of seventeen years in the Health Department, insisted.

I could see that even the nurse in charge was vacillating between common sense and bureaucratic training.

"Suppose he was in contact with a gonorrhea?" I said. "Weren't you lately in contact with a suspicious woman?" I asked the middle-aged Puerto Rican, who was sitting there impassively.

"Sorry, no speak English well," He said, smiling politely.

"You see, he's a typical G 90 and qualifies for a preventive shot of penicillin!" And I gave him the shot.

I felt like the Boy Scout who has done the required good deed for the day.

POSTSCRIPTUM. I may as well stop here. If there was a point to be made I must have made it by now.

Some years ago I gave up smoking. I was smoking over three packs a day and felt miserable. Once I caught myself trying to light a cigarette while a half-smoked Camel still dangled from the other corner of my mouth. That gave me the needed shock. I understood that, in reality, I was seeking something else, that tobacco was only a substitute, which obviously did not satisfy me.

I get the same impression now from all these singles, couples, and triangles, young and old, hetero- and homosexuals, these wives, husbands, lovers, and mistresses: they are after something else, and sex is only a substitute, which, apparently, does not satisfy them. It is the job of a teacher, a philosopher, or physician to make this clear to every pupil, neighbor, or patient that comes his way.

Every time I stick in my needle I feel: penicillin is not enough!

Chapter Twenty-One

Raphael Soyer

BORN IN 1899 IN RUSSIA, Raphael Soyer came to New York with his family in 1912 where, along with his twin brother Moses, he began to study drawing and painting in the art institutes of the city. He had his first one-man show in 1929. For the better part of this century much of his work has continued to capture his special perception of urban life. "Art is local," he quotes; his cityscapes and their people, his portraits of friends, relatives, and fellow artists all echo that insight. In 1962 the Whitney Museum gave the first retrospective of Soyer's work.

Diary of an Artist is one of several that Raphael Soyer has kept during his later years. It serves as a delightful antidote to any caricature we might still hold of some mad genius at his easel. It also might point to the possibility that artists are among the luckiest of men. Their work is theirs, their reflections and feelings are expected to inform it, and their freedom even to fail is secure.

Filled with his thoughtful appreciation of old and new masters, continuing assessments of his own work and esthetics, the difficulties of his task and the solutions he chooses, Soyer's diary might also show any working man simply going about his daily business in an engaged way. But with this difference: While at it, this most accomplished artist often displays all the innocence of the beginner. With another empty canvas before him, the problem seems every time new, as is his surprise when he happens to look again at his finished work. At such times his humility seems the source of his genius.

1963

JANUARY. I am planning a large painting, "Homage to Eakins." What inspired me to attempt this project was "homage à Delacroix" and the Eakins exhibition in Philadelphia, which I went to see twice. I felt it would be good to make a painting honoring this great American realist. Also, for many years I've had a gnawing desire to do a large group portrait.

I contacted a few artists and Lloyd Goodrich, the biographer of Thomas Eakins. I wrote first to Edward Hopper, saying, "I'm writing to you first because I cannot conceive this composition without you in it. In other words, I consider this projected painting not plausible unless I have you in it."

I promised to use as little of their time as possible, to make a quick oil sketch of each artist, and then to compose the large canvas with Eakins's "Gross Clinic" in the background. All the artists agreed to pose, but since each one was involved with his own work, it was difficult, as I had thought it would be, to fit their schedules with mine. . . .

1964

FEBRUARY. I'm finally at work on the large version of "Homage to Eakins." . . .

When the large canvas was brought up to my studio I was appalled by its size and by the raw whiteness of its surface. For two weeks it stood propped up against the wall without my approaching it, as if I were trying to ignore it, to pretend it wasn't there. I busied myself with other canvases. . . .

As soon as I began I was immediately confronted by the following problems (which, frankly, I had anticipated): On the large canvas I had to make the figures on the first plane, in the foreground, somewhat bigger than life, the size I painted them in the preparatory studies, so that the figures in the back should not appear too small. But the main difficulty I found to be copying my own work. I was amazed by what had gone into the making of the portraits, how meaningful each seemingly haphazard brush stroke was, how expressive was every varied patch of color. These were not definitive studies that could be accurately transferred to the final composition; they lacked absolute rendition. They were tentative, nervous, personal, calligraphic, immediate reactions of the artist to his subject. They became art works in themselves rather than functional studies for a larger work. And therefore difficult to copy. But I did copy them, realizing at the same time that it was impossible to maintain the spontaneity of the sketches, to copy each brush stroke as it was done originally, almost automatically.

JUNE. The canvas is all covered. All the figures and faces are at last painted in their first state. I found a place for my self-portrait, for which I had made three studies in different positions on one canvas. I have also indicated a figure of a woman serving a tray with drinks, for which my daughter promised to pose. Now and then when I step back to look at this painting, I find it rather impressive. The composition seems to satisfy me. But it's a long way from being finished.

My goal is to make the whole painting as living and intense as each individual portrait of the artists. Will I be able to capture the tremor in the temples of Jack Levine's portrait, the anxious face of Moses Soyer? Or the aura of aloneness about Hopper? However, although I have hardly begun to dig into these portraits, their being next to one another seems to help to point up their individual likenesses.

It got around that I was doing this group portrait of the artists, and people frequently ask me how it is getting along. This worries me. It is still in its initial state, and its final realization is questionable. I am never certain of a painting until the very last brush stroke is applied. About this particular one I have often a very uneasy feeling that I simply am struggling with something beyond me for which I have not enough technical knowledge. Such paintings are not done today. The secret of doing big group paintings has been lost. Probably Fantin-Latour and Eakins were the last portrait painters of this type. It is impossible to paint that way now. The portraits painted today are fragmentary, personal, capricious, nervous, tentative. They are incomplete, accidental, at times full of inaccuracies. But they are fascinating—revealing the artist more than the subject he paints. If ever completed, my paintings should have some of these characteristics.

1967

OCTOBER 24. Fifteen minutes before my exhibition opened to the public Rebecca and I were admitted to the Whitney. The first glance of rooms-opening-upon-rooms filled with my paintings was startling. It is hard to describe my feelings upon suddenly being confronted with so great a part of my lifework. I was engulfed in a panorama of canvases.

Looking at all these pictures I didn't know whether to be pleased or distressed by the sameness, the thread of continuity I found there. Though the men and women who people my canvases cover a span of forty years and more, they have changed a little. Their costumes may differ slightly, but their bearing, their gestures, the atmosphere emanating from them, are hardly changed. There is the same detachment, the same disassociation even when grouped together, the same withdrawal, the same involvement with oneself. From the first to the last canvas there is no abrupt or sudden activity, no drama. On the whole, I was struck by a sense of the static, of repose. The gestures are restrained, the arms never too far away from the body. Even the walking figures and those engaged in work have an air of arrested motion. This is true even of my latest compositions ("Pedestrians," "Village East"). Like stills from some contemporary film; sitting, standing, walking, there is a feeling of waiting for something that is not even expected to come. Beckett's *Waiting for Godot* suddenly came to my mind.

All these paintings were done in New York, of its people, its streets, of myself, the members of my family, my friends. "Art is local," I said to myself, quoting from my favorite aphorism by Derain: "Stupidity is national, intelligence is international, art is local." I recalled the paintings I saw this morning at the Metropolitan Museum by Rembrandt, Degas, Eakins. "Art is local," I repeated to myself.

OCTOBER 25. Yesterday morning, before my exhibition opened, I was invited to look at my paintings installed on the walls of the Whitney. I was tempted to go but was filled with trepidation. Instead I visited the Metropolitan Museum, to which I retreat whenever I need reassurance. There, absorbed in the paintings of the masters, my own work became less important and I felt ready to face my retrospective.

1968

Paris, JUNE 14. ... I stood for a long time in front of Delacroix's study for his masterpiece "Massacre at Scio"—that of the wounded and dying woman with a child clinging to her breast. This study recalled to my mind my conversations with the Israeli artist, Naftali Bezem. I agreed with him then that today artists could not adequately depict the massive horrors of our civilization. This live child, however, clinging to a dying mother, makes me retract what I said then. In such a detail it is possible to express a Vietnam or an Auschwitz. All the modern media of communication notwithstanding, one would wish to conjure up a Daumier, a Delacroix.

Paris, JULY 17. . . . I think I'm one of the few who paint directly from nature today. My palette is a wooden rectangle. There is a self-portrait of Rembrandt in the outskirts of London in which he holds a palette like mine. When Edward Hopper once showed me the oversized easel he had made himself, I exclaimed, "Why, its like the easel used by St. Luke painting the Madonna and the Child in medieval Flemish pictures!"

How primitive are the tools with which I paint! How ancient is the art of painting as I know it! Can it still be the art for our times? Such thoughts are always with me while I work, for better or for worse.

How autobiographical my art is. All these portraits of myself, my parents, the members of my family; the pictures of the artists with whom I came in contact; the city I have known, and its people; the few landscapes of Maine—I have revealed myself in them long before this rambling chronicle was conceived, not only by the usual automatic revelation of the artist's personality, but through the subject matter which is my life.

1969

Paris, SEPTEMBER 29. . . . Manet was the first who began to discard the elements that gave epic character to painting: story-telling, emotion, three dimensionalism, light and shade, etc. He flattened his paintings, minimized expressiveness. Nevertheless there is still enough humanism, reality, even characterization in his figures. The nude in "Déjeuner sur l'herbe," while it lacks the fullness, the warmth of Bathsheba, is earthy and real. But this trend begun by Manet was continued by Gauguin, Matisse, Braque, Picasso, and painting has become increasingly abstract, till it has reached today the "'ad absur-dum," the "minimal" in art.

I am omitting much in this rambling, and historically, what I am writing is full of gaps, but what I am trying to say is that painting has become so thin, so pallid since Courbet, so unrecognizable. Nothing but sheer esthetics, pure, like sterilized water.

I recall Arshile Gorky's last visit to my studio, a few weeks before his suicide. In a particularly melancholy mood he pointed to a newly stretched-bare canvas and said: "This is art, anything done to its surface in color or charcoal will destroy its innate beauty." In other words, he reached a point of no art. But the very masters whom he admired—El Greco, Ingres, Goya, Poussin, Degas, among others—destroyed the purity, the whiteness of the raw canvas, molded, stained it, underpainted it before composing their pictures. The original canvas was no more, it became something else, absorbed within the painting.

NOVEMBER 28. I finally managed to get to see the "American Painting 1940-1970." In a small room were some Hoppers, Milton Averys, and a couple of semi-abstract Stuart Davises, serving as a sort of introduction to the Jackson Pollocks, to the Rothkos, to the de Koonings, and so forth—on to the Olitzkis, Rosenquists, Rauschenbergs, Warhols. These paintings occupy the walls upon which used to hang Rembrandts, Veroneses, the Flemish masters, the Cezannes, the Manets, the Degas. The rooms are large, the light exceptionally good, and the brightly colored canvases seem ever brighter than they are. But all this glitter cannot hide the unbelievable shallowness, flatness, and sterility of this show.

There is a theory today that with our advances in science, in technology, in exploration of space, in psychology, and with the discovery of new materials and new techniques, there are possibilities for a much deeper, more varied and unusual art than has ever existed. How wonderful it would be if this were so. But the paintings here that claim to be the products of such advances belie this contention. There is nothing in these huge canvases, but raw paint, chaos and void.

1976

JUNE 10. I decided that my posthumous portrait of Moses Soyer is finished. I painted it from snapshots, from several sketches, and from memory. It was difficult. . . . My first idea was to paint him posthumously sitting in his studio with a nude model in the background and a suggestion of his studio furnishings. But in the process of work I eliminated the figure of the model and everything else, just leaving Moses against gray walls.

I could have painted his face, ravaged by illness, more expressionistically, but I held back for reasons I cannot fully explain. Perhaps it was too painful to reveal the physical deterioration of his once magnificent head, which I liked to paint many times. . . .

JUNE 11. Moses was a sociable man. He had many friends. Students, models, fellow artists, owners of his paintings were in close contact with him after [his wife] Ida's death. But he was lonely. In the last portraits I did of him I felt and tried to express the loneliness of his last years. Gradually I think, he began to accept his solitude, even to like it. He spent most of every day in his studio, and when not painting he would occupy himself with translating Russian poems into English. . . .

We would phone each other every day and speak in Russian, a language we both loved.

. . . He told me that since Ida died he thought of death every day. He died while he was painting the young dancer, Phoebe Neville. His last words were, "Phoebe, don't frown." Some of his last paintings are among his best.

London, JUNE 23. How interesting that Irving Howe, in his now famous book *World of Our Fathers* chooses my painting, the "Dancing Lesson," which I did fifty years ago, as a basis for discussing the question ". . . Is there a distinctive, contemporary Jewish art?". . .

Shahn, Walkowitz, and Weber were poetic, imaginative artists. They did not paint Jewish subjects from their own experience, from life, but from knowledge derived from their cultural heritage. I have trained myself from childhood to draw and paint from life only, what I see, never trusting my memory or imagination. I witnessed my sister teaching my twin brother Moses to dance, with other members of the family in the background, and that became a painting. They posed for me.

I was moved by Howe's description of it, and I now recognize that it "communicates something about the immigrants' experience," that "the postures of its figures are a little fearful and clumsy. These immigrant postures held through decades seem now to be shaping the very contours of the picture." While I was painting it, however, I was not aware that I was doing something so meaningful.

It is surprising that after having so perceptively interpreted the "Dancing Lesson" Irving Howe should accept the schmaltzy comments by the art critic Harold Rosenberg about my other painting discussed in World of Our Fathers. It is a simple portrait of my parents revealing their environment and their daily mood. There is no "Friday night dinner" there, no celebration or any ritual. I painted it directly under the influence of Degas's "Absinthe Drinker," which may make it a "French painting." The "golden glow as of chicken soup," which according to Rosenberg "permeates the picture," is nothing more than cheap yellow varnish. The painting has now been cleaned and restored to its original gray tonality, to its mood of everydayness.

JULY 31. I hold my breath when I open the door of my studio, this always happens after being away for a long time. A feeling of mystery and familiarity comes over me as I enter the silent room. The smell of turpentine and oil, the diffused light. The canvases I was working on before I left are neatly stacked against the wall. The completed paintings, recent and old, are safe in the racks. The several easels, usually in constant use, stand empty and seem to be resting. The originally white walls, which haven't been painted in ten years, are stained and patinated by time.

Here and there on the walls are groups of reproductions and original drawings, some thumbtacked, some scotch-taped: reproductions of a famous photograph of the old Delacroix; of the etched self-portrait of Degas; of a caricature of me by David Levine; an astrological crayon drawing made for me by Gregory Corso; several drawings by George

Grosz, and Lambro Ahlas's self-portrait in gouache. Also a drawing in pencil of me and of himself by Isaac Bashevis Singer. He drew it especially for me.

Here is the old wooden, clumsy furniture that follows me from studio to studio: the chairs, the desk, the table, the cot with its striped, sagging mattress. No matter how many times I move, my studios assume that same character—bare, no comforts, just a place to work in. The old sink is encrusted with paint and oil from washing brushes. On the floor, dust. "There's so much dust under the cot," a model said, "you can plant there."

I prop up unfinished canvases against table and chairs, adjoining one another—a one-man show all to myself. I examine them. Am I pleased? Am I disappointed? I take from the racks of old paintings done in the thirties, forties, and fifties and put them alongside the recent ones—a retrospective exhibition. Have I progressed? Have I changed?

SEPTEMBER 8. Yesterday I had lunch with my dealer, Bella Fishko. The conversation, of course, was about the New York art world, the economic outlook of the coming season, not a bright one. As in the last year or two, Bella pressed me to have a one-man exhibition, and as usual, I voiced my reluctance.

. . . Then Bella suddenly said that it would be an interesting idea for a museum to do, perhaps a joint exhibition of the works by Hopper and myself.

Well, this struck me as preposterous and inappropriate. I never saw an affinity between his works and mine. I once saw a collection of still lifes, street scenes, interiors by Hopper, Sheller, Spencer, O'Keefe, and others. Not a human figure in any of those cold, precious, prophylactic pictures. I remember having at one time called this group of artists, somewhat resentfully, "the aristocrats of the so-called indigenous American art." I consider myself in the other stream of American art, formed by those who came with cultures from Europe that added to the pluralistic culture of this country.

Bella's suggestion, however, worries me. I knew Hopper well and visited him in New York and Truro. He posed for me several times, and I was fond of him and admired his intelligence and integrity. I came home and looked at the two books by Lloyd Goodrich about Hopper and me, and began to see, to my surprise, some basis for Bella's idea. There is an element in the work of this Anglo-Saxon American that is also found in my work—an element of loneliness. A different kind of loneliness, naturally, differently depicted. There may be a basis for comparison.

1977

Washington, MAY 23. . . . To my pleasant astonishment there was my large painting, "Homage to Thomas Eakins" at the entrance leading to the exhibition of the Hirschorn Museum's Thomas Eakins Collection.

I like such exhibitions. There were only several of his great portraits, the greatest of them, that of his wife, Susan Hannah Macdowell; . . .

No matter how often I look at this portrait of Eakins's middle-aged wife, it never fails to make me wonder how he was able to put so much in a face. It is so penetrating. It not only pictures her features, but also reveals her state of mind. The way her eyes are painted gets me—the irises, the pupils, the red-rimmed eyelids, the highlights in the pupils. All this naturalism, however, is miraculously transcended.

Eakins was the least ingratiating of artists. In a sense, he was the least esthetic. The blood on the hand of Dr. Gross is not the blood so harmoniously blended in Delacroix's battle scenes. It is real blood, sticky, thick.

Attended talks by Lloyd Goodrich and Evan Turner on Thomas Eakins. They showed slides. . . . The slides were at times breathtakingly beautiful, but I couldn't help thinking, deceptive, for they are transparent, lit up from within, whereas the original paints are not luminous. They have an opaque quality of their own. . . .

It was Turner who pointed out that Eakins was not appreciated in his lifetime. He mentioned contemporaries of Eakins who were praised and constantly placed before the public eye: Sargent, of course, Chase, and the now completely forgotten Celia Beaux.

I did not attend the afternoon session of this symposium, but took a plane back to New York, went to my studio, and examined closely my own paintings.

Part Five

Explorers

Chapter Twenty-Two

Richard E. Byrd
1888-1957

E VEN AS A BOY Richard Byrd wrote in his childhood diary of his wish to reach the North Pole. His imagination fired by the polar explorations of Admiral Perry, the dreamer and fighter in young Byrd helped him to fashion a lifetime of firsts for himself, which included his being the first to fly over the North Pole (1926) and the South Pole (1929). Aviator, explorer, and inspired organizer, Admiral Byrd spearheaded five expeditions to Antarctica, though no expedition was more important for him than the second.

In 1933 from his home base at Little America, Byrd moved 123 miles closer to the South Pole to spend seven months all alone at an advance base in order to keep meteorological equipment in order and to transcribe their measurements. Though this too was a first, his critics noted that Byrd failed here as a leader for giving up his command to fulfill a personal ambition. Never denying his individualism, Byrd also claimed practical expediency as a motive, and a need to experience a certain welcome solitude after his years of public service and social demands.

What he did not bargain for were the physical and spiritual trials of that confining Antarctic winter. Again and again his experiences with the darkness, cold, and isolation suggest how the nature of one's environment determines the nature of one's life, how our thoughts and feelings are influenced by the condition of our bodies. As a spiritual harmony born of confidence in his own powers and the beauties of the night give way to the chaos of that dark "evenness" and eventually to his near-death from carbon monoxide poisoning due to a faulty stove duct, the oneness with the universe that Byrd seeks to regain is envisioned through a more authentic sense of his own insignificance in the scheme of things. In *Alone,* the reconstructed story of this adventure, Byrd liberally used his diary to dramatize the inner exploration that led him to live the rest of his life "more simply . . . and with more peace."

1933

APRIL 7. The six months' day is slowly dying, and the darkness is descending very gently. Even at midday the sun is only several times its diameter above the horizon. It is cold and dull. At its brightest it scarcely gives light enough to throw a shadow. A funereal gloom hangs in the twilight sky. This is the period between life and death. This is the way the world will look to the last man when it dies.

APRIL 14. . . . Took my daily walk at 4 P.M. today, in 89° of frost. The sun had dropped below the horizon, and a blue—of a richness I've never seen anywhere else—flooded in, extinguishing all but the dying embers of the sunset.

. . . The day was dying, the night being born—but with great peace. Here were the imponderable processes and forces of the cosmos, harmonious and soundless. Harmony, that was it! That was what came out of the silence—a gentle rhythm, the strain of a perfect chord, the music of the spheres, perhaps.

It was enough to catch that rhythm, momentarily to be myself a part of it. In that instant I could feel no doubt of man's oneness with the universe. The conviction came that that rhythm was too orderly, too harmonious, too perfect to be a product of blind chance—that, therefore, there must be purpose in the whole and that man was part of that whole and not an accidental offshoot. It was a feeling that transcended reason; that went to the heart of man's despair and found it groundless. The universe was a cosmos, not a chaos; man was as rightfully a part of that cosmos as were the day and night.

APRIL 17. Another important event occurred today. The sun departed for good. It peeped above the horizon at noon, and with that hasty gesture set for the last time. I am feeling no particular reaction over the loss of the sun—not even envy for the men at Little America, who have an appreciably shorter winter night. Wondering why, I concluded that the long period of preparation—the lingering twilight, the lengthening nights—had put me in the mood for the change. If you hadn't lost the sun, I told myself, you would have had something serious to think about, since that would mean that the earth's axis was pointing the wrong way, and the entire solar system was running amok.

APRIL 21. The morning is the hardest time. It is hard enough anywhere for a man to begin the day's work in darkness; where I am it is doubly difficult. One may be a long time realizing it, but cold and darkness deplete the body gradually; the mind turns sluggish; and the nervous system slows up in its responses. This morning I had to admit to myself that I was lonely. Try as I may, I find I can't take my loneliness casually; it is too big. But I must not dwell on it. Otherwise, I am undone. . . .

APRIL 22. . . . The silence during these first minutes of the day is always depressing. It seems real, as if a gloomy critic were brooding in the shadows, on the verge of saying something unpleasant. Sharing his mood, I merely grunt a good morning. My exercises help to snap me out of this. Stretched out flat on the bunk, I go through fifteen minutes of various kinds of muscle stretchings. By the time I've finished the water is hot. I brew about a pint of tea in a big porcelain cup, and dump in lots of sugar and powdered milk. After a sip or two, I put the cup over the flame, and hold it there until it gets piping hot; so hot, in fact, that it burns the mouth and throat. Thus fortified, I am ready for the observations. . . .

MAY 3. . . . I again saw in the southeast, touching the horizon, a star so bright as to be startling. The first time I saw it several weeks ago I yielded for an instant to the fantastic notion that somebody was trying to signal me; that thought came to me again this afternoon. It's a queer sort of star, which appears and disappears irregularly, like the winking of a light.

The wind vane has been giving quite a bit of trouble lately. I've had to climb the pole once or twice every day to scrape the contact points. The temperature is holding pretty steadily between 50° and 60° below zero; and I must admit that the job is chillier than I bargained for. Freezing my hands, nose, and cheeks, separately or all together every time I mount the pole is an old story by now; today, for a change, I froze my chin. But all this is not as bad as it sounds. . . .

MAY 6. . . . Curiosity tempted me to ask Little America [by Morse Code] how the stock market was going. It was a ghastly mistake. I can in no earthly way alter the situation. Worry, therefore, is needless. Before leaving (home) I had invested my own funds—carefully, I thought—in the hope of making a little money and thus reducing the expedition's debt. This additional loss, on top of ever-mounting operating expenses, may be disastrous. Well, I don't need money here. The wisest course is to close off my mind to the bothersome details of the world.

MAY 9. . . . I have been persistent in my effort to eliminate the aftersupper periods of depression. Until tonight my mood has been progressively better; now I am despondent again. Reason tells me that I have no right to be depressed.

. . . It is really essential that I take careful stock of my situation because my enemy is subtle. This doesn't mean that I have become too introspective or that I am taking myself too seriously. My thoughts have been objective enough. But, if something is poisoning or otherwise afflicting my body, what effect will this have on my peace of mind? Certain types of physical ailments have a definitely depressing effect. The question is, how much can this effect be overcome by disregarding or even denying its existence? Suppose the disorder is organic and lies in a deep-seated complaint. Suppose it comes from bad food, from germs, or from the gases given off by the stove. How much resistance, then, can my mind impart to the body if the mind is properly directed? . . . Which is it, then? My mind or my body or both? It is of vital importance that I find the truth. . . .

MAY 11. 12:15 A.M. It is late, but I've just had an experience which I wish to record. At midnight I went topside to have a last look at the aurora, but found only a spotty glow on the horizon extending from north to northeast. I had been playing the victrola while I waited for the midnight hour. I was using my homemade repeater and was playing one of the records of Beethoven's Fifth Symphony. The night was calm and clear. I left the door to my shack open and also my trapdoor. I stood there in the darkness to look around at some of my favorite constellations, which were as bright as I had ever seen them.

Presently I began to have the illusion that what I was seeing was also what I was hearing, so perfectly did the music seem to blend with what was happening in the sky. As the notes swelled, the dull aurora on the horizon pulsed and quickened and draped itself into arches and fanning beams which reached across the sky until at my zenith the display attained its crescendo. The music and the night became one; and I told myself that all beauty was akin and sprang from the same substance. . . .

10 P.M. Solitude is an excellent laboratory in which to observe the extent to which manners and habits are conditioned by others. My table manners are atrocious—in this respect I've slipped back hundreds of

years; in fact, I have no manners whatsoever. If I feel like it, I eat with my fingers, or out of a can, or standing up—in other words, whichever is easiest. What's left over I just heave into the slop pail, close to my feet. Come to think of it, no reason why I shouldn't. It's rather a convenient way to eat; I seem to remember reading in Epicurus that a man living alone lives the life of a wolf. . . .

. . . I find, too, that absence of conversation makes it harder for me to think in words. . . . Today, for instance, I was thinking of the extraordinary effect of the lack of diversions upon my existence; but describing it is beyond my power. I could feel the difference between this life and a normal life; I could see the difference in my mind's eye, but I couldn't satisfactorily express the subtleties in words. That may be because I have already come to live more deeply within myself; what I feel needs no further definition, since the senses are intuitive and exact. . . .

. . . How I look is no longer of the least importance; all that matters is how I feel.

. . . In civilization my necessarily gregarious life with its countless distractions and diversions had blinded me to how vitally important a role they really did play. I find that their sudden removal has been much more of a wrench than I had anticipated. As much as anything, I miss being insulted every now and then, which is probably the Virginian in me.

MAY 25. . . . I am finding that life here has become largely a life of the mind. Unhurried reflection is a sort of companion. Yes, solitude is greater than I anticipated. My sense of values is changing, and many things which before were in solution in my mind now seem to be crystallizing. I am better able to tell what in the world is wheat for me and what is chaff. In fact, my defintion of success itself is changing. . . .

. . . When a man achieves a fair measure of harmony within himself and his family circle, he achieves peace; and a nation made up of such individuals and groups is a happy nation. As the harmony of a star in its course is expressed by rhythm and grace, so the harmony of a man's life-course is expressed by happiness; this, I believe is the prime desire of mankind.

"The universe is an almost untouched reservoir of significance and value," and man need not be discouraged because he cannot fathom it. His view of life is no more than a flash in time. The details and distractions are infinite. It is only natural, therefore, that we should never see the picture whole. But the universal goal—the attainment of harmony—is apparent. The very act of perceiving this goal and striving constantly toward it does much in itself to bring us closer, and therefore, becomes an end in itself.

JUNE 10. . . . During my rare "up" moments I compel myself to draw all my fuel from the farther drum in the tunnel. The roof is caving in again at that end, and I haven't the strength to shore it properly. These few extra steps I may presently be unable to take, and I want a full drum nearby. Even now I sometimes can hardly reach the nearer drum.

I dare say that every ounce of egotism has been knocked out of me; and yet, today, when I looked at the small heap of data in the tunnel, I felt some stirrings of pride. But I wish that the instruments did not always make their inevitable demands, even though they require little actual strength. How pitilessly resolute and faithful they are. In the cold and darkness of this polar silence they steadfastly do their appointed jobs, clicking day and night, demanding a replenishment I cannot give myself. Sometimes, when my body is aching and fingers won't obey, they appear utterly remorseless. Over and over they seem to say, "If we stop, you stop; if you stop, we stop."

JULY 4. I was greatly encouraged over finding myself able to level some of the drifts. Yet, I had to drive myself, for the temperature was in the minus 50's; and, animal-like, I seem to shrink instinctively from anything that hurts. It's odd that I should have changed so much. The cold never used to bother me. I rather liked it for its cleansing, antiseptic action. But now I seem to have very little resistance. . . .

. . . I have always valued life, but never to the degree I do now. It is not within the power of words to describe what it means to have life pulsing through me again. I've been thinking of all the new things I'm going to do and the old things I'm going to do differently, if and when I ever get out of here. . . .

JULY 7. Everything—myself included—is saturated with cold. For two solid weeks the red thermograph trace has been wandering through the minus 40's, 50's, and 60's. . . .

. . . I am still in wretched condition. My brain seems unspeakably tired and confused. Last night was agony. This morning was one of my worst. The gloom, the cold, and the *evenness* of the Barrier are a drag on the spirits; my poise and equanimity are almost gone. . . .

JULY 9. I've been feeling like a joke without a laugh or, more apt, like a tortoise on its back. This damnable evenness is getting me. It has been impossible to read or wind up the phonograph lately. I must pull out of it somehow, and the only way I can do it is by invoking help from my faith, which I depended upon last month. For I have lost almost entirely the inner peace which I had almost achieved then, and which I know pulled me through. I must somehow win this inner harmony back. Somewhere I must have got off the track.

JULY 11. . . . I was at low ebb last night. My brain was not only tired but confused. The thirst for light was so intense that in spite of my resolve I finally lighted the pressure lantern and drank in its bright light for half an hour. It was almost like seeing sunlight again, for the gloom went out of the corner, and there was a respite from the everlasting dimness and flickering.

The trouble with me, I have decided, is that I've been thinking words without feeling their meaning; that I've been repeating my convictions about the universe without feeling their significance. That is how I have wandered from the track. If I could feel as well as assert the truth, I should regain inward peace. . . .

Chapter Twenty-Three

Tobias Schneebaum

BORN AND BROUGHT UP in New York City, Tobias Schnee-baum served in the army as a radio mechanic during World War II, after which he studied art under Rufino Tamayo. Later, he continued to paint and teach in Mexico for several years before a Fulbright Grant in Art took him to Peru in 1955. During his time there, Schneebaum descended the eastern slopes of the Andes into the jungle, where he disappeared for nearly a year to live with a cannibalistic tribe, the Akaramas. Subsequent travels have taken him to Africa, Tibet, Borneo, and New Guinea, where other civilizations have continued to inform his search for a greater sense of wholeness in his own nature.

Unlike Richard Byrd, it is not solitude that Tobias Schneebaum seeks, but a more fulfilling sense of community. Among the Akaramas of Peru he finds just that—though on their terms alone. Is this Utopia or nightmare? As Schneebaum shares the rituals of love and war among his new brothers, he comes to experience both the ecstasy of communion and his own heart of darkness. His journal, *Keep the River on Your Right*, allows us to share this odd adventure while perhaps disturbing your own moral and social assumptions, those arbitrary living arrangements we so often assume to be life's immutable laws.

the tone of his whispered words were enough. It is only weeks now that I have been here, but I can translate his words. "You have come a long way and you will rest with us. . . . We are content that you have come and you will remain." Now I can answer, "I have come a long way and I am happy to rest with you." . . .

How much time, for how many weeks, have I been here? The moon can tell me, I know, yet I look at the moon only for itself, for the light by which I walk, for the glow it sets within me as I lie on leaves. Ooooo-ooooo; it whispers, and Ooooo-ooooo I whisper back.

I lay down in my compartment with the other men, thinking of the sketches I had done and watching Michii brush his hair with a densely thistled pod. Darinimbiak began to giggle and slapped Michii on the back and thighs and took up his penis and pulled at it and caressed the testicles. He leaned over and slapped my leg, pulled at the end of my penis and pointed to the woman who had given birth that afternoon and shoved at Michii's back, and hugged him from behind, telling me that Michii had become a father. Michii himself gave no sign of pride or pleasure, and though the mother and child were no more than ten feet away, at the edge of the nearest fire, he made no move toward them. After we had eaten, he got up and went out, passing his child on the way, glancing down for only an instant.

We live apart here, the men and the women. There are children and pregnancies. Yet in the middle of the night no one moves from his partition to seek out a partner. A partner is there next to you, huddled up to you, arms and legs around you.

Last night, after we came back from a hunting trip, Michii presented me with a bow and six arrows of two types, four wide-bladed bamboo arrows for animals like monkeys and ocelots, and two made of ebony with notched shafts and sharpened ends for birds. This morning he and Darinimbiak led me out to a field and began to teach me how to use them. I had thought that the day they both sat me by the river and painted me with the same designs they wore themselves, the day also that Michii scraped off the hair on my body, for the first time, with a nutria's tooth, that somehow I had then, with no other ceremony, become a member of the tribe, had become within that short time as close as possible to being an Akarama, to accepting myself as the being I had always dreamt myself to be. Until the bow and arrows were offered, they gave me everything: laughter, food, themselves, time; but with that presentation came also the need to learn their use, a sympathy for the weapons themselves, as if without them it was only my mind that lived here, and my body, even with all its pleasures, had remained in other worlds. But oh! what a fiasco I made of that first lesson! . . . There was no impatience as time passed, only a lessening of the laughter, and I improved and finally was able to send an arrow straight and somewhat close to its hoped-for distance. For me it was as if I had conquered an earthly element, and there was a glow on their faces that held me staring from one to the other until they placed the bow and arrows in my hand and back we went to the hut and lay down to sleep, one upon the other.

. . . I walk within my world a man, I think, and every day confirms my need to live it out with all my senses. . . . My friends are real and solid, to be slapped and bitten, friends to race with along the jungle floor to shoot an arrow into food. . . . No day of death has yet entered me and I see my friends as proof of my own aliveness, no reflection of them, but a response all my own that wakes me up with no alarm ringing in my ears and takes me through the day with no dream thoughts to tell me what I hope will come. . . .

. . . What had I released from inside me that day I first set foot inside a jungle and I could not see the violence of those strangling vines, of plant life fighting for a bit of sun, nor insects sending forth venom? Instead perhaps a dybbuk entered me, the spirit waiting for the day I crossed a threshold of unknown self, lying dormant all these years in patience until a time it knew would come, the time perhaps when I prepared myself with practice every morning with my friends, to shoot my bow and arrows till I felled a flying toucan, two wild turkeys, and another bird they called a mee-ekana, with orange breast and wide black wings. For years I had practiced on a violin, making music heard by none but me; for weeks I practiced with a different bow and those birds that I impaled were sources for a hundred joys that covered me with gooseflesh and sent sensations through my groin. . . .

. . . The smell of smoke drifted toward us and I heard the muffled sounds of a village, not our own. My companions, twenty-three of them, went on in single file, and then broke into groups as the forest opened into a clearing, each group moving toward one of the several

1955

It was the fourth day and I was walking along munching on fried bits of yuca that I had soaked in a stream to soften. . . . I made out a group of men, their bodies variously painted in black and red, looking tiny against the gigantic backdrop of the jungle that stretched so high above them. No one moved; no one turned his eyes away or looked anywhere but straight at me. They were frozen in place. They were squatting tightly together, chins on knees, arms on one another's shoulders, leaning over resting heads upon another's knee, or thigh or flank. They continued to stare, moving neither a toe nor an eyelash. Smiles were fixed upon their faces, mouths were closed, placid. Some had match-like sticks through their lower lips, others had bone through noses. Their feet and toes curled around stones and twigs in the same way that their hands held vertically bows and long arrows, and axes of stone tied to short pieces of bough. Long, well-combed bangs ran over their foreheads into the scarlet paint of their faces and hair covered the length of their backs and shoulders. Masses of necklaces of seeds and huge animal teeth and small yellow and black birds hung down from thick necks and almost touched the stones between their open thighs. . . .

Still no one moved, still no one made a gesture of any kind, no gesture of hate or love, no gesture of curiosity or fear. My feet moved, my arm went out automatically and I put a hand easily upon the nearest shoulder, and I smiled. The head leaned over and briefly rested its cheek upon my hand, almost caressing it. The body got up, straightening out and the frozen smile split open and laughter came out, giggles at first, then great bellows that echoed back against the wall of trees. He threw his arms around me, almost crushing with strength and pleasure, the laughter continuing, doubling, trebling, until I realized that all the men had got up and were laughing and embracing each other, holding their bellies as if in pain, rolling on the ground with feet kicking the air. All weapons had been left lying on stones and we were jumping up and down and my arms went around body after body and I felt myself getting hysterical, wildly ecstatic with love for all humanity, and I returned slaps on backs and bites on hard flesh, and small as they were, I twirled some round like children and wept away the world of my past. . . .

. . . From behind me someone had finally pulled out my shirttails and was pushing the shirt up and pinching my skin, then rubbing it with the flat of his palm. A cold tongue licked at my back and then came around to my hand and licked again. I unbuttoned the last of the buttons of my shirt and took it off. I removed my trousers. Hands were all over me again, pulling hard at the hair on my chest, pulling at the hair of my groin, lifting my penis and whispering Ooooo-ooooo, spreading the cheeks of my buttocks, and hugging, always hugging me. They each had a turn at touching my whole body, and some came up and held their penises alongside mine, comparing them. My nipples ached from the pinching and it seemed that my body hair would soon be removed, painfully. At last we all squatted down and they spoke to me as if I understood their language fluently.

This was the beginning of my meeting with the Akaramas, and now, living within their lives, I have become what I have always been and it has taken a lifetime, all of my own life, to reach this point, where it is as if I know finally that I am alive and that I am here, right now. . . . To become Michii, I must not only rid myself of the need to write, but also of the very knowledge that writing exists. Whatever self I have opened within me is one which forever must retain a sense of another world. In my hand at this moment is a pen and it is making marks on paper. On my hand is the black paint that comes from the fruit of the huito tree. There are designs painted over my body and I have scraped away with a bone knife all hair below my shoulders. So I sit here writing, naked. Was I in the same way naked before them, before I had removed my shirt and trousers? Had I bared my soul before my body? How is it that they did not kill me? How is it that I was not frightened of them? . . .

. . . An old man came up to us and squatted down. There was a hole where one eye was missing and his face had deep wrinkles as if cut in with a knife. His name was Yoreitone, he said. He was the chief, and he had come to me now to tell me how happy he was at my arrival. I did not need to understand his speech to know what it was he was saying. The expressions on his face, the movements of his hands, and huts. . . . Great cries of EEEE-eeee!! hit the air and ears as we ran into a fire-lit hut and animal arrows in front of my eyes were used as spears, and axes split into skulls. I stood and watched, no word or sound from me, but shaking, trembling with cold, my breathing coming in gasps. No time was passing, but seven men lay there dead, bellies and chests open, still pouring out hot blood, heads crushed and dripping brain, while women huddled far in a corner, chanting in deep moans and holding the fright-filled faces of their children into the red paint of their breasts. . . . Michii took an arrow from my hand and plunged it through an inert breast. With another arrow he sliced through the string that held a penis stiff against an abdomen, and the penis curled and slipped between its thighs. Outside, my stomach turned upside down, but I went on with them to look in other huts, where other dead lay in other positions, and against the background of the unending moaning of the women, the crying of the children, was the laughter of my people. Not one had a scratch on him, it was over so quickly, and once, even I laughed with them. . . .

We did not sleep that night, but walked on until the early morning, when we reached our river, where we washed, and then we rested. In the light of day, in the thoughts that run through me, I could not sleep, but rested my head on Michii's chest, with Darinimbiak's legs woven with mine. It was evening, and I had dozed at times before I felt Michii move out from under me and we three got up and crossed with all the others to where fires were burning in the open and human flesh was already roasting. . . .

. . . They danced without tiring, sometimes undulating and sway-ing, the long plumes blurring from their backs in flight, and when I entered the circle, I was hypnotized by movement always up and down, kaleidoscopic lights that flickered through my iris, a chant that soon became a roar that drained out thoughts that came my way, and hours later when I sat with Michii and Darinimbiak, the three of us alone at the fire with others dancing, singing around us, I took a piece of meat that Michii held out and ate and swallowed and ate some more, and entered the circle again to dance. Mayaarii-há, Mayaarii-há!!

. . . Four got up, one picked a heart from the embers, and they walked into the forest. Small groups of others rose, selected a piece of meat, and disppeared in other directions. . . . Michii looked up at the moon and showed it to the heart. He bit into it as if it were an apple, taking a large bite, almost half the heart, and chewed down several times, spit it into a hand, separated the meat into six sections and placed some into the mouths of each of us. We chewed and swallowed. He did the same with the other half of the heart. He turned Darinimbiak onto his stomach, lifted his hips so that he crouched on all fours. Darinimbiak growled. Mayaarri-há! Michii growled. Mayaarii-há!, bent down to lay himself upon Darinimbiak's back and entered him.

I am a cannibal.

That four-word sentence doesn't leave my head. No matter into what far corner of my mind I push those words, they flash along the surface of my brain like news along the track that runs around the building at Times Square. So thoughts of death are natural now as love, I tell myself, and I repeat it on and on, hoping some impression will be made. It is a simple truth of this life, and Michii and Darinimbiak can live in no other way that would keep them as they are, the way in which I continue and will forever love them. What monster do I become that I can write and think so cruel a combination of words! Better let me lie sleepless again another night like last, when I chanted to myself Shema, Hear, Ysroel, O Israel, Adonoi, The Lord, Elohenu, our God, Adonoi, The Lord, Echod, is One. There was a certain element of comfort thinking out excuses for those killings, but none would hold in any way, and I cannot help but judge myself even in the role of onlooker, helpless for a moment, yes, helpless to react, but later surely taking part. In that past life of mine in which I could not live the norm and take an ordinary job, marry and have children, I set myself apart, seeing no pleasure in the marriage covenant, or in a TV set or bridge or in owning any kind of car. And then I came out here and for the first time joined a real community, immersing myself within their lives as best I could, not deeply enough I see now to go deeper into their whole way, to become an honest one of them, not thinking back to that other day on which I wrote I'd always necessarily have knowledge they could never know or feel, but going even where I never thought to travel into inner consciousness and asking my flesh and blood to turn my centuries back to their beginnings. This is a limitation of my own, not theirs, and if I sit in judgment on myself, it must remain only me whom I judge, for I have come here into a new world, from a world as strange in other ways, a world which always troubled me.

"Fill the emptiness!"

Those words of Yoreitone's come back to me now with such clarity and meaning for myself as if always before my coming here I had searched for some filling, as if there had been within me such a vast emptiness that my whole being, my whole physical self and my soul, were together in search of some region then not known to me, perhaps a people, a manner of living with hardship, primitive ways; as if for some reason primitive life, I don't know how, but somehow could not wash me of what had passed for my life within civilization, but could enter and flow through my veins with a new kind of blood that would circulate throughout my system and pump new energies through my heart; in all the emptiness of my days and years there had never been anything that touched my soul that had in any way compared with my past wanderings, wanderings in areas difficult to survive. . . .

. . . Must (I) always be, nothing more than a seeker? I came into a jungle to live a new incarnation and now discover that I am more a part of the family of Man than a part only of those men with whom I spent such days and nights of love. It is not possible, for I have seen it, felt it, lived it, denied it, dreaded it, it is not possible for oh! I know it now, to step out of the skin I've worn for most all my life and grow or put on a new one. . . . I begin to see things now with all my past and all my present confused and intermingled with importance and without, but all of pieces that strangely fit together and I learn only now, or maybe I always knew it but only now can I sense its truth in everyday reality, I learn that my self is made of all my selves, not only of the parts I wish to show, the parts that can be seen from outside, but there is also that interior that so often cries my agony and denies me all my rights, denies me all the things I also am. . . .

I took a walk alone and I carried with me all my back would take of food, and here I am now back at my beginning in Pasñiquti, sitting on a hard bed as soft as softest feathers, writing under netting made for mosquitos and vampire bats, having eaten a piece of homegrown cow I cut with knife and fork, and bread spread with cold butter, beer I drank that came from Holland. . . . I did not blush and hide myself when men in clothes stared, and shrank back, and when I told them who I was, there was a shock of recognition and a fear of me at first, a strange, wild man with faded paint on his nude body, looking like a savage, though none had dared before to come to this place, but then with clean face, with trousers, shirt and shoes to cover me, all borrowed articles, they offered me beer and food and talk and listened quietly to my tale. . . .

Chapter Twenty-Four

Thomas Merton
1915-1968

WITH THE 1948 PUBLICATION of his autobiography, *The Seven Storey Mountain*, the Trappist monk Father Louis—better known by his secular name, Thomas Merton—captured the imagination of the whole world. But the inspiring story of his spiritual journey toward a place in the Cistercian order did not end with the taking of his solemn vows. After his ordination as priest at the Abbey of Gethsemani in Kentucky in 1949, Merton continued to refine for himself and his readers the significance he found in Christianity and the contemplative life.

Though he remained within the relative seclusion of the monastery, his reputation as a spiritual writer continued to grow through his published poems, journals, essays, and religious inquiries. In touch with many prominent people, he was drawn more and more toward the world's increasing concern for interracial justice and political peace. Vatican II and the larger spirit of ecumenism within the Catholic Church moved Merton even further away from his earlier conservative posture toward an exploration of his faith through the complexities of the modern world.

Always an explorer through his study and writing and prayer, Merton, after twenty-seven years at Gethsemani, made a pilgrimage to the East in 1968 to address a conference of Asian monastic orders in Bangkok, and to try to experience something more of the contemplative dedication of his Buddhist counterparts. While in Bangkok a bizarre accident ended his life, but not before his journal had recorded a portrait of this sensitive traveler and tireless seeker, who reaffirmed his own monastic loyalty while becoming more deeply attuned to a spiritual unity beyond the practice of any religion.

1968

OCTOBER 19, *Calcutta.* When we landed in Calcutta the customs gave two utterly lovely—and haughty—Indian girls in saris a rough time. I got through quite fast though with no rupees yet, and Susan Hyde, a secretary to Peter Dunne, was there to meet me with a garland of flowers: "Welcome to India." V.I.P. treatment. I felt confused, trying to talk sense to Susan about religious affairs. The Indian darkness was full of people and cows. Rough roads on which cars sped toward each other head-on. It takes some time here to discover which side anyone is driving on—he may take either side, right or left. Then into the big, beat-up, hot, teeming, incredible city. People! People! People! Campfires in the streets and squares. Movie posters—those Asian movie posters with the strange, enormous faces of violent or demented Western gods, the enormous gunners, surrounded by impossible writings. They are a crass, camp deification of the more obvious emotions: love, hate, desire, greed, revenge. . . .

The situation of the tourist becomes ludicrous and impossible in a place like Calcutta. How does one take pictures of these streets with the faces, the eyes, of such people, and the cows roaming among them on the sidewalks and buzzards by the score circling over the main streets in the "best" section? Yet the people are beautiful. But the routine of the beggars is heart-rending. The little girl who suddenly appeared at the window of my taxi, the utterly lovely smile with which she stretched out her hand, and then the extinguishing of the light when she drew it back empty. I had no Indian money yet. She fell away from the taxi as if she were sinking in water and drowning, and I wanted to die. I couldn't get her out of my mind. Yet when you give money to one, a dozen half kill themselves running after your cab. This morning one little kid hung on to the door and ran whining beside the cab in the traffic while the driver turned around and made gestures as if to beat him away. Sure, there is a well-practiced routine, an art, a theater, but a starkly necessary art of dramatizing one's despair and awful emptiness. Then there was the woman who followed me three blocks sweetly murmuring something like "Daddy, Daddy, I am very poor" until I finally gave her a rupee. OK, a contest, too. But she *is* very poor. And I have come from the West, a Rich Daddy.

OCTOBER 29.   The mandala concept accepts the fact that cosmic processes (maya) express themselves in symbols of masculine and feminine deities, beatific and terrifying. It organizes them in certain schemas, representing the drama of disintegration and reintegration. Correctly read by the initiate, they "will induce the liberating psychological experience.". . .

And yet I have a sense that all this mandala business is, for me, at least, useless. It has considerable interest, but there is no point in my seeking anything there for my own enlightenment. Why complicate what is simple? I am reading on the balcony outside my room. Five green parrots, then eight more fly shrieking over my head.

OCTOBER 30.   For the Tibetans, every conceivable sound is both music and mantra. Great brasses. Trumpets snoring into the earth. They wake the mountain spirits, inviting canyon populations to a solemn rite of life and death. The clear outcry of gyelings (shawms), the throb of drums, bells and cymbals. The "sonorous icon" with its unending trance of atonal sound repels evil. But a huge mask of evil is pressing down close. The deep sounds renew life, repel the death-grin (i.e., ignorance). The sound is the sound of emptiness. It is profound and clean. We are washed in the millennial silent roar of a rock-eating glacier.

NOVEMBER 2, *Dharamsala.* . . . Sonam Kazi is a lay Nyingmapa monk. He has had several good gurus and seems far advanced in meditation. He is of course full of information but also of insight. He thinks I ought to find a Tibetan guru and go in for Nyingmapa Tantrism initiation along the line of "direct realization and dzogchen (final resolution)." At least he asked me if I were willing to risk it and I said why not? The question is finding the right man. I am not exactly dizzy with the idea of looking for a magic master but I would certainly like to learn something by experience and it does seem that the Tibetan Buddhists are the only ones who, at present, have a really large number of people who have attained to extraordinary heights in meditation and contemplation. This does not exclude Zen. But I do feel very much at home with the Tibetans, even though much that appears in books about them seems bizarre if not sinister.

Sonam Kazi is against the mixing of traditions, even Tibetan ones. Let the Kagyudpa keep to itself. He suggests that if I edit a book of Tibetan texts, let them all be *one* tradition. A fortiori, we should not try to set up a pseudocommunity of people from different traditions, Asian and Western. I agree with this. . . . Now, since seeing the books the other night in Canada House, I am curious about re-exploring the Romanesque artistic tradition and the 12th Century writers in Christian monasticism in relation to the Eastern traditions . . . i.e., in the light thrown on them by the East.

Sonam Kazi spoke of acting with no desire for gain, even spiritual—whether merit or attainment. A white butterfly appears in the sun, then vanishes again. Another passes in the distance. No gain for them—or for me.

Sonam Kazi condemned "world-evasion," which he thinks ruined Buddhism in India. He would be against an eremitism entirely cut off from all contact, at least for me. But in another context he admired the recluses who severed all contacts, seeing only a few people or perhaps none at all, reserving special contacts only for a restricted list. Harold asked whether others would respect this arrangement. Sonam Kazi thought they would. When a hermit goes on full retreat he places a mantra, an image, and a seal on the outside of his cell, and the mantra reads: "All gods, men, and demons keep out of this retreat."

Cocks crow in the valley. The tall illuminated grasses bend in the wind. One white butterfly hovers and settles. Another passes in a hurry. How glad I am not to be in any city.

NOVEMBER 3. What is important is not liberation from the body but liberation from the mind. We are not entangled in our own body but entangled in our own mind.

NOVEMBER 4. . . . The way in which I have been suddenly brought here constantly surprises me. The few days so far in Dharamsala have all been extremely fruitful in every way: the beauty and quiet of the mountains, my own reading and meditation, encounters with lamas, everything.

. . . Trying to get a better perspective on the earlier part of this year, there is a lot I cannot quite understand. And perhaps do not need to understand. The last months have been demanding and fruitful. I have needed the experience of this journey. Much as the hermitage has meant, I have been needing to get away from Gethsemani and it was long overdue.

This evening the lights in the cottage went dead for a while. I stood out in the moonlight, listening to drums down in the village and looking up at the stars. The same constellations as over the hermitage and the porch opening in about the same direction, southeast toward Aquila and the Dolphin. Aquarius out over the plain, the Swan up above. Cassiopeia over the mountains. . . .

NOVEMBER 5. Buddhist dialectic and "alienation" might be a good theme for my Bangkok conference. Like Marxism, Buddhism considers that a fundamental egocentrism, "providing for the self" (with possible economic implications in a more modern context) leads to dogmatism about the self—either that it is eternal or that it does not exist at all. A truly critical attitude implies a certain freedom from predetermination by economic and sociological factors. The notion of "I" implies the notion of "mine." I am "my property"—I am constituted by what separates me from "not I"—i.e., by what is mine "and not anybody's else."

As long as "I" assert the "I" dogmatically there is lacking a critical awareness that experiences the "I" dynamically in a continuum of cause and effect—a chain of economic or other causations and coordinated interrelationships. . . .

. . . Last night I dreamed that I was, temporarily, back at Gethsemani. I was dressed in a Buddhist monk's habit, but with more black and red and gold, a "Zen" habit, in color more Tibetan than Zen. I was going to tell Brother Donald Kane, the cook in the diet kitchen, that I would be there for supper. I met some women in the corridor, visitors and students of Asian religion, to whom I was explaining I was a kind of Zen monk and Gelugpa together, when I woke up. . . .

NOVEMBER 6. . . . There I was riding through Lower Dharamsala, up the mountain, through McLeod Ganj, in the Dalai Lama's jeep, wearing a snow-white Cistercian robe and black scapular. Smiles of all the Tibetans recognizing the jeep. Namaste gestures (palms raised together before the nose), stares of Indians. Am I part of it? Trying to fit into an interrelation, but on my own terms? Trying to find a dogmatic solution to this contradiction? One must provisionally at least, experience all roles as slightly strange, ridiculous, contrived. Wearing my monastic habit because Marco Pallis strongly urged me to—and it is right, I guess, thoroughly expected. Yet recognizing that it is at odds with my own policy of *not* appearing as a monk, a priest, a cleric, in "the world." The role of "tourist" is less offensive. However, I have the feeling that everybody here knows all about everything and that as an "American lama" I am a joyful and acceptable portent to all the Tibetans. Smiles everywhere. Every Tibetan lights up, even when I am in no jeep, no habit, and only in corduroy pants and turtleneck jersey. . . .

NOVEMBER 7. The contemplative life must provide an area, a space of liberty, of silence, in which possibilities are allowed to surface and new choices—beyond routine choice—become manifest. It should create a new experience of time, not as stopgap, stillness, but as "temps vierge"—not a blank to be filled or an untouched space to be conquered and violated, but a space which can enjoy its own potentialities and hopes—and its own presence to itself. One's *own* time. But not dominated by one's own ego and its demands. Hence open to others— *compassionate* time, rooted in the sense of common illusion and in criticism of it. . . .

NOVEMBER 12. Returning to Calcutta, I have a completely new impression: greater respect for this vast, crumby city. There is a kind of nobility in its sordidness: the sheer quantity of everything. . . .

. . . Buildings. Crowds. Rags. Dirt, laughter, torpor, movement. Calcutta is overwhelming: the elemental city, with no room left for masks. Only the naked truth of overpopulation, underemployment, hunger, disease, a mixture of great vitality and permanent exhaustion— but an exhaustion in which the vitality renews itself. How does it happen that the skinny men in bare feet trotting with rickshaws don't all drop dead? And maybe many do! . . .

. . . Somehow the crime gets lost in the sheer massive poverty and exhaustion—the innocence of despair. The place gives no impression of wickedness. For the masses of Calcutta, you dimly begin to think, there is no judgment. Only their misery. And instead of being judged, they are a judgment on the rest of the world. Yet curiously nonprophetic . . . nonaccusatory. Passive. Not exactly resentful. Not yet. . . .

How long before it explodes? What will the explosion mean?

One imagines an enormous, elemental, thoughtless, confused violence like that of a sweeping storm of rain after a sultry summer day. Will it cleanse anything? Clear the air? Will the city simply go on stifling in its own steam? It breathes, sprawls, broods, sweats, moves, lies down, and gets up again.

NOVEMBER 16. ... We went looking first for Chatral Rimpoche at his hermitage above Ghoom. ...

Chatral looked like a vigorous old peasant in a Bhutanese jacket tied at the neck with thongs and a red woolen cap on his head. He had a week's growth of beard, bright eyes, a strong voice, and was very articulate, much more communicative than I expected. We had a fine talk and all through it Jimpa, the interpreter, laughed and said several times, "These are hermit questions . . . this is another hermit question." We started talking about dzogchen and Nyingmapa meditation and "direct realization" and soon saw that we agreed very well. We must have talked for two hours or more, covering all sorts of ground, mostly around about the idea of dzogchen, but also taking in some points of Christian doctrine compared with Buddhist: dharmakaya . . . the Risen Christ, suffering, compassion for all creatures, motives for "helping others,"—but all leading back to dzogchen, the ultimate emptiness, the unity of sunyata and karuna, going "beyond the dharmakaya" and "beyond God" to the ultimate perfect emptiness. He said he had meditated in solitude for thirty years or more and had not attained to perfect emptiness and I said I hadn't either.

The unspoken or half-spoken message of the talk was our complete understanding of each other as people who were somehow *on the edge* of great realization and knew it and were trying, somehow or other, to go out and get lost in it—and that it was a grace for us to meet one another. . . . He told me, seriously, that perhaps he and I would attain to complete Buddhahood in our next lives, perhaps even in this life, and the parting note was a kind of compact that we would both do our best to make it in *this* life. I was profoundly moved, because he is so obviously a great man, the true practitioner of dzogchen, the best of the Nyingmapa lamas, marked by complete simplicity and freedom. He was surprised at getting on so well with a Christian and at one point laughed and said, "There must be something wrong here!" If I were going to settle down with a Tibetan guru, I think Chatral would be the one I'd choose. But I don't know yet if that is what I'll be able to do—or whether I need to. . . .

NOVEMBER 18, *Mim Tea Estate.* I'm glad I came here. All morning alone on the mountainside, in the warm sun, now overclouded. Plenty of time to think. Reassessment of this whole Indian experience in more critical terms. Too much movement. Too much "looking for" something: an answer, a vision, "something other." And this breeds illusion. Illusion that there *is* something else. Differentiation—the old splitting-up process that leads to mindlessness, instead of the mindfulness of seeing all-in-emptiness and not having to break it up against itself. . . .

. . . I am still not able fully to appreciate what this exposure to Asia has meant. There has been so much—and yet also so little. I have only been here a month! . . . Meeting the Dalai Lama and the various Tibetans, lamas, or "enlightened" laymen, has been the most significant thing of all, especially in the way we were able to communicate with one another and share an essentially spiritual experience of "Buddhism" which is also somehow in harmony with Christianity. . . .

. . . This deep valley, the Mim Tea Estate, above Darjeeling: it is beautiful and quiet and it is right for Martin Hall, the manager, and his wife, who are in their own way hermits and appreciate my need for a couple of days of silence. Yet it has nothing I could not, essentially, have found at Needle Rock or Bear Harbor—nothing I did not find there last May. Or did I find an illusion of Asia that needed to be dissolved by experience? *Here?*

What *does* this valley have? Landslides. Hundreds of them. The mountains are terribly gashed, except where the forest is thick. Whole sections of tea plantations were carried away six weeks ago. And it is obviously going to be worse the next time there are really heavy rains. The place is a frightening example of anicca—"impermanence." A good place, therefore, to adjust one's perspectives. I find my mind rebelling against the landslides. I am distracted by reforestation projects and other devices to *deny* them, *forbid* them. I want this all to be *permanent.* A permanent post card for meditation, day dreams. The landslides are ironic and silent comments on the apparent permanence, the "eternal snows" of solid Kanchenjunga. . . .

NOVEMBER 19, *Mim Tea Estate.* . . . Kanchenjunga this afternoon. The clouds of the morning parted slightly and the mountain, the massif of attendant peaks, put on a great, slow, silent dorje dance of snow and mist, light and shadow, surface and sinew, sudden cloud towers spiraling up out of icy holes, blue expanses of half-revealed rock, peaks appearing and disappearing with the top of Kanchenjunga remaining the visible and constant president over the whole slow show. It went on for hours. Very stately and beautiful. Then toward evening the clouds cleared some more, except for a long apron of mist and shadow below the main peaks. There were a few discreet showings of whorehouse pink but most of it was shape and line and shadow and form. O Tantric Mother Mountain! Yin-yang palace of opposites in unity! Palace of anicca, impermanence and patience, solidity and nonbeing, existence and wisdom. A great *consent* to be and not-be, a compact to delude no one who does not first want to be deluded. The full beauty of the mountain is not seen until you too consent to the impossible paradox: it is and is not. When nothing more needs to be said, the smoke of ideas clears, the mountain is SEEN.

Testament of Kanchenjunga. Testament of fatherless old Melchizedek. Testament from before the time of oxen and sacrifice. Testament without Law. NEW Testament. Full circle! The sun sets in the East! The nuns at Loreta kept asking me, "Have you seen the snows?" Could they have been serious?

DECEMBER 4, COLOMBO. . . . The path dips down to Gal Vihara: a wide, quiet, hollow, surrounded with trees. A low outcrop of rock, with a cave cut into it, and beside the cave a big seated Buddha on the left, a reclining Buddha on the right, and Ananda, I guess, standing by the head of the reclining Buddha. In the cave, another seated Buddha. The vicar general, shying away from "paganism," hangs back and sits under a tree reading the guidebook. I am able to approach the Buddhas barefoot and undisturbed, my feet in wet grass, wet sand. Then the silence of the extraordinary faces. The great smiles. Huge and yet subtle. Filled with every possibility, questioning nothing, knowing everything, rejecting nothing, the peace not of emotional resignation but of Madhyamika, of sunyata, that has seen through every question without trying to discredit anyone or anything—*without refutation*—without establishing some other argument. For the doctrinaire, the mind that needs well-established positions, such peace, such silence, can be frightening. I was knocked over with a rush of relief and thankfulness at the obvious clarity of the figure, the clarity and fluidity of shape and line, the design of the monumental bodies composed into the rock shape and landscape, figure, rock and tree. And the sweep of bare rock sloping away on the other side of the hollow, where you can go back and see different aspects of the figures.

Looking at these figures I was suddenly, almost forcibly, jerked clean out of the habitual, half-tied vision of things, and an inner clearness, clarity, as if exploding from the rocks themselves, became evident and obvious. . . . The thing about all this is that there is no puzzle, no problem, and really no "mystery." All problems are resolved and everything is clear, simply because what matters is clear. The rock, all matter, all life, is charged with dharmakaya . . . everything is emptiness and everything is compassion. I don't know when in my life I have ever had such a sense of beauty and spiritual validity running together in one aesthetic illumination. . . . This is Asia in its purity, not covered over with garbage, Asian, or European, or American, and it is clear, pure, complete. It says everything; it needs nothing. And because it needs nothing it can afford to be silent, unnoticed, undiscovered. It does not need to be discovered. It is we, Asians included, who need to discover it.

Chapter Twenty-Five

Howard Nemerov

IN A SEASON MADE DARK by the death of his father and his fears for the loss of his sexual and creative powers, Howard Nemerov—American poet, novelist, critic—attempted to turn this condition into some ordered notes for a novel. The notes soon yielded instead a novel form of self-exploration. Nemerov's *Journal of the Fictive Life* became his singular adventure into his own psyche, recording and analyzing his dreams and memories with all their present and past associations—and especially those sharp mental links that were made during the very act of keeping his journal.

Though Nemerov's journey is more cerebral than visceral, his refusal to flinch before even the most shocking of unearthed material may inspire any serious diarist to stay with what hurts, ails, confuses, and shames in order to come to know himself better. But perhaps not without a price for such self-knowledge: As link after link in his psyche is looked at, Nemerov sees this self-reflection knotting up into associative nets that are finally "endless, and endlessly intricate." A Jungian might claim other meanings for some of Nemerov's Freudian reductions, but that might also suggest what Nemerov finally comes to feel, too—that after all his "analytics," "there is no self, there is only an echoing emptiness within."

---

25 VII

DREAMS. 1. A list of titles of home movies, of which I remember only a few scattered words: ruby, spy, secret, spider. Vague association of "a Negro neighborhood."

2. I am at an airport. We take off, and though I am a passenger I can see ahead, and have a sort of telephone receiver at hand through which I am able to hear the pilot; he is saying we are late. We arrive at another airport; instead of a bus there is a truck, and it is crowded. Also hard to get into because so high off the ground. But I find a stirrup on one side and climb up; the pilot approves. Before this, on the way out of the terminal, I farted, but the fart became shit and dropped down my trouser leg to the ground, whereon I reflected comfortably that I would not stink much and therefore need not be embarrassed.

3. A list of ice-cream flavors and amounts and prices, apparently issued to a child or to children, saying how much allowed for individual consumption, for two, for parties.

The man I wrote of a couple of days ago, who found his life turning into an art work, is myself, and the notion is a phantasy about this self-examination; that is, I was taking pleasure in the idea that it might be interminable, but was already being compelled to understand the consequences: that inevitably I should actually make some discoveries about myself, that these would give this writing a species of form, that this developing form would dictate one day a conclusion. . . . and with four dots I leave that sentence endless.

Dreams this morning seem impenetrable. I observe that I very much wanted to leave out the last detail in dream 2 (shit, in childhood, by the way, was known as Number Two), so that I forgot it until after its proper place in the narrative; also I put it in the past tense as though to emphasize its distance from me (putting it *behind* me?). But as soon as I wrote it down the memory became silly rather than sinister. Maybe for some people writing has quite often this function of reducing the magical power of the word to nothing, to a joke? For surely the word 'fart,' in my childhood, was more shameful, and if possible more forbidden, than all the other words (nothing one ever put to the test with a grownup around, though). Even now, though 'fuck' and 'shit' have become permissible, and even rather popular, one much more rarely hears the word 'fart'—except around my house, where because of my son's fascination with this phenomenon we have grown perfectly accustomed to using the word without embarrassment. So part of my embarrassment about writing down the dream episode has another reference, and the first one I think of is this: What I am writing now is private, or even secret. But I have the idea of it as one day being published as a book. So I resist writing details that will get in the way of its being published.

A further thought. To "shit oneself" (childhood expression) was always a shameful thing, something one tried to conceal on those unfortunate occasions when it helplessly happened. In the dream episode it happens to me when I am a grownup, and seems to say that in this respect I am a mere child again, or still. And the "purely spiritual" fart surprises me by turning into purely material shit; I can't help viewing this as an emblem of this writing itself, which began with the contemplation of imaginative fiction and turned into the exploration of my own more or less real life. Yet the incident has a reassuring termination: The accident, instead of fouling me up, passes away and is left behind.

Dreams 1 and 3 have in common the being about lists (home movies, of course, came from the memory of one related yesterday). Dream 2 seems to stand apart as an exception. Dreams 1 and 3 perhaps imitate what I have been doing recently in writing of memory, that is, making lists of items belonging in a single category, analyzing these items by means of their inter-references with one another, much as if you were to isolate 'the meaning' of a word by noting what was common to a number of usages of it.

Ruby, spy, secret, spider. In connexion with the associated "Negro neighborhood," Ruby is a stereotyped Negro name. Conrad Aiken wrote a poem, "Blues for Ruby Matrix," where the surname brings in the idea of Mother again. "Who can find a virtuous woman? for her price is above rubies." (Proverbs 31:10.) So this part of the dream somehow relates to the home movie in which Mother made love to another man, and the associations seem to protest that she wouldn't do that (one notes, however, that in the proverb a virtuous woman does have a price, though it is rather high).

Spy may relate to yesterday's thoughts about seeing, as may secret. Spider, again, contains spy, though it comes up perhaps because I was reading about spiders the other day, about their web-building technique.

"Dreams this morning seem impenetrable." They still do. But I observe that whatever I have been able to say has come less from the dream than from the criticism of my method in narrating it. This has to do, once again, with fiction, the original subject of these notes. The statement that dreams seem impenetrable relates to the statement in Dream 2: "hard to get into."

I remembered on waking this morning something I said about the age of ten, in a crowded bus full of children, to the effect that girls did have penis and scrotum too, but kept these in a "streamlined case." I had hoped for laughter and approval from this remark, and made it several times, but to no effect, for the others were talking about something else. I was also impressed with the daring of this speculation, for I was generally rather priggishly clean of speech, even though (evidently) containing the complete cesspool of thoughts in silence. The bus in this memory relates to the truck (instead of bus) in the airport dream, and "streamlined case" is from flying, which was my passion for many years dating from Lindbergh's Atlantic flight when I was seven.

Still, these associations seem to me rather random and remote; they are still such a divergence from the dream(s) rather than converging upon the meaning. . . .

8 VIII

. . . A long time ago, near the beginning of these notes I mentioned an identification of Negro with feces, and said I had been too embarrassed to record the dream that gave it me. Not true. It is recorded in my Notebooks for 18 III 63, and I repeat it, with its related comment, here.

Following R into town, we go by a steep way which turns into a swamp full of rotting logs. He leaps lightly across and turns to help me, but I say I can make it but want to go slowly. Later, I am walking alone on the other road into town; it is night. I overtake a Negro, who wants to be sure this is the easy road; I am able to reassure him, and we proceed together. I realize that he is just as frightened as I am.

Concerning this I wrote at that time: "I remember thinking several times recently how the problem for the Negro in America is tragically related to the white man's problem with his own feces, hence could never be resolved by reasonable discussion, law &c. And I made up the slogan which said that our question was not integrate or segregate, but integrate or disintegrate.

"The basis for my strange assertion concerning the Negro might be found in the rule of life which seems to say, in the South, that the Negro's place is always at the back, at the back of the bus, the back door of the house, the back of town. The servant's quarters, of course, gain symbolic force of this kind by being quite literally the place whence garbage is disposed." (Hindquarters; hind-servant, slave.)

A confused, or condensed, memory of a much earlier dream about a Negro, amounting in effect to a terrified religious revelation. One memory says that in this dream a Negro was killed and hung upside down on a butcher's hook in a refrigerated room; another memory says that a giant Negro, naked to the waste, (I have to leave 'waste' for 'waist' as appropriate; I almost never misspell words.) had done the killing and hung the flayed corpse (white?) on a hook, and now came at me with a cleaver. Waking, I thought first, What a terrible man that Negro is, and, immediately after, There was no Negro, there was only yourself; you were the Negro, the corpse, the murderer; probably you provided the hook and the refrigeration as well.

Now I am well aware of my temptation to ease off the pressure by referring to poems instead of memories; on the other hand, in poems I do frequently put together my iterative imagery in a somewhat illuminating way, so that I cannot resist entering the following rich combination, which oddly enough took me several minutes to find; I had to look through three of my own books.

The poem is called "A Picture," and describes a newspaper photograph of white people running down a street, "hunting down a Negro, according to the caption." The white people are metaphorically seen as cattle headed for the slaughterhouse, with "the serious patience of animals/ Driven through a gate by some/ Urgency out of the camera's range," and, in an ironic conclusion, as "Obedient, it might be, to the Negro,/ Who was not caught by the camera," &c. Segregation, butchery, seeing, the camera, are put together with a mocking expression of religious feeling: the faces of the whites "Expressed a religion of running," and so on.

But perhaps all this is no more than to say I am about what I am about, my concerns at one time are my concerns at another time. . . . Still, what the poem tries to say is something like this: The camera is false art, one cannot tell what these people are doing except by means of a caption, after one is told one doesn't want to believe that people actually do anything like that, and the camera leaves out the very object of all this senseless activity, that is, presents an incomplete view of reality. Therefore the white people who appear in the picture are "caught by the camera," it 'took' them in the sense of 'took them in,' while the Negro victim, however he may have suffered, was at any rate not the victim of their illusions, which (the poem did not explicitly add) show the world as 'black and white.'

Another poem, arbitrarily placed next to that one, is also about newspapers and relates the Negro question to sexual questions by speaking of "the segregated photographs/ Of the girls that marry and the men that die." I remember thinking that another example of segregation in our society appears in the signs Men and Women, but that no one crusades for integration here. And, a funny rider to that one, M confessed to being embarrassed while we were in the South by something that had never bothered her, or even occurred to her, before: that when you went to the Laundromat you naturally 'segregated' the white clothes and the colored.

Bathrooms, washing, keeping clean (being 'white' in the sense of pure), food (the butchered corpses), killing and being killed, ritual sacrifice, clean clothing, sexual relations, privacy (as in 'privy'), all run together with (cannot be segregated from) the dream about defecation and dirt that began this cluster of associated images.

Offhand, I have very few memories of Negroes, have known very few. Yet it appears to me as though the Negro people exemplify some of my worst fears and most shameful secret thoughts. It horrifies me to have to discuss the subject, because consciously I want to see our society integrated (instead of destroyed), regard American treatment of Negroes, both in North and South, as shameful (using, I see, the same word about the public as about the private motif) and absurd. But if I do not discuss the subject, I fail at what so far is the nearest to an ultimate confrontation these notes have presented, and so I fail at their object. So discuss, and don't be so timid.

The statement, whether true or not, that "I have very few memories of Negroes," &c., immediately offers a reason for their possibly symbolizing something very nasty, mean, and secret in myself. What one doesn't know is a good territory for the growth of phantasies. And the more you don't know something, the more reason you find for not getting to know; avoidance itself becomes a motive for avoidance. The Negro is 'strange' and 'dark.' In a characteristic metaphor, he is a photographic negative of the white man, and allegorically is victimized by being made to represent evil in all contests of black and white (even ambiguously and ironically, as in such a contest represented on the stern of the vessel in Melville's *Benito Cereno*).

Like any number of well-intentioned white people, I am ill at ease with Negroes. First, because I am aware that as a white I owe them something; they represent my bad conscience. Second, becuse I know that they are aware of this, hence have the power of seeing through my politeness, amiableness, and self-consciousness about these. I do not like for people to be in a position which allows them to see more irony in life than I am able to (which is, after all, a fair lot). Third, because they so often appear as servants, and the position of servant is always a position of immense power, hence a threat (just as the Devil characteristically appears as a servant). It goes with this that I disliked and rather feared servants in childhood (few if any of these were colored), and I remind myself that a child's relation with the parents' servants is an extremely precarious one; if they are below the parents they are nevertheless above the children; their power to love or withhold love, or even to punish, threaten, be cruel or mean or unfair, is perhaps not greater than that of the parents but is surely more continuous and constantly present—and may effectively be greater, at that. The relation is ambiguous, because the child has a power too, the power of telling on the servant, and this is an economic power connected with shame; that is, if you got the maid fired (and especially during the Depression) you would have to feel that you had unintentionally produced an effect disproportionate to the cause, and that you had been a sneak. Also, servants always knew what you were doing, and even when they couldn't or were disinclined to punish you for it, they might laugh at you, which is worse.

In a more secret set of notions, Negroes smell different, they represent poverty, hence filth, and they are entitled to represent 'envy from the depths,' or the fear of revolution; again they are my bad conscience about being white (clean) which relates to my boyhood bad conscience about being rich. All this was carried on during College, too, where I was ashamed of being rich, where ever so many people said, as it was fashionable to do then, that the son of rich parents could never be a poet. Easy to see why I respond with unquestioning assent to the Freudian equation between money and feces, it is a sorites involving an economic relation of servant and master, the unconscious identification of poverty with filth with 'the depths,' that is, the sexual and excretory arrangements of the body. Which may be why my few meetings with Negroes are infected by my self-consciousness and my awareness of their knowledge of it, by my masochistic wish to see myself as a victim, expressing itself in attitude as my putting myself out to be pleasant, &c.: "See how well I am behaving, see how good (what a good boy) am I!"

It seems extremely likely that the rich red inside of the Negro's mouth, with its very white teeth, shown in laughter, is my secret image for the female genital. But I have no memory to go with that.

Oops, I'm afraid that is not quite so.

> *Little Jack Horner*
> *Sat in a corner*
>
> *He stuck in his thumb*
> *And pulled out a plum*
> *And said what a good boy am I!*

This relates to the Negro by means of my earliest memory. A little boy
fell off his tricycle on the sidewalk. He bled from the mouth.
"Grandma," I cried, running into the house, "there are plums coming
out of his mouth." Stewed plums, stewed prunes, early aversions, no
wonder at it. Additional relations: the imagery about horns, minotaur,
unicorn, &c., a few days ago; and what has been said this morning
about 'Jack.' Probably I once was little Jack Horner, and now I am Big
Jack Horner, but not out of trouble even so. (Jack = the penis, jack off
= jerk off.)

Addenda—8 VIII

. . . Imagining the Negro as filth, his mouth as symbolizing the
female genital, it is worth remarking how many correspondences relate
those thoughts to the poem about the mud turtle (a creature of chiefly
Southern associations anyhow, like that turtleish-looking white TV
editorialist in Virginia, who L said was called The Mouth of the South).

The turtle was seen as black, dark, bearing filth on his back; he
comes up from beneath (the South, the underworld). His teeth are
emphasized, and his claws; red comes in where the toes have been torn
off one foot.

I have tried to keep this inquisition reasonable in tone, certainly
not to hoke it up by getting rhapsodic, or by the usual literary claim
that all this showed great courage on my part, and *therefore* must be
very grand literature. A tone scientifically dispassionate need not prevent my occasionally saying, however, that I would rather not be

compelled to write down these things, would prefer not to look any further into my nature, and perhaps most of all wish I did not need to make remarks which an injudicious public might take in the literal sense as outwardly directed, toward the world; whereas their sense is symbolic, they are Allegory addressed to the Intellectual Powers, and as such, according to the vocabulary of this book, they are determined from within and diagnostic, if at all, only of the writer himself and the child he was and is.

Chapter Twenty-Six

Frederick S. Perls
1893-1970

A MONG THESE EXPLORERS in search of themselves, none knew better than Fritz Perls the easy escape routes along that difficult way. A Berlin-born Freudian analyst, Perls founded the South African Institute of Psychoanalysis in 1935. Later, after immigrating to the United States, he established the New York Institute for Gestalt Therapy in 1952, and the Cleveland Institute for Gestalt Therapy in 1954. During the last years of his life, he and his wife Laura were associated with Esalen, the California institute of Big Sur that remains dedicated to the study and practices of the Human Potential Movement.

Always the innovator, Perls turned the principles of gestalt psychology, with its understanding of the formation of perceptual configurations, into new approaches to practical therapy. His appreciation of phenomenology, eastern philosophy, and the theater plays as much into these therapeutic endeavors as do his Viennese masters.

When once again Perls was urged to write something for the record about his own life, he did so according to his own methodology. Inevitably, the very act of writing became an essential part of the process by which he stays "in touch" with himself and his material. *In and Out the Garbage Pail* is the book that eventually resulted from this task, a unique blend of biography, theory, and the techniques of gestalt therapy—techniques that might also point the diarist down more novel and dramatic avenues of self-exploration.

———————————————————————————————

My name is Friedrich Salomon Perls, in American: Frederick S. Perls, usually called Fritz or Fritz Perls, sometimes Doctor Fritz—writing this down I feel somewhat light and officious. Also wondering for whom I am writing this annd most of all, how honest I will be. Oh, I know, I am not called upon to write true confessions, but I would like to be honest for my own sake. What do I have to risk?

For me, one of two "problems" of mine belongs under the heading "showing off." The other—the problem of smoking and poisoning myself—can wait. As for the first one, the frequent experience of being bored is connected with "showing off." How it is connected I hope to find out in the course of this writing. I often ask for approval, recognition and admiration during conversations. As a matter of fact, often I push myself forward or bring the talk around to subjects not in order to be brilliant or shine, but to boast about the recognition I, or what I consider the same, Gestalt Therapy is getting.

Boredom also often drives me (see the disowning of responsibility for *my* producing *my* boredom!) to be obnoxious to people or to do some "gloom-casting" or to start flirting and sexy games. This will require more discussion in a different context. One boast belongs here. The *Nation* wrote in an article on Esalen: "And all the girls agree; nobody kisses like Fritz Perls."

I am still stuck and determined to get through this impasse. I am too easily inclined to give up and let go. But to force myself to do something against my inclination likewise does not work out. Thus, suspended between the Scylla of phobia, avoidance, flight, and the Charybdis of chore, strain and effort, what is one to do?

I would not be a phenomenologist if I could not see the obvious, namely the experience of being bogged down. I would not be a Gestaltist if I could not enter the experience of being bogged down with confidence that some figure will emerge from the chaotic background.

And lo! the theme emerges. Organismic self-control versus dictatorial control, authentic control versus authoritarian control. The dynamic of gestalt formation versus the superimposition of manufactured goals. Dominance of life versus the whip of moral prejudices, concerted powerful flow of organismic involvement versus the drag of *shouldism*. I am returning to the human split: the animal versus the social, the spontaneous versus the deliberate.

Topdog: Stop talking about Reich. Follow your intentions and stick to your theme, the oral resistances.

Underdog: Shut up. I told you a few times, this is my book, my confessions, my ruminations, my need to clarify what is obscure to me.

Topdog: Look! Your readers will see you as a senile, loquacious rambler.

Underdog: So, we are back again to my *self* versus my *image*. If a reader wants to look over my shoulder, he is welcome, even invited to peep. What's more, I have been more than once prodded to write my memories.

Topdog: Fritz, you are getting defensive.

Underdog: And you are wasting too much of my and the reader's time. So sit still and bide your time and let me keep *you* waiting. Let me be just as I am, and stop your chronic barking.

Topdog: O.K., but I'll be back again when you will least expect me and you *need* guidance from your brain: "Computer, please, direct me."

Once something happened that really scared me. Many patients "retroflect" their aggression and take it out on themselves, for instance by choking themselves. I used to let them choke *me* instead. Until one day a girl meant business. I had not realized her schizoid personality. I had already begun to lose consciousness, when at the last moment I pushed my arms between hers and tore them apart. Since then I just give them my *arm* to choke. This is sometimes pretty painful too.

There are quite a few stranglers in the world. With patients who have a good fantasy, a cushion will serve the purpose.

I myself have very little tendency to get violent without adequate provocation. I might get angry, and twice I have thrown people physically out of a seminar if they were unmanageably destructive and refused to leave. I hit back hard when attacked. I have a few times become violent with jealousy, but am mostly satisfied to torture my beloved with questions and relentless requests for detailed confessions.

As for the sex games, in the baths and otherwise, reticence does not apply to me. Freud would call me a polymorph pervert. I even learned to enjoy intimate kisses of some man friends. I used to enjoy screwing for hours, but now, at my age, I enjoy mostly being turned on without having to deliver the goods. I like my reputation as being both a dirty old man and a guru. Unfortunately the first is on the wane and the second ascending.

Friend, don't be a perfectionist. Perfectionism is a curse, and a strain. For you tremble lest you miss the bull's-eye. You are perfect if you let be.

Friend, don't be afraid of mistakes. Mistakes are not sins. Mistakes are ways of doing something different, perhaps creatively new.

Friend, don't be sorry for your mistakes. Be proud of them. You had the courage to give something of yourself.

It takes years to be centered; it takes more years to understand to be *now*.

Until then, beware of both extremes, perfectionism as well as instant cure, instant joy, instant sensory awareness.

Until then, beware of any helpers. Helpers are con-men who promise something for nothing. They spoil you and keep you dependent and immature.

It feels good to play preacher and enjoy a pompous Nietzsche style.

. . . Zen had attracted me as the possibility of a religion without a God. I was surprised to see that before each session we had to invoke and bow before a Buddha statue. Symbolism or not, to me it was again a *re*ification leading to a *de*ification.

"Sitting" was not a great strain, as we interrupted the two or three hour session with some walking. We had to breathe in a certain way and keep the attention on the breathing in order to minimize the intrusion of thoughts while the master was strutting up and down, occasionally correcting our posture. Each time he came close to me, I got anxious. This, of course, threw my breathing out of gear. He only hit me very few times. He had very strong stomach muscles which he liked to show off. I had the impression that his muscles mattered more to him than his enlightenment.

I was there for two months. There was not time to be properly introduced to the *koan* game. He only gave me one childishly simple *koan*: "What color is the wind" and he seemed to be satisfied when, as an answer, I blew in his face.

I am stuck again. I looked over the last two paragraphs and found them rather garbled and jumpy in parts. What will the editor do? For by now I see that this writing wants to become a book. That falsifies my original intentions to write only for myself, to sort myself out to investigate my smoking and other remaining symptoms. It falsifies my honesty, too. Not only did I catch myself twice in the sin of omission, but, what's more, I began to hesitate to bring in living people. Fear of being sued, and that sort of thing. Well *que será será*. Whatever will be, will be, as Edith Piaf sings.

Through the mobilization of the writing excitement, I feel better throughout. I am getting and giving more and more love. The dirty old man gets somewhat cleaner. But what can I do if more and more beautiful young and not-so-young girls and frequently this or that man are hugging and kissing me?

My serenity, humor, and therapeutic skill are on the increase, as is my happiness. Interestingly, I feel in the last few years that I am no longer condemned to, but blessed with, life.

Topdog: Stop, Fritz, what are you doing?

Underdog: What do you mean?

Topdog: You know very well what I mean. You're drifting from one thing to another. You are starting something like identification, then mention confluence. Now I already see that you are ready to plunge into a discussion on repression.

Underdog: I still don't see your objection.

Topdog: You don't see my objection? Man, who the hell can get a clear picture of my therapy? . . .

Underdog: So what do you want me to do? Stop letting the river flow? Stop playing my garbage bin game?

Topdog: Well, that wouldn't be a bad idea, if you would sit down and discipline yourself like Paul did and write:

1. your biography
2. your theory
3. case histories, dream work, etc.
4. poetry, if you must

Underdog: Go to hell. You know me better. If I try to do something deliberate and under pressure, I get spiteful and go on strike. All my life I have been a drifter. . . .

This afternoon I had a filmed dialogue with an Indian swami, Maharishi. His thing was a rather stereotyped getting in touch with the "infinite" to develop one's highest potential. As he played deaf or, at best, gave me a cackle that probably meant to be a laugh, I could not find out what that potential was, and how his meditation compares with our simpler coping/withdrawing technique. Still, he has good eyes and beautiful hands. I personally think he is a drag and I would not care to play a saint for all the fame and money in the world. His game and role is frozen, though I suspect that there must be situations where he would be capable of other roles.

I am up early, look over this section. I don't like "it." It reads stuffy, like a school composition—oral and anal zone—stuffy, stuffy, stuffy. Why can't you just say: Freud you have a mouth and an asshole. And a big mouth; so have I. And you are an asshole and so am I. We both are pompous asses, taking us so seriously. We have to produce big theories for mankind.

I've had enough. Let's throw the whole garbage pail into a super garbage bin and have done with it.

Topdog: Fritz, you can't do this. One more unfinished manuscript! Readers or not, publisher or not, you have excitements, new insights, and discoveries. What if others profit by it?

Underdog: This is not the point. I am getting obsessed with words and I am becoming selective. What I see, think, and remember is being put into words viewed from a writer's point of view. This morning I felt close to insanity. Words were crawling all over me like termites.

Topdog: All the more I suggest you go on. You had times where words, feelings and thoughts came together in poetry. If you are stuck between the verbal and the non-verbal, then look at your impasse, use your theory.

Underdog: Disciplining and forcing myself is not my preaching.

Topdog: Who speaks of preaching? You yourself said over and over that any mental illness is the result of phobic behavior. You declare over and over that Freud could not finish his work, in spite of all his discoveries, because he had severe phobias. Now you are becoming phobic yourself. Now you are avoiding the pain of drudgery or a possible slight to your vanity.

Underdog: You are right and you are wrong. Sure I am phobic when it comes to insanity. I don't want to go crazy.

Topdog: Stop that nonsense immediately! You know that you are a near borderline case. You know that you had the courage to go a few times closer to the border of insanity. You know that your dreams are schizy. You want to explore schizophrenia. You know how with all your pathology you managed to develop into a being of which many, many are jealous. And most of all your role on earth is not finished! You are beginning to assume a place in history, at least in psychology, perhaps in philosophy.

Underdog: Blah, blah, blah, blah, blah.

Topdog: Now Fritz, don't make me angry. And don't play the spiteful brat.

Underdog: Ha, ha, ha, ha! I got you. I can play teacher, I can play sexpot, but I must not play spiteful brat.

Topdog: Well, you are too sharp for me. So do what you want to do!

Never mind. I will. And I feel better after this conversation. I will pretend that there is no atomic bomb in the background and that I will live forever. This, at least, will take some pressure off my writing. . . .

I begin to realize that I am much more complicated than I expected.

I begin to realize the tremendous difficulties I will have finishing, even continuing, this writing.

I begin to realize the amount of struggle I feel between reporting and planning on the one hand and a spontaneous flow on the other.

It is getting more and more difficult to be honest and to involve living people.

Compared with that, it is easy to live in abstractions, to make up theories and play fitting games.

Does this word fit the fact? Does this gown fit the occasion? Does this accessory fit the gown? Does this theory fit the observation? Does this behavior fit the mother's wishes?

Does this shell fit the gun? This president this state? This program my potential? Fitting, fitting, fitting. Fitting and comparing. What other games are there to play? Does my living fit your expectations? Compare me with your other lovers. Am I tops? . . .

. . . Very peculiar morning. I felt in a desperate mood—silly, unnecessary demands. Smoked a lot, lots of heartbeats missing. Wanted to withdraw, sent Teddy away. The film people who did the Fritz-Maharishi encounter were back for shooting additional footage to another scene. . . .

I was glad about that pulling me out of my whirl. Here was something simple to do.

It was a minor instance of what I had felt when I volunteered for the army. Unexpectedly the training was a great relief from responsibility. I was told how to greet an officer, how to march, make a bed, etc. No choices, no decisions.

I am yawning, yawning. I am avoiding going into my anal difficulties and the fight with my mother about my constipation. I only know that she gave me suppositories made from soap and I hated her for that. The rest is conjecture.

I am yawning, yawning, yawning. It's still early, not even eleven o'clock. Often I write until two o'clock or even later.

Top dog, you are right. We have some mopping-up operations to do. The pieces that come up—Freud, Ida Rolf, constipation, loss of excitement, a premature going into social relations—don't form a gestalt yet.

Teddy said that the previous writing went zigzag, in schizy-like associations.

"She is right. Let's find out where we are."

As soon as you say that I start groping, searching, yawning, sluggish, though I slept nine hours. I've got to wait until something comes up, or in shit language, until something comes out.

Yawning, yawning. This begins to become a symptom. Boredom? I started this book as an antidote to boredom. I got excited, released much energy. I am getting excited with the idea: Does this new wave of boredom herald another source of energy? Is this state of boredom an implosive state? . . .

The fertile void is boiling. The sterile void, the world of boredom is gone. How to harness the richness of the fertile void? This is more than a garbage pail, more than just obsolete stuff coming up.

But it is too much: thoughts, emotions, pictures, judgments. Too much excitement. Gestalt formation is in danger; schizophrenic-fractionalism, chaotically manifesting its right to be, overwhelms me.

Stay in touch, take your tiredness to dampen the hysteria of too many voices screaming for attention. Simmer down. Stay with Heisenberg's principle: observed facts change through being observed!

Tiredness, I took you, like boredom, for my enemy. I took you for something that wants to deprive me of a part of my life. You know how greedy I am. More and more and more.

I am in real trouble. I am producing sentences on paper, having them typed, xeroxed, proofread. And all the time I don't even know to whom I am talking.

I am anxious to get some feedback.

When I am "thinking," I am also in fantasy. I talk to somebody and I don't know to whom I am talking. I don't really hear myself thinking, except in verse.

Sometimes I feel different. When I split myself up into topdog and underdog, I feel some communication. When I am playing a lecturer and demonstrate my theories, I am addressing a class. When I am attacking somebody, be it Freud or the Prussian lieutenant, I have a reader as witness of my courage and viciousness. In either case I am not alone.

When I am writing these sentences I am alone and . . .

Just now I had a sudden experience. I was dictating those sentences to myself and I am also the recorder who has to watch grammar and spelling.

I can conjure up purposes and other justifications: to write a book, to exhibit myself, to satisfy the curiosity of my friends, to sort myself out. I am still alone and lost.

Where are you? Who are you to whom I want to speak? No answer. . . .

Part Six

Aging, Old, and Dying Men

Chapter Twenty-Seven

James Dickey

A s a man grows older, he feels little joy in the fact of his aging. If he has been lucky or smart, maturity has deepened his appreciation of love and work; even so, the machinery he uses for both is slowing down. Though appetite has not abated, opportunity is beginning to. He fears his middle age. He resents it. He toys with that ancient choice: Which is better, the short and glorious life or the long, mediocre one—growing bearded and decrepit, but still alive?

"The main thing is to ride the flood tide," James Dickey claims in his late forties, though this desire is equalled by his wish to face his coming years with grace, without the "facile overemotionalism" he feels he has been using "as a substitute for youth." A vigorous life, filled with varied successes, Dickey's position is made all the more poignant by this continuing need for intensity.

Born in 1923, James Dickey was educated at Vanderbilt University, where he was also a star athlete in football and hurdles. During World War II and in Korea, he was a night fighter pilot, credited with over 100 missions. A successful advertising executive, a husband and father, a woodsman, an archer, a guitarist, and a most unlikely poet, Dickey's literary successes include his award-winning collection *Buckdancer's Choice* and the popular novel *Deliverance*.

His journal, *Sorties*, is aptly named. Each entry reads like a sudden attack from a defensive position. Though these swift forays cover a wide range of topics—poetry, music, sports, love—skirmishing throughout is that man of "muscular sensibility" who is unwilling to surrender to age though he knows that time is calling all the shots.

The body is the one thing you cannot fake. It is what it is, and it does what it does. It also fails to do what it cannot do. It would seem to me that people would realize this, especially men.

Miserable day at the range yesterday. I was almost 100 points below the scores that I have been shooting lately. This inconsistency is the worst thing about my archery, and comes, I am quite sure, from the fact that I am of an extremely nervous and explosive temperament, and standing still and being calm about things and doing them in a routine manner, as one must do in archery, is as unnatural to me as anything could possibly be. And yet the fact that I have shot scores up to 430 indicates that I *can* shoot well; the point is to find a way to enable myself to do it consistently. The trouble is with my release; there is that hysteria. I do not seem able to get a consistently relaxed release, and when the right hand snaps open something also happens in the left hand: I throw the bow either to the left or the right or up. All this can be taken care of with a lot of practice and concentration. . . .

The longer I live, the longer and better the whole perspective of possibility becomes, and the more I see how necessary it is to *throw* one's self open to the least chance impulse or stimulus coming from anywhere. Who knows where that "anywhere" comes from or is? It can be the slightest thing, it can be something immortal in literature or art, it can be the way a high jumper takes off his warm-up pants. No wonder Whitman is the poet who opened up America for us: he was open to *all* kinds of possibilities. A man sawing a plank was a great man to Whitman and imminently worth watching and learning from.

The sadness of middle age is absolutely unfathomable; there is no bottom to it. Everything you do is sad. If you look at a football game, you are only a middle-aged man looking at a football game. If you eat a sandwich in a public place, it is sadness beyond any ever conceived of in the Lamentations of the Old Testament. And if you look at a girl on the street, she makes it a point not to look back, and this is sadness also. The only possibility lies in the past: if you are middle-aged, and aging, then your strength lies in what those years have given you. The only excuse for old age is mastery, and this depends on many years of devotion to the thing that you have mastered. But without mastery, middle age is a joke and old age is Hell itself, the inferno.

Mediocre day at the range today. But I *can* shoot well. It is all a matter of concentration, and of *willing* the body into a state of relaxation, from which the arrow leaps. It is all so amazingly easy when one does what one should do.

How sad it all is, this trying to be Immortal, this desperate attempt to say something memorable. But I, like Yeats, would cast all that out. If I did not believe that the whole literary effort was a hell of a lot of fun—exciting, perhaps superhuman fun—I would not do it. I had rather go for some big archery trophy, and spend my time practicing my release.

There is a time in the aging process when a terrible, reverse miracle seems to have happened. You see people that you know from day to day, and they scarcely seem older at all. But you have an image of people in your mind, and if you are removed from them for a certain period—say a couple of years, a number of years—*then* you see them, an extremely awful, even metaphysical change seems to have taken place in them. You look at them and you can scarcely recognize them. Nor they you.

I would like it said of me that I had a muscular sensibility.

There is always this thing in me between doing the thing of the maximum physical pleasure and that of the maximum physical difficulty, toughness. How long will I hang between these two? For the rest of my life probably, or for as long as I hold out.

The skin all over you is getting old. You can look at your foot, in an off moment, and it is not the foot you ever had before.

Hard, intense work of the body—work that includes fatigue and the sense of defeat—is the most conclusive evidence of our own being that we could possibly have. Thank God for it. It must be pursued wherever it lies and in any form in which it appears; on water, on land, or in the air.

With age, the only thing that matters is one's perversions. Let the world say what it will. Any human being who has ever lived a life on this planet knows that this is so.

I cannot stand myself when my belly is full of food.

If I slowed my life down, and lived more like an ordinary person, I might live a very long time and this is supposed to be the desired object of all human life. But it is not. The main thing is to ride the flood tide. Only a few get a chance to do this and one year of it is worth a thousand years of mediocrity.

Guitar playing very good, especially when I am sober. In about another ten years I will be able to do whatever I want with the instrument. At that time I will be fifty-seven years old. But so what? Gary Davis is about seventy-two and he is by far the best guitar player around, particularly of the kind of guitar playing that I like best. I look forward to the bearing of the fruits of the long, devoted discipline. This is something I love very much; it is as close to me as any mode of action there is. The only thing that worries me is some kind of injury to my hands, or arthritis. But that will be as it will be. Meanwhile, I will keep on playing as though nothing were going to happen. Probably it won't, anyway.

Ecstasy, and the continual need for it via alcohol and the insistence on living on the so-called "higher planes" of existence, killed James Agee. Ecstasy is a drug; one must learn the virtues and the creative possibilities of boredom. Likewise, Randall Jarrell was killed by his own intelligence, by overconcern for things, by frustration brought on by these matters, and by the aging process, which intelligence made more intolerable for him than it need have been. There are lessons here, there is no doubt. I must learn to reject the ecstasy that I have longed for all my life and have only recently learned how to attain, sometimes with alcohol and sometimes without. I must go through a slowdown period, and try to become slower and deeper, and operate on more of a consistent human psychological level than being very high or very low allows me to be. I should think this would give a certain number of advantages which I have not yet been able to understand fully.

Hunting season coming up again, and there is always the strange excitement. Bought Kevin a bow, some field points, and myself a bow and another kind of bow quiver. There is nothing like the excitement of the perennially unsuccessful hunter! But the idea of getting out in the fields again, a thing I do only once a year, of walking all day, of finding deer tracks, and the rest, is unbelievably exciting to me. If a biographer or someone else knew the horrible extent of my unsuccess, my so-called hunting activity would seem ludicrous, and could be made to seem pathetic, which in some ways, I guess, it is. That does not matter to me at all. I know how I feel, and what I want to do, and what I feel right doing, and consequently what I *will* do.

I am uncommonly terrifed when our basketball team loses. I find myself unable to explain this. I could see it would be normal to be depressed, but not frightened. Strange.

I know, it's very God damn strange. I don't believe I could do *anything* I would approve of.

Will it ever be given to me to attain that large, free, effortless, and essentially *simple* thing that I have wanted all my life? But at times I have sensed it, and have been close. I wonder if this will ever be true again. Perhaps in death itself. Perhaps not.

I hope that I am through with the facile overemotionalism that I have been using for the last few years as a substitute for youth. There are far better things, deeper feelings.

At the age of forty-eight, one becomes aware of a singular, distressing, strange, and exhilarating thing: the world and experience gets going faster and faster. Life is speeded up, the lid comes off, and one has no recourse but to go with bodily desire, imaginative abandon, delight, frustration, and death.

I am beginning to look old, and I feel, faintly, the cold breath of the void, for such a look is one of the bodily things that nothing can be done about. But I feel great, and I am down under 215 pounds. It has always been easy for me to lose weight and I think I will go down now to 185 just to see what happens. I will really be a rail at that weight. Still, my tennis game may pick up, and I could surely do a great deal more physically than I can at 215. This should take until about the middle of the summer, with a lot of tennis and running.

Very good guitar these last few days. Quite a heartening experience. In another five years I can do what I want with the instrument, and that is something to look forward to when you are middled-aged.

I was never really young, because my generation went into the war. I found my true youth in middle age, and it is much better than the actual youth that I had. It is good to think of this.

Chapter Twenty-Eight

Gamaliel Bradford
1863-1932

Is it true, as often is said, that as we grow older we only become more like ourselves? If so, the journals of Gamaliel Bradford seem intent upon proving the point. Almost every day of his last sixteen years, this New England Brahmin—a direct descendant of Governor William Bradford of Plymouth—typed out exactly one more page in his journal. Each entry was approximately three hundred and fifty words long. "Pre-written" during nights of insomnia or daily lulls on his hammock, this methodically kept journal was only part of the strict schedule of Bradford's assiduous life: so many minutes given to reading, to studying yet another new language, to playing the piano, to taking notes and writing the next "psychography," his popular psychological studies of historical figures.

Unfortunately, his systematic diligence, the habit of a whole lifetime, never brought Bradford the rewards he most craved. His prodigious efforts at poetry, novels, and playwriting invariably met with little success. And not until his forty-ninth year did he win some renown with the publication of *Lee the American*, a biography that characterized the method of his future works, *Portraits of American*

Women, Damaged Souls, Darwin, The Quick and the Dead, Daughters of Eden, among many others.

Though central to his enthusiasm, writing and study were not all that occupied Bradford's careful use of his time. His journal reflects a wide range of interests and activities enjoyed with his family and friends—baseball, movies, theater, gardening, boating, his home in Wellesley Hills, the cultural affairs of Boston. All too often, however, we read of these pleasures being curtailed by a lifetime of physical problems—long weaknesses, ear troubles, seizures of vertigo—or worse, chronic depressions, unreasonable worries, self-doubt. When the common complaints of old age compound these old ills, the later entries of Bradford's journal turn very gloomy.

Yet, always there is a valiant return to his delight in the nearby natural world, his nourishing memories, his intellectual engagements, the will to go on with his work. If we add to all this his strong sense of historical continuity, his pleasure in other people's achievements, emotional warmth, and a concern for ethical and artistic values beyond his own immediate interests, then these "consolations of age"—as Christopher Lasch has recently defined them—show us a man whose last years are filled with the deepest kind of success.

1924

JUNE 24. Today out of doors just as I might have been three years ago, and the wonder of it! . . . And this afternoon . . . walked actually over the hill; not to the extreme further side, but through the deep and lonely woods on the northern slope to the Reservoir and so down again over the open field. No great walk in itself, but a priceless adventure for me, after these seven months of prison confinement in the four walls of my own room. I am an independent creature by temperament, and to get out into the absolute solitude, alone on my own feet and with my own soul, is very wonderful and delightful, to feel that if I fall over and die no one will be the wiser, for some hours at any rate. . . .

AUGUST 20. Oh, the wild world, the puzzling, inextricable world, the perplexing, seducing world, the dissolving, elusive world, which slips away into incomprehensible nothingness when you try to grasp it. . . . And where is God in it all?—the old, old question, which it seems as if I might be weary of asking. I have not asked it of late so much in this Journal, but I am always asking it in my heart. . . .

OCTOBER 4. Afternoon . . . walk over the hill. . . . All last winter I feared I should never do it again. But never was it more beautiful than this afternoon. The heavenly silence of those autumn woods with the low sunlight streaming, throbbing through them, and everywhere the manifold tender murmur of the insects, accentuating the holy silence. The lingering flowers, especially the delicious, cold, melancholy purple of the asters, mingled with the warm yellow of the persistent snapdragons. And the October light, the incomparable easterly haze, clothing all the distant hills with dreamy mystery, filling my soul with the mystery and revery which are now my greatest delight, as they have always been, with far off flashes of vague possible glory flitting through them.

DECEMBER 27. In the night . . . thinking of my sins . . . it struck me what a famous thing it would be for me to take hold in the beginning of the New Year and build my life over. This was what . . . T, the neurologist, said was all he could see to do when I expounded to him the various nervous drawbacks and inhibitions under which I labored. How grand it would be to get control of my soul, to live with hope instead of fear, to see the rose instead of the gray over everything, to shake off these maddening, haunting worries over everything and nothing, which make my life a burden and a misery and always have— to change altogether, in short. . . . How grand such a change, and such a working over of the spirit, would be—and how extremely improbable!

1925

JULY 18. Trip down the river with M. . . . Not having touched a paddle for three or four years, and being one mass of lameness from my neck to my feet, was not sure what exercise of that kind would do to me. But after all there is no exercise that is gentler or less exhausting, and I managed to paddle mildly for an hour to an hour and a half with little fatigue at the time and scarcely any increase of lameness today. The river was extraordinarily beautiful; not a touch of air all the time, and reflections that were incomparable. Everywhere were the July flowers, the pickerel weed and the nightshade, if it is nightshade, the fireweed and the button-bush, all the pale bloom that we used to see along those shores together fifty years ago. And it is astonishing how little the shores have changed; where we went hardly an alteration in the general features of the landscape, simply the growth and disappearance of a few trees here and there; but the wide meadows stretch in their perennial green and yellow as they did then.

1926

JANUARY 1. Strange that in such an utterly dull and uneventful life there should be such a crowding conflict of emotions and experiences. But thus it has ever been: I live in a perpetual tempest, and the rending and shattering keeps me a withered wreck just tottering on the edge of the grave, though, alas, never falling. This morning . . . Darwin. Oh, what a book it should be! Such an incomparable plan, and material in richness beyond all imagination! How I am ever going to use a tithe of the significant, magnificent passages I have marked, I cannot imagine. And is the undertaking going to be altogether beyond my feeble nerves and failing powers? . . .

FEBRUARY 19. Finished this morning the first chapter of the *Darwin*, five weeks after beginning it, a much longer interval than I like to have and one would think not calculated to improve the quality. Odd, these milestones, as they always seem, in the road towards the grave, milestones so conspicuous and prodigious as I pass them, and so quickly forgotten. What a fever I was in the last summer over the *Moody*, and now it has all passed away. . . . So I suppose the *Darwin* will be completed, and forgotten, in the same fashion, if I live.

MARCH 9. . . . My attitude towards life has always been one of question, not one of assertion. Now Emerson's attitude is that of assertion always. And what is more, the assertion always seems to me unreal. . . . It is a perpetual bellowing repetition of confidence, as a child bellows it, because it knows if it stops bellowing the terrible silence will oppress and overwhelm it. How Emerson would have resented that imputation! Yet I cannot help feeling so. And I will not bellow, I will not assert, one way or the other. I hate questioning. It wearies me beyond expression; but, as I have said often before, questioning came I into this world, and questioning shall I go out of it.

NOVEMBER 28. Four days in New York. . . . Simply the old story of travel. I should be glad enough to have spent hours in the Metropolitan Museum, to have gone to the theatre twice a day, or merely to have wandered aimlessly about the streets. But the intolerable fatigue which haunted me from the start made any such diversions sheerly impossible. Every bone about me ached. The last afternoon I walked up Fifth Avenue, from Forty-second to Fifty-fifth, and back. But all the time it seemed as if my back would collapse, and as soon as I got to the hotel I subsided on to the bed, which indeed was by far the most agreeable thing I found in New York at all, though far inferior in comfort to my bed at home. We did go Thursday afternoon to *Iolanthe*, which was admirably done, and was very delightful. And my great enjoyment, as last year, was to sit in the great dining-room in the evening, and watch the dancing, which filled my heart with the strange longing and fascination that dancing always gives. But I think I will never leave home again.

1927

NOVEMBER 11. Still a ragged wreck and in such a state of general apprehension that all sorts of disagreeable possibilities suggest themselves as sequels of all the surgical disturbances that I had had. Ah, how impatient my father used to get in my childhood—'always seeing lions in the path,' he said—and it appears to me that there is little or no improvement since. On the contrary, a wider experience helps me to see a whole menagerie, and to have them howling and growling around me at all hours, seasonable and unseasonable. For which, of course, the only proper and reliable remedy is work. . . .

1928

JUNE 11. Slowly and painfully recovering a certain amount of tone, but it seems impossible to get back the elasticity of life.

JULY 26. . . . The depression has no definite spiritual cause, takes no definite spiritual shape; it is simply a desperate indifference to living and disgust with it, a hopeless incapacity for meeting the tasks and the efforts of life, and even worse, a sense that they are in no way worth meeting. The only consolation, the only salvation is work, and, while it is possible that the work itself is injurious, I think the value of it must far outweigh the injury. . . . On the other hand, the subjects that I happen to be dealing with do not particularly tend to dissipate depression. The real, the genuine George Sand was always in despair and always crying out for suicide, and now Julie de Lespinasse cries out for death perpetually as the greatest possible good.

1929

APRIL 6.   After all, my real life, the little I have left, is in the passionate succession of all these people I am dealing with, and I cannot get over the extraordinary hold they take upon me for the time and the extraordinary swiftness and completeness with which they depart. And it is exactly the way I like it and apparently I was created to have ephemeral friendships such as these, which glide away from me into eternity. There is nothing stable, nothing solid, nothing substantial about me, a mercurial creature, all passing emotions and temporary and superficial response. The strange thing is that with such extreme, absurd fluidity, there should be such permanence also. For, as I look back over the past and read the journals and letters of fifty years ago, I am more than ever impressed with the strange identity on which I am always insisting. I am in all essentials just what I was as a boy of twenty. I do not think there has been any vital or material change whatsoever, nothing but the slight modification that age necessarily introduces into the powers and the aspirations. And yet, no, by God! I think these latter are as intense and violent as they ever were. As to the powers— that is another matter. . . .

JUNE 26.   Working along steadily every day, in spite of the miserable lameness, and it is amazing how much steady work, even if it is very little, will accomplish. Have already copied half of the *Daughters*. . . . The rest of the morning in the exquisite hammock, digging at *Borgia* and listening to the wood-pewee, which, I am happy to say, still sings across the street. Think I shall shortly write an editorial for *The Herald* on the three sounds which to me are most characteristic of woodland solitude, the songs of the red-eyed vireo, the oven-bird, and

the wood-pewee. Needless to say, they are none of them great sing-
ers. . . . But have each a peculiar note, which begins to thrill and throb
about you so soon as you lose yourself in the silence and loneliness of
the June and July woods. At least they are all full of exquisite association
to me, and above all the wood-pewee. . . .

Some tearless tragedy of old despair—that is the suggestion that
still comes to me, as I lie in the hammock and hear the slow, delicate,
monotonous wail, echoing lightly in the oak woods over across the
street.

SEPTEMBER 2. Am I getting even more infirm of purpose, as
age comes upon me, even more incapable of making up my mind, of
taking any definite stand with regard to anything or anybody? Or is it
that I used to be more satisfied with a quick and superficial grasp of
things, whereas now I am getting more and more the habit of probing
deeply, so deeply that I get lost in morasses and quagmires and can
never extricate a clear and sharp judgment at all? But what shall I do
with this man Coolidge and how shall I come out? It seems to me that
my view veers with every book and article I read. Will it be possible for
me to make any firm and definite portrait that will in any sort of way
cohere? I am immensely curious to see. This morning I picked up
Damaged Souls and glanced through the *Paine* and the *Burr*. I was
utterly discouraged. How did I ever manage to do such work as that
and can I ever do it again? Am I doing anything like it now? It may not
be so good as I think it is, but somehow it seems as if I should never
again be capable of that clear-cut power, that firm and substantial grasp
of what I am at any rate trying to do. Well, one does what one can.

NOVEMBER 22. Another unspeakably wretched night, caused
by equally unspeakable folly in allowing myself to get nervous over
listening to my clock, by which I try to time my stupid insomnia. I
have always forced myself to lie perfectly quiet on one side for a half-
hour, then for a half-hour on the other. Now that I am getting deaf in
one ear, I cannot hear the clock strike and I strain my nerves in the
effort to listen, with consequent disaster to my sleep. All inexpressibly

silly, but I set it down because it is of a piece with the incredible folly of my psychological life, so overgrown and overcrusted with childish habits which I find it difficult to shake off. . . .

1930

JULY 31. This afternoon had an exquisite ride with H. of some seventy miles to Scituate and back. It was a northerly midsummer day, with the most delicious floating masses of what I call Constable clouds, so different from Corot's. The color of the water with the white sails flitting over it everywhere was beyond any expression of mine. But my wretched back—oh, how it did ache after the first half-hour and how I twitched and fretted in my seat to ease it—quite in vain. But why remember that?

1931

FEBRUARY 25. Saturday, after I finished writing, was sitting quietly reading in the library, when I was overcome with an attack of vertigo which struck me like a hailstorm, in the old-fashioned way of ten years ago. Had just time to call H., who fortunately was about and got me down gently flat on the floor, where I had to remain till the mad revolution of the universe came to an end. Luckily the attack was brief, and in ten or fifteen minutes I was able to crawl upstairs on to the bed. I had three or four more attacks the next day and feared the old condition was returning permanently. . . . But I., who came out Sunday, assures me that the antrum is wide open and that any return of the chronic disability is most unlikely.

SEPTEMBER 21. Byron's Italian epitaph, *implora pace, implora eterna quiete*, becomes more alluring than any heavenly kingdom whatever. That is, I think so, I think so; for where is the use in denying that, as I approach it, death, unillumined by any conception of any sort of future, becomes more and more repulsive and disagreeable. I hate life; I am weary of it and sick of it. How could one be anything else, when life is mainly composed of refractory ears and unresponsive stomachs? Yet with Madame du Deffand, than whom no one ever found life more detestable, I shudder and shrink at the thought of death, and find the best refuge to be not to think of it, knowing that, when it comes, one will probably sink into it with complete and utter indifference.

OCTOBER 11. . . . Try to work now in the mornings out on the balcony, as I am told the sun and fresh air are good for me. But while to lie and swing gently in the hammock on the summer piazza is the most exquisite relaxation and repose I know, I detest wrapping myself up in the cumbrous fur coat and climbing out on to the balcony. Last winter I simply refused to do it, and in the spring I was a wreck as I have been ever since. This year I will try to fight along on the balcony as I did winter before last, but I hardly think my patience will hold out. . . .

OCTOBER 21. . . . These divine October days try to get back to my old lovely walks. Yesterday wandered a little on the hill, though too weak and lame to get very far. But the light, and the color, and the delicate tones of the withered grasses—altogether unutterable. Today walked much farther—perhaps too far—nearly an hour on the old Park walk which I have not taken for some time, and again the color and the light so penetrating, delicious, that I can find no words for them. If only I did not get so deadly tired with it all. But even through the fatigue the light and the color are restful to remember. I suppose I might get more of it by driving, but the driving always seems spectacular and theatrical. What I want is the slow, quiet, silent, meandering through the varied deliciousness.

NOVEMBER 1. Oh, so tired, so utterly exhausted, spiritually and physically, so many little, irritating ills, and so wearily difficult to move or stand or work or do anything but lie flat on the bed! It makes the grave seem singularly peaceful—*implora pace, implora eterna quiete.* Yet all the time, when it comes to dying, I somehow want to get one more book done, and one more. . . .

NOVEMBER 6. Immensely impressed with the advantage of having a lifework that can be done in spite of difficulties. So many men, when they are hampered and crippled by old age, are cut off from the active pursuits which they have followed eagerly all their lives, and are obliged to hang about at home with nothing to do but dwell upon their miseries and complain of them. It may well be that my infirmities incapacitate me, so that what I do is far inferior to what I have done in the past. But at least I can keep on working and the most absorbing and exquisite of occupations does not fail me. . . .

1932

JANUARY 2. Pretty draggy days, especially when, like today, they are so thick with storm that one can hardly see to read or write even by the window. And every mite of elasticity and energy gone out of me. I make desperate efforts to get about daily a little more, but it is always an effort, and so great and so wearisome that there is no satisfaction in the result. However, keep busy as far as the darkness will let me.

Chapter Twenty-Nine

Angelo Roncalli
1881-1963

Pope John xxiii, the beloved "Pope of the People," reigned for only four and a half years. But during his brief time as Pontiff of the Roman Catholic Church, this dynamic old man, always so traditional in his own piety, initiated a more liberal attitude in a conservative Curia, reorganized the Vatican administration, made unprecedented calls outside the Holy See, spoke out to the world on secular issues, and successfully organized the Second Vatican Council with its far-reaching reforms.

Born into a peasant family of Bergamo, Angelo Giuseppe Roncalli received his First Communion at the unusual age of seven. The assortment of notes that comprise his posthumously published *Journal of a Soul* were begun as a young seminarian at the age of fourteen. For sixty-seven years he returned to these bundles of paper and copybooks to record his most intimate spiritual reflections as he moved into the priesthood, through his years of hard work as a papal diplomat in Bulgaria, Turkey, and France, then on to Patriarch of Venice, and finally into the Papacy. Despite all the pomp and circumstance of his various offices, Roncalli always insists on simplicity for himself, and at times almost a Lear-like stripping away to the essentials of faith. Revealed throughout his diaries is a full life of service dedicated to the attainment of spiritual perfection.

Nowhere is Roncalli's unshakable faith, with its sustaining vision of God, more profoundly called upon than during his contemplation of his old age. But not without its own irony. For, as he begins to consider his aging, and later anticipates his inevitable death, we remember that he is still fulfilling the most inspiring offices of his life.

1945–1952
Papal Representative in France

1945

. . . 2. I must not disguise from myself the truth: I am definitely approaching old age. My mind resents this and almost rebels, for I still feel so young, eager, agile, and alert. But one look in my mirror disillusions me. This is the season of maturity; I must do more and better, reflecting that perhaps the time still granted to me for living is brief, and that I am drawing near to the gates of eternity. This thought caused Hezekiah to turn to the wall and weep. I do not weep.

3. No, I do not weep, and I do not even desire to live my life over again, so as to do better. I entrust to the Lord's mercy whatever I have done, badly or less than well, and I look to the future, brief or long as it may be here below, because I want to make it holy and a source of holiness to others. . . .

1948

. . . 4. The more mature I grow in years and experience the more I recognize that the surest way to make myself holy and to succeed in

the service of the Holy See lies in the constant effort to reduce everything, principles, aims, position, business, to the utmost simplicity and
tranquility; I must always take care to strip my vines of all useless
foliage and spreading tendrils, and concentrate on what is truth, justice
and charity, above all charity. Any other way of behaving is nothing
but affectation and self-assertion; it soon shows itself in its true colours
and becomes a hindrance and a mockery. . . .

1950

HOLY SATURDAY: *My Future.*   When one is nearly seventy, one
cannot be sure of the future. 'The years of our life are three score and
ten, and even if we are strong enough to reach the age of eighty, yet
these years are but toil and vanity; they are soon passed and we also
pass away.' (cf. Psalm 89: 10–11). So it is no use nursing any illusions:
I must make myself familiar with the thought of the end, not with
dismay which saps the will, but with confidence which preserves our
enthusiasm for living, working and serving. Some time ago I resolved
to bear constantly in mind this reverent expectation of death, this joy
which ought to be my soul's last happiness when it departs from this
life. I need not become wearisome to others by speaking frequently of
this; but I must always think of it, because the consideration of death,
the *judicium mortis,* when it has become a familiar thought, is good
and useful for the mortification of vanity and for infusing into everything a sense of moderation and calm. As regards temporal matters, I
will revise my will once more. I am poor, thank God, and I mean to die
poor. . . .

I must comfort myself with the thought that the souls that I have
known, loved and still love are now almost all in the other world,
waiting and praying for me. Will the Lord call me soon to the heavenly
fatherland? Here I am, ready. I beg him only to take me at a good
moment. Has he perhaps reserved for me many more years of life? I
will be grateful for them, but always implore him not to leave me on
this earth when I have become an encumbrance and of no further use

to Holy Church. But in this also the Lord's holy will, that is
enough. . . .

1953–1958
Cardinal Patriarch of Venice

1953

. . . 3. I am beginning my direct ministry at an age—seventy-two
years—when others end theirs. So, *I find myself on the threshold of
eternity.* O Jesus, chief Shepherd and Bishop of our souls, the mystery
of my life and death is in your hands, close to your heart. On the one
hand I tremble at the approach of my last hour; on the other hand I
trust in you and only look one day ahead. I feel I am in the same
condition as St Aloysium Gonzaga, that is, I must go on with what I
have to do, always striving after perfection but thinking still more of
God's mercy. . . .

8. Sometimes the thought of the short time still left to me tempts
me to slacken my efforts. But with God's help I will not give in. 'I
neither fear to die nor refuse to live.' The Lord's will is still my peace.

The arc of my humble life, honoured far beyond my desserts by
the Holy See, rose in my native village and now curves over the domes
and pinnacles of St. Mark's.

I want to add to my will the request that I should have a resting
place reserved for me in the crypt of the basilica, near the tomb of the
Evangelist, who has now become so dear and familiar to my soul and
to my prayers. Mark, son to St Peter, and his disciple and interpreter.

1955

2. The thought of death has kept me good, if melancholy company
since the day of my nomination as Cardinal and Patriarch of Venice.

In seventeen months I have lost three dear sisters; two of them especially dear because they lived solely for the Lord and for me; for more than thirty years they looked after my house in tranquil expectation of spending their last years with their brother the Bishop. Losing them has been a great blow to me; it is my heart, not my reasoning mind, that has grieved. Although I never cease praying for them, I love to think of them in heaven praying for me, even more delighted than of old to help me and await me there. O Ancilla, O Maria, now reunited in the joyous radiance of eternity with the other two, Teresa and Enrica, so good and God-fearing all four of you, I remember you always, I mourn for you and at the same time I bless you.

Now I clearly see that this separation too was decreed by the Lord so that, as I devote myself to the spiritual welfare of my Venetian children, I may seem to them to be like Melchisedech, with 'no father, no mother, no genealogy.'

1956

. . . 2. With regard to practical proposals for the year I have confirmed my renewed resolution to achieve what has been the object of so many of my efforts, so frequently repeated, to improve my spiritual life: the perfection of mildness, patience and charity in my prayers as a priest and in my work for souls and for Holy Church, day by day. And this at all costs, at the risk of seeming to be and being considered a person of little worth, with little to give.

3. This sense of my own insufficiency, which is always with me and preserves me from vanity, is a great gift from the Lord: it keeps me simple and saves me from making a fool of myself.

I would not mind being thought a fool if this could help people to understand what I firmly believe and shall assert as long as I live, that the Gospel teaching is unalterable, and that in the Gospel Jesus teaches us to be *gentle and humble*; naturally this is not the same thing as being weak and easy-going. Everything that smacks of pretentiousness and self-assertion is only selfishness and comes to nought. . . .

1957

1. 'Give me more light as evening falls.' O Lord, we are now in the evening of our life. I am in my seventy-sixth year. Life is a great gift from our heavenly Father. Three-quarters of my contemporaries have passed over to the far shore. So I too must always be ready for the great moment. The thought of death does not alarm me. Now one of my five brothers also has gone before me, and he was the youngest but one, my beloved Giovanni. Ah, what a good life and what a fine death! My health is excellent and still robust, but I cannot count on it. I want to hold myself ready to reply *adsum* at any, even the most unexpected moment.

2. Old age, likewise a great gift of the Lord's must be for me a source of *tranquil inner joy*, and a reason for trusting day by day in the Lord himself, to whom I am now turned as a child turns to his father's open arms.

3. My poor life, now such a long one, has unwound itself as easily as a ball of string, under the sign of simplicity and purity. It costs me nothing to acknowledge and repeat that *I am nothing* and *worth precisely nothing*. . . .

4. I think the Lord Jesus has in store for me, before I die, for my complete mortification and purification and in order to admit me to his everlasting joy, some great suffering and affliction of body and spirit. Well, I accept everything and with all my heart, if it is for his glory and the good of my soul and for the souls of my dear spiritual children. I fear my weakness in bearing pain; I implore him to help me, for I have little faith in myself, but complete faith in the Lord Jesus. . . .

1958–1963
Pope

1961

STILL 11 AUGUST, *The Afternoon of Forgiveness*. Holy confession, well prepared and repeated every week on Friday and Saturday, still remains a solid foundation for the progress of sanctification; and it gives me peace and encouragement as I hold myself ready to make a good death at any hour and any moment of the day. This serenity of mine, this readiness to depart and appear before the Lord whenever he wills, seems to me to be such a sign of trust and love as to deserve from Jesus, whose Vicar on earth I am called, the final gesture of his mercy.

So let us continue moving slowly towards him, as if he stood waiting with outstretched arms. . . .

14 AUGUST, MONDAY—*Six Maxims of Perfection.* Considering the purpose of my own life I must:

1. Desire only to be virtuous and holy, and so be pleasing to God.

2. Direct all things, thoughts as well as actions, to the increase, the service and the glory of Holy Church.

3. Recognize that I have been set here by God, and therefore remain perfectly serene about all that happens, not only as regards myself but also with regard to the Church, continuing to work and suffer with Christ, for her good.

4. Entrust myself at all times to Divine Providence.

5. Always acknowledge my own nothingness.

6. Always arrange my day in an intelligent and orderly manner.

. . . O Jesus, here I am before you. You are suffering and dying for me, old as I am now and drawing near the end of my service and my life. Hold me closely, and near to your heart, letting mine beat with yours. I love to feel myself bound for ever to you with a gold chain, woven of lovely, delicate links. . . .

As I have already indicated in these pages: if and when the 'great tribulation befalls me,' I must accept it willingly; and if it delays its coming a little longer, I must continue to nourish myself with the Blood of Jesus, with the addition of all those great and little tribulations which the good Lord may send me. The short Psalm 130 has always made, and still makes, a great impression on me: 'O Lord, my heart is not lifted up, my eyes are not raised too high; I do not occupy myself with things too great and too marvellous for me. But I have calmed and quieted my soul, like a child quieted at its mother's breast.' Oh, how I love these words! But even if they were to lose their comfort for me towards the end of my life, Lord Jesus, you will strengthen me in my suffering. Your Blood, your Blood which I shall continue to drink from your chalice, that is, from your Heart, shall be for me a pledge of eternal salvation and happiness. 'For this slight momentary affliction is preparing for us an eternal weight of glory, beyond all comparison' (2 Cor. 4:17).

15 AUGUST—*Feast of the Assumption.* . . . In fact, this life of mine, now nearing its sunset, could find no better end than in the concentration of all my thoughts in Jesus, the Son of Mary, who holds him out to me in her arms for the joy and comfort of my soul.

So I shall concentrate with great care and intimate joy on these three highly significant and glorious words which must summarize my efforts to attain perfection: piety, meekness, charity.

I shall go on trying to perfect my pious practices: Holy Mass, the Breviary, the whole rosary, and a great and constant friendship with Jesus, contemplated as the Child and as the Crucified, and adored in the Blessed Sacrament. The Breviary at all times uplifts my soul; Holy Mass sanctifies it in the Name, the Heart and the Blood of Christ. Oh what tenderness and love and what refreshing happiness I find in my morning Mass!

The rosary, which since the beginning of 1953 I have pledged myself to recite devoutly in its entirety, has become an exercise of constant meditation and tranquil daily contemplation, keeping my mind alert in the vast field of my teaching office and my ministry as supreme Pastor of the Church and common Father of souls.

As my retreat draws to an end, I see very clearly the substance of the task which Jesus in his Providence has allowed to be entrusted to me.

'Vicar of Christ'? Ah, I am not worthy of this name, I, the humble child of Battista and Marianna Roncalli, two good Christians to be sure, but so modest and humble! Yet that is what I must be; the Vicar of Christ. 'Priest and victim,' the priesthood fills me with joy, but the sacrifice implied in the priesthood makes me tremble.

Blessed Jesus, God and man! I renew the consecration of myself to you, for life, for death, for eternity.

Chapter Thirty

William
Soutar
1898-1942

MAYBE IT'S BEST to let William Soutar have the last entry in this section for, after years of chronic illness, this Scottish poet faced his death in a more common way, the way a great many of us come to face it, without the support of any orthodox faith or any transcendent perception.

Born in the Scottish burgh of Perth in 1898, Soutar was brought up in a pious family of farmers and craftsmen who were devoted to emotional and intellectual honesty and to a kindly concern for other people. Soutar's special delight in the sensual world around him was added to these simple, learned virtues, and are all well-reflected in the vernacular poetry he wrote throughout his life.

During World War I, however, while serving in the British Navy, Soutar suffered from food poisoning, which resulted in spondylitis, an inflammation of the vertebrae caused by his infected bowel. Mis-diagnosed as rheumatism, this degenerative concretion of the spine came to proper attention too late for any cure. Although Soutar entered the University of Edinburgh in 1919 to study medicine, and later, the liberal arts, his physical condition began to deteriorate, leaving him a semi-invalid for the rest of his life. In 1929 he also contracted pneumonia, his long confinement affecting the use of his right leg, a paralysis that failed to respond to surgery.

During the 1930's, the scope of the diaries that Soutar had been keeping since adolescence enlarged. His invalidism hardly his deepest concern, the world outside was brought into his bedroom through his varied studies, his family, and a wide circle of friends. But in 1942, when another bout with pneumonia affected his lungs, he began to keep his *Diary of a Dying Man*, which records his feelings and reflections regarding his imminent death, a death that occurred less than two days after the last entry here. Soutar's attention to the simple details of this process during his last months, and the honest examination of his emotions, might again suggest that our experience with dying is designed by the way we have lived our lives.

1942, July

MONDAY 5. . . . Yesterday at 11:30, while I was yet dressing after my Sabbath ablution, D.B. Low came in to sound my chest—now a corrugated wheeze-box. After roaming all regions, he came back to a spot at the top of my right lung. It must have been a slightly ludicrous scene as I lay with my shirt collarless and my head encased in a blue beret set at an acute angle while David invited me to whisper one, one, one, one. The whispering definitely certified a cavity—and I suppose David realized, as surely as myself, that he was listening-in to a grave. I had a fleeting impulse to ask: "How long do you think I may live?" but refrained as I considered it was rather premature, and also because I was not quite certain that I wished to know just yet. . . .

SATURDAY 10. D.B. looked in to let me know the report on the sample of sputum which he asked for lately—the finding was positive, of course: yet to have this unquestionable proof brought the certainty of death into clear focus: there is now no longer any scope for fanciful hopes. When D.B. was sounding me I asked if he'd any idea how long I might last. Why do the doomed always ask this question: probably in order to complete what may be completed within the period: yet is it not a useless query, since the doom, though certain, is nevertheless centred in uncertainty; D.B. could not say which was the proper answer. . . .

SUNDAY 11. When I looked out on the garden this morning and saw the "blue bells" I said to myself spontaneously, "I wonder if I'll see these next year?" This is the first time the thought has presented itself: the awareness of the certainty has gone deeper. . . .

MONDAY 12. . . . We are strange creatures who can find cause for exhilaration even in disaster. As I lifted this diary yesterday I was sensible of such a reaction to misfortune: is it not a distinctive state of living to be under a doom and yet with time enough to contemplate the implications of such a state? Few are privileged by environment and temperament to explore without hastening the last reaches of the journey which ends in silence; to note, with what fidelity is ours, the thoughts and emotions which are dulled or stimulated by the close companionship of death; to sense in some measure the mystery of life and death in their mutuality, so that in approaching the final halt we no longer ask who is our guide. . . .

FRIDAY 16. With death in the breast, it is necessary for the body to conserve its remaining strength; it draws into itself, avoiding unnecessary contacts and expenditure of energy; its duty is now to sustain as long as possible the contemplative mind, that it may gather-in the last gleanings of experience which, in their turn, sustain the imagination. The body must come home to itself, but still it is the sanity of the spirit to go forth, forgetting the doom that is upon its flesh and the lassitude that at last will silence all communication. It is this conservation of the fated flesh which explains why in the past three months I have ceased to think about women, or indulge in amorous imaginings. This abstinence has not been aided by any moral resolutions which the nearness of the grave might have called up: the only exercise of will power has been to cut short any day-dream tending towards sensuality, and this ascetic gesture has been made but very rarely. How many reformers who condemn the licentiousness of others may be unconscious hypocrites, having never known desire in its full potency.

MONDAY 19. I recall but rarely that I am under the shadow of death, and this is natural behavior, for the day is full of the abundance of little duties and distractions, and the bright presence of life turns our attention to the movement and inter-relationship of the ordinary sights and sounds which pass across the small orbit of our tangible world. Situated as I am, still almost at ease, only the perversity of a morbid spirit could withhold a normal response, in contact with earth and one's fellows: and while strength is yet sufficient there will remain an alertness ready to recognize a transitory manifestation of beauty, and to find emblems of everlastingness in familiar meetings. And when debility brings a dullness over the sense and the selfhood draws back farther and farther from the shining day, even in the increasing darkness remembrance may still remain, to assure that each day dawns in praise and departs in expectancy.

TUESDAY 20. How trifling as yet the inconveniences which trouble me. A prolonged spell of coughing to dislodge an obstruction only four or five times a day; the waking in a night-sweat (not excessive) three or four times; the breathlessness and palpitation after exertion; and a few racked muscles. These indications of illness do not disturb, and rarely remind me of catastrophe: it is the look of my face that sometimes makes me wonder if I may have time to complete what I have planned: though I eat quite well, and the most sustaining fare, the hollows in the cheeks and at the temples remain the same. Before settling for sleep I draw the sheet high up each side of my head to cover the ears, and I am reminded, unmorbidly, of John Donne in his shroud.

FRIDAY 30. The other day, the thought came to me that I no longer whistle or sing; but this is no indication of depression, its cause is poor respiration: the singing often comes up in the silence. However, we have here yet another proof of how dependent is the spirit upon the expressiveness of the flesh.

August

MONDAY 2. . . . So far, I find few if any indications of that growth into serenity which I surmised would follow the confronting of premature death. Actually, during the past week or two I have been cursing and swearing more and more, due to an increase in bony irritation and the impossibility of coming upon a restful position that remains comparatively comfortable for more than half an hour. Sometimes I am shamed by the childish desire to roar in anger when a shift in position brings a tortuous pressure on a spinal ridge. Even a night of hardly-broken sleep fails to refresh the body; tiredness still remains in the morning, and drowsiness steals too many minutes from the working day. But the cursing ought to come under better control, lest from habit one begin to cry too readily at the touch of pain. The time will come when weakness may lessen the power to endure; then the body itself would seem to moan and murmur; and the tendency to such a subjugation of the will were increased by peevish outcries and curses while yet the mind was unclouded.

SUNDAY 8. Many of my dreams now belong to that type in which one is endeavoring to resolve something. All are most indefinite and hazy in setting, and are accordingly rarely remembered. Whatever the problem, and it may be as simple as arranging lines of writing in correct order, the task is never completed; but there is never a feeling of anxiety or anger at the frustration—though I believe on some occasions there has been a sense of increasing tiredness. . . . Apart from the lack of liveliness, there are one or two particular reasons for my forgetfulness as regards dreams. Now that circumstance has given a certain definiteness to the future, and now that I rarely think of women, there is a large elimination of tension and intensity both from day-dream and dream. Not only is there a curtailment of emotional "subject matter" for dreams to work upon, with the consequence (which we may assume with assurance) that there will be fewer dreams, but the weakness of the accompanying emotion must leave only a faint impression on the mind.

TUESDAY 10. How difficult, when invalidism is known to be progressive and finally fatal, to avoid an increasing consideration of the self. The therapeutic precautions in themselves are often limitations which others must·share—hence they become concessions made to the individual. Already I begin to meet the temptations of self-pity, by which one looks at himself against the background of the invalid state and not the normal day; with the implication that normality must be adapted to keep the abnormal in comparative comfort. So one might easily slide into complete egocentricity, relating all happenings not to general existence but to the particular corner of existence in which a life dwindled. This condition of a growing self absorption is at this hour of time less excusable than in peace, when throughout half the world millions are in destitution, hunger and slavery, and millions are being mutilated or slaughtered. How easily a small inconvenience can cover the sun and make us forget the misery of a universe; and the tragic element in self-pity is this, that at last the power of maintaining proportion between the world and the self is lost, and is not known to have been lost, since what is now a world is within the deathly confines of a wholly involved self.

WILLIAM SOUTAR

September

MONDAY 6. The coughing has become more of a nuisance since last I wrote, and about every hour I have to perform a clearing out process which in accumulation wastes a lot of time. The actual coughing isn't, so far, much of a strain, but my muscles inserted into the groin region have become strained and any sudden cough produces a most painful reaction; this makes me swear involuntarily. Fortunately as yet, my sleep is little disturbed; and I am wakened but once or twice by the need to get rid of phlegm. One accepts the coughing as a nuisance, but breathlessness is an aggravation. The feeling of helplessness and frustration during a spell of breathlessness hurts one's pride and one grows angry. In our temporary weakness we tend to become childish; and not a few times my face has automatically puckered up as if I were about to cry: in the humiliation of extreme weakness one might actually cry like a child.

The curse of a cough is not that it curtails one's speech only but also one's laughter; the involuntary expression of mirth becomes guarded, and full enjoyment is modified. This condition would seem to react upon the feelings, and one begins to note fewer occasions for laughter: it is in one's sense of humour as a gradual diminution of memory.

SATURDAY 18. . . . I fancy I noted somewhere lately that an obvious sign of my increasing weakness was the satisfaction which I found at the end of the day in the thought that I would soon be asleep. This anticipation is not wholly explained by tiredness or restlessness, but has an element in it, however small, of the desire for a period of complete stillness and forgetfulness; a thought which can hardly be explained otherwise than deathwardly: we sigh to return to our earthly silence. And even from the very qualified urgency of this wish we can appreciate the welcome which the severe sufferer gives to the moment which brings his narcotic, and of the ultimate cry of the whole being for oblivion. The desire is wholly human, and most natural, as it originates in the body and is a cry from the flesh rather than the mind: it is not calculating, but causal. So long as the senses can appreciate the world with a modicum of gladness, so long the wish to live remains, if the mind it not unbalanced; but when pain has grown so strong that the mind and senses are withdrawn from outward contemplation into a core of mere endurance, then the mind through the misery of sense asks the question: *If the world is now a nothingness let us pass away from it?*

TUESDAY 21. This morning about 8:30 I had a most disturbing experience. I began to cough, and a lot of phlegm gathered. I kept on coughing but could dislodge nothing, and after I was pretty well exhausted I found that my windpipe seemed nearly blocked. I began to cough again, but to no purpose—the matter merely coming up so far and then going back again. Suddenly I felt I was choking, and for a while a spasmodic coughing and gasping for breath went on, with the continued up-and-down shifting of the phlegm. Just when I thought I was to be deprived of breath altogether, a slight passage was cleared and I was able to rest: by now my heart was pounding fiercely, and it was a good while later before I was able to clear my throat properly.

I had not thought of how far I had lapsed from the vitality of youth until I looked on Ian Black yesterday afternoon and had shaken hands with him. Ian certainly looks the part of athletic youth in its prime freshness. He has a mop of bright fair curly hair, his complexion clear and fresh. He is at least 6 ft. 1 in., and solidly built with strong bones, but not too large; as he bent over the bed to shake hands I sensed the glowing strength of youth.

SUNDAY 26. I wonder if breathlessness reduces one to childish behavior more readily than other forms of weakness. To-day when my pillows at the weekly changing required far more readjustment than usual, I displayed a peevishness which, in retrospect, was most humiliating. It seemed incredible that a man of my age should act like a bairn and be brought by frustration to the verge of tears. I must be weaker than I know, surely; and as weak in will as in body—for there is no indication yet of this increasing stoic calm that I imagined I would gradually achieve. . . .

October

WEDNESDAY 6. How snail-like the tempo at which I seem to be living now—and yet my days are hurrying out of the world. I do not think any of my friends suspect as yet that I am under the sentence of death; and it will be fine if they continue for a good while yet to imagine that I have a touch of bronchitis, or something like that: when at last they know, an undefinable restraint will come between the free interchange of friendship.

Desire, if one may use so strong a word, has been completely transferred from the thought of women to considerations of "what we shall eat, and what we shall drink." The other evening it came to me almost as a relief that for many months the attractiveness of women no longer disturbed me; that neither in dream or day-dream was I fretted by images of passion. Everything in my life is being quieted; and the great orbit of life is moving in from the bounds of the universe like the gradually diminishing circle of light from a wasting flame. Whether the mood adapts itself to the environment, or whether I have somehow achieved a sense of proportion which adapts itself readily to the inevitable, I am scarcely touched by regret or anxiety, but derive even an element of satisfaction from being able to stand back and watch myself busied or idling under the shadow of a doom which is but rarely remembered. So much can wither away from the human spirit, and yet the great gift of the ordinary day remains; the stability of the small things of life, which yet in their constancy are the greatest. All the daily kindness; the little obligations, the signs of remembrance in the homely gifts: these do not pass, but still hearten the body and spirit to the verge of the grave.

TUESDAY 12. Yesterday's experience of coughing for three hours without clearage . . . was a most wearing one and left me very limp indeed. . . . From this incident I can guess that many very unpleasant experiences are awaiting me; and one of the most unfortunate consequences is the loss of time. The breathing remains exceptionally shallow, and one has to make an effort with some care to avoid bodily inconvenience. How quickly one may be brought down by this sort of thing is seen in my temporal hollows, which have slightly deepened in the past two days. Of course, all the abdominal muscles are on a strain and tend to remain so for a while, affecting appetite in a negative way. To-day I have been controlling my coughing with care whenever possible. Phlegm continues to be watery, but the sweetish smell is less apparent. However, if one is not clearing, one must be collecting more and more: it is not a satisfying choice, either way.

WEDNESDAY 13. Writing in the forenoon: G.G., with the concern of an elder brother, trotted in to find if I was more settled this morning: I could say that I was, but that that was due in the main to the fact that I wasn't attempting to get rid of the phlegm. The stuff was accordingly accumulating—and could not but be a factor in the increase of breathlessness and palpitation: thus one is threatened from all around, by night and by day: whichever way one may turn, the net is closing and cannot be evaded.

Permission continued from copyright page.